IN THE EYELINE
OF FURTHERANCE

John Howard

FISHER KING PUBLISHING

In The Eyeline of Furtherance

Copyright © 2022 John Howard

Fisher King Publishing Ltd,
The Old Barn
York Road
Thirsk
YO7 3AD
England.

www.fisherkingpublishing.co.uk

A CIP catalogue record of this book is available from the British Library

Print ISBN 978-1-914560-14-9
Epub ISBN 978-1-914560-35-4

Throughout this book names may have been changed at the discretion of the author.

Unless otherwise stated all lyrics are copyright of the author.

For Neil. My husband, friend, confidante
and never-wavering supporter.

Chapter One

We Are

In early June 2000, I lay by the pool at the Ibiza Finca where my husband-to-be, Neil, and I were staying, listening to the gently swishing sound of the palm trees overhead. They shaded us from the midday heat and, although we were miles from the sea, their fronds blowing in the gentle warm breeze mimicked undulating waves perfectly.

"I know the sun's a long way off setting over the yard arm," I heard Neil say through my dozing, "but I fancy a G & T. How about you?"

"Mmm!" I replied through the slats of the straw hat covering my face. "Lovely idea."

Neil padded off to the pool bar, where seconds later I could hear the cooling chink of ice into crystal glasses, the glug-glug of the gin pouring in after it and the 'pssht!' of the tonic bottles being opened.

The Finca ran a great pool bar system, built entirely on trust. There was no barman, one simply helped oneself to an array of spirits and beers from the cupboard beneath the bar and wrote one's name in the little notebook hanging on a piece of string. At the end of each week, you'd be given a bill by Ebbe, the Swedish owner of the Finca, and pay him for what you'd had.

"Hola Ebbe!" I heard Neil shout. The air carried their chatter towards me in that lazy warm afternoon way. At one point, I heard Ebbe shriek with laughter at something Neil had said, which I hadn't caught. As I felt myself falling once more into a contented snooze, my mobile rang.

"Bloody thing!" I grouched.

I brushed my hand underneath the sunbed to locate it, vowing to change its merrily plink-plonked 'Edelweiss' a la Wendy Carlos to something less embarrassing.

It was Patsy, my former manager's wife, and I knew why she was calling.

"Patsy, darling," I purred, "lovely to hear from you."

"Where are you, John?!" she demanded, panic in her voice.

"Ibiza, darling," I replied, in a tone which implied I'd already told her.

"*Ibiza*?! What are you doing *there*?" she cried. "I rang your office this morning and they told me you'd left. But not for Ibiza!"

"I have left, Patsy. For good."

"But *why*? You *loved* that job!"

"They sacked me, Patsy."

Her voice went from outrage to sympathy within a nano second.

"Oh God! You poor thing! How are you, John?"

"I'm okay!," I said brightly, sitting up for my G & T which Neil had brought me.

'Patsy?' he mouthed, to which I nodded.

"You don't *have* to say you're okay, you know, John," Patsy was saying, adopting her familiar, affectionately scolding tone. "You *can* say how you really feel. If you feel terrible there's no need to hide it from *me*. You know that."

The truth was, I felt great. I'd just agreed a very nice pay-off from my former employer, Reader's Digest, which my solicitor had niftily negotiated on the grounds of Constructive Dismissal. I'd had to sign a confidentiality agreement, but I knew my former boss was no doubt already breaking that. He was unable to be confidential about anything.

"I know you always want to portray a positive image to the world, John," Patsy continued, "and that's laudable. But sometimes, you simply have to let the screen down and show how you really feel!"

I supped my gorgeously cold gin and smiled as Patsy poured out her usual dose of motherly love and support. Mrs Reid had been like a second mother to me, ever since I'd landed in London in 1973 and signed a management deal with her husband, Stuart. The three of us had enjoyed some truly exciting times over the first couple of years. I'd written the theme song for a Peter Fonda movie, been signed to CBS Records in a wave of anticipation and expectation, and recorded my debut LP at Abbey Road studios. The world had seemed our oyster.

However, following increasing failure, disappointment and finally a frustrating vacuum of acceptance, by the end of the decade inspiration had even deserted the usually upbeat and optimistic Stuart. He no longer had any more ideas as to how to achieve the success he'd once believed inevitable for me, and which was so resolutely refusing to materialize.

After breaking my back in 1976 and eventually attempting a failed comeback to recording, by the early 1980s it was clear something new had to come along to prevent me freefalling into despair.

My move into working in the music business supplied the lifeline I needed. I found a new way of channelling my love and knowledge of popular music through the music of others, enjoying a kind of success I hadn't expected or aimed for.

Although I'd severed my business partnership with Stuart and Patsy in 1979 for the sake of our friendship, Mr and Mrs Reid became lifelong pals as they watched my burgeoning new career with a joy and pride which impressed me and warmed my heart.

"So, what will you *do?*" Patsy was asking me, as I waved at a sleepy-eyed neighbour coming out of one of the Finca rooms. A true Ibiza party animal, he often stayed out for several days, getting wrecked at various raves, then crawling back to sleep it off, before leaving for yet another seventy-two-hour marathon in the Old Town.

"Retire, darling," I told Patsy, which elicited a loud huff from Mrs Reid.

"Retire?! But you're still young!" I was forty-seven. "Plenty of new challenges ahead for you, John! Stuart never retired, until he had to."

Alzheimer's had crept up and nabbed her husband ten years earlier, to everyone's surprise. A bright, cheery, intelligent man, always younger than his years and a lover of life and people, we all thought Stuart would go on following his dream of one day managing a star. Sadly, the agile and curious man we all loved was slowly sinking into an often angry state of confusion.

His bereft wife now looked to their showbusiness friends to give her some respite, some exciting news to lift her out of the daily grind of dealing with a man slowly falling away from her. I decided to give her the next bit of my news as gently as possible.

"Neil and I have put our house on the market, Patsy."

"Really? Where are you moving to?"

"Pembrokeshire."

"*Pembrokeshire*?!" She almost spat the word out. "But you *love* Oxfordshire! And it's so near to London! There's *nothing* in Pembrokeshire!"

"Apart from beautiful countryside, lovely people, and a house to die for which we found last weekend, I guess not!"

I tried a chuckle. It failed. All I could hear were gasps and huffing.

"But what will you *do* there?" she demanded.

Dear Patsy. She still lived in a bygone world where only London offered a career and a reason for living.

"No idea, darling," I told her, trying another chuckle. "Possibly open a little second-hand bookshop, or do cream teas from our balcony, overlooking half an acre of apple trees and rose bushes."

Decidedly unimpressed, she guffawed down the phone. I could imagine her shaking her head, as she stood in the hall of her North London flat, surrounded by the memorabilia gathered through the years when she and her husband travelled the world together, accompanied by various pop stars and million-selling songwriters of the day.

"Why don't you start writing and recording again, John?" she suddenly said, as though her brilliant idea had appeared out of nowhere. "You had such a talent; it breaks my heart that you gave it up! It's a terrible waste that you no longer sing or play." She sighed heavily. "If you lived in London, you could do that again."

"I couldn't afford a garage in London, Patsy."

"You could rent a nice little one-bedroomed flat in Soho, and be, well, around."

"Around what?"

"The *record companies*, John!" she almost yelled. "You need to be on the *scene*, where you can... you know... do some networking!"

I smiled at how only Patsy could make 'networking' sound so arcane. And I sighed at her complete lack of understanding of who I now was, and of what my life now consisted.

In truth, Patsy still thought of me as twenty-one, single, and with a burning ambition to be a pop star. My life with Neil was kept somewhere in the bottom drawer of her mental filing cabinet. The fact that we'd been together for almost fifteen years, which was a damn sight longer than many of the marriages of her music business friends, meant very little to her. She liked Neil but he was never going to rank as one of her 'Dear People', one of the members of her exclusive club of treasured souls.

I'd been welcomed through those hallowed doors ever since the night in 1973 when Stuart, Patsy and I had first met at a music club in Oxford Street. Her waves of love and affection had been almost tangible across our table as I'd nattered on about my ambitions to be a recording artist. But any partner who'd entered my life thereafter inhabited a world outside of her acknowledgement. She still had trouble even remembering Neil's name.

"We'll talk when you get back," she said, as though, having had time to reflect on her suggestion, I'd want to discuss it with her in more detail on my return home. "But keep your pecker up, boy, don't let the buggers grind you down, as my mother used to say. And give my regards to… er… your friend."

"*Neil* sends his best to you too, Patsy."

With her usual kisses down the phone sign-off, she was gone and I lay back and sipped my gin. I reflected happily that it was those very buggers who my solicitor and I had well and truly ground down.

I could faintly hear the sound of Rachmaninov's 'Rhapsody On A Theme of Paganini' floating from Neil's Walkman and, checking my tan-line beneath my wristwatch, I settled down for a lovely do-nothing day.

I drifted off, remembering that night in July '86 when I'd first met Neil. I had no idea then that he would be my partner, my husband and my protector for the rest of my life.

'My,' I thought, as the palm fronds above swished like the ocean and lulled me into a hazy snooze, 'an awful lot has happened since then…'

Neil

Chapter Two

You Breathed New Life Into Me

In early May 1986, I walked into my new job at Pickwick Records, feeling ready for anything. It was just as well. I was immediately thrown into the deep end and then some.

The company had just signed its first licensing deal with MCA/Universal, owner of recordings by everyone from Bing Crosby to Guns 'n' Roses and a great deal in between. Pickwick's Marketing Director, Gary Le Count, strode into my office and gave me a thick wodge of papers, incorporating MCA's complete licensing catalogue.

"John! Can you go through that, mark the artists you think would be good for us to release, and then join me and M.L. in a meeting tomorrow morning?"

M.L. was Gary's moniker for our Chairman and owner of Pickwick, Monty Lewis, who'd set the company up in the '70s as a budget record label, specialising in cover versions of the latest hits – the *Top of The Pops* series, which had sold millions of LPs. He'd helmed the growth of Pickwick into a successful multi-media giant, handling records, CDs, a massive catalogue of BBC, MGM and Warner Brothers videos as well as the UK's best-selling range of children's spoken word cassettes, Thomas The Tank Engine, narrated by Ringo Starr.

As I perused the MCA licensing catalogue, it was clear that the bulk of the available repertoire was from their 1940s, '50s and '60s roster, with a few interesting things from the '70s and early '80s. There was nothing from their Universal or Geffen catalogue on offer such as Cher and Guns 'n' Roses. The biggest names were Buddy Holly & The Crickets, Bing, Ella Fitzgerald, Brenda Lee, Judy Garland, Patsy Cline, Satchmo, The Mamas & The Papas, Bill Haley, Chuck Berry, Nik Kershaw and Kim Wilde. Also in there were several one-and-two-big-hit wonders like Danny & The Juniors, Tony Christie and Fontella Bass, who would provide good inclusions on multi-artist compilations. I made notes on each artist I fancied and typed out a list, ready for the meeting with M.L and Gary.

* * *

"This is *brilliant!*" Gary shouted, looking through my list and handing it to Monty, who studied it with no expression on his face at all.

"Yes, it's certainly an interesting list," he said to Gary, sucking on his pen.

"M.L.," Gary continued enthusiastically, "I think we should send John down to meet the licensing guy at MCA, have lunch with him and build up a working relationship as soon as possible."

"Is that necessary?" Monty asked, still not looking at me. "Why don't you and I go over there, Gary, once John has compiled the albums we want?"

"Because, ML, with all due respect, it's becoming a young guy's game. John should be the conduit for the music licensing side of our business!"

Monty licked his lips and pondered unhappily.

At that point, his secretary, Stevie, came through and said he had another meeting in five minutes.

Gary and I got up and readied to leave.

"Well, thank you Gary, Monty!" I said, beaming at them both. "This is going to be a great catalogue to work with!"

As though time had stopped, I felt the room freeze. No-one moved. As Monty's face turned a bright red, he stared at me as though I'd just called him a fucking idiot. Gary seemed to shudder slightly and Stevie did a little cough. But, as no-one actually said anything, I smiled, nodded at everyone and went back to my office.

I was just starting to make a few more notes on the MCA list when Stevie's smiling face popped around my door.

"Erm, do you mind if I tell you something?"

She wandered in, closed the door and sat down.

"No-one here *ever* calls Mr Lewis 'Monty'. *Ever!* We all call him Mr Lewis. Only Gary gets away with calling him 'M.L.', and that took years."

"I thought something was wrong," I said. "I thought he'd had a sudden embarrassing moment!"

She giggled.

"Isn't it rather archaic?" I said. "Expecting us to doff the proverbial cap? This is the 1980s! It's the music business, for God's sake! One of the least stuffy industries on Earth. I've always called the MDs of companies I've worked for by their first names. They've actually insisted I do!"

"You're probably right, John, but if you're to get on with him, you'll have to play by his rules. Who knows, maybe one day you'll get to call him 'M.L.'!"

When Stevie had gone, promising to bring me a cuppa, I mulled over our strange conversation. Maybe it was this kind of thing which my previous boss, the MD of Conifer Records, Alison Wenham, had warned me about when she'd reacted with such horror as I'd told her where I was moving to? The days of being on equal terms with everybody I worked with and for were obviously over, while I remained at Pickwick anyway.

During convivial evenings at my old friend Terry's, where I was staying until my solicitor completed on my studio flat in Hammersmith, conversation inevitably came around to life with my recently ex-partner, Bayliss. I was always happy to talk about it; it acted as a kind of therapy, shaking off doubts, bringing things into perspective, confirming for me that I'd done the right thing in leaving him after seven years together.

One of the episodes which occurred when we were on holiday in

Ibiza a couple of years earlier fascinated Terry's guests as I recounted it...

We'd just returned from the beach and, while Bayliss was in the shower, I got on with unpacking our bags. Unbeknownst to me, he'd wrapped his brand new Walkman in his beach towel before putting it in his back-pack and - of course - I gave it a good shake over the balcony.

The Walkman tumbled out like a dead bird, plummeting to the ground and smashing into pieces on the tiles by the pool. As Bayliss was singing away in the bathroom, I ran downstairs and frantically scooped up the bits from the ground.

Rushing back upstairs, I laid the pieces on the dresser and was attempting a hasty reassemble job when Bayliss marched in full of the joys of Spring.

"I'll put something on while I'm getting dressed!," he said happily, picking up the Walkman. "What do you fancy, Babyki -"

We both stared in horror as it disintegrated in his hand.

"It was in your towel!" I shouted. "I didn't *know*!"

Even after I'd offered to buy him a new one when we got home, he hardly spoke to me for the rest of the evening and bitched about it to anyone who'd listen for the rest of the holiday.

Now, sitting in Terry's flat telling friends about the episode, I was surrounded by laughter.

"You're *adorable*!" one of the guys shouted.

"Bayliss clearly disagreed!" I replied.

"Then he's a stupid asshole!"

Yes, I thought, he is. Fuck him.

***

One night in early July, after being a 'stay-at-home divorcee' for almost three months, I felt the need to get out somewhere, go to a club, maybe even meet someone.

However, I knew that if I went to any of the places I used to frequent with Bayliss, I risked a torrent of abuse from my ex. So, I got a copy of the latest Gay Times from Terry's Canterbury and scanned the ad pages. Finally, I found somewhere which looked perfect - The Back Street Club. It was in the Mile End Road *and* a Leather Bar. Bayliss would never been seen dead in either of them.

At the bottom of the ad it read in bold lettering, 'Strict Leather/ Uniform Dress Code!'.

'Hm,' I thought, 'I wonder… '

Terry was out wining and dining clients of his printing company, so I had a quick look through his wardrobe and found a black leather jacket and some slightly torn jeans which fit okay. While I didn't have the pre-requisite black boots I decided my brown leather shoes would do.

I checked myself in Terry's full-length mirror, did a quick scowl, and decided I passed muster. I checked my watch, it was nine o'clock. Arriving at a quarter-to-ten seemed about perfect, so off I went.

Forty-five minutes later, I got out of the car and, vanity prevailing, took off my glasses before venturing along the dingily lit road towards the club. The brick wall alongside it was painted black so, in my myopic state, I literally felt my way until I detected a door. Finding the bell, I rang it and waited.

A small hatch opened and a pair of eyes stared out at me, eyeing up my bare chest and leather jacket. A lock clunked and the door was pulled ajar.

"Hi!" I said brightly to the unsmiling guy in chains and leather chaps, immediately regretting sounding so queeny.

I went to the pay-window, gave the half-naked pierced chap my two pounds and sauntered off in the direction of the throbbing music.

"Excuse me!" a loud rasping voice said to my retreating back.

I turned around and Chain Boy was pointing at my shoes, tutting and shaking his head.

"*Brown* shoes! They are *not* allowed!" he growled at me.

"They're all I've got tonight," I explained, trying to sound pathetic. "I'm staying with a friend and left my black boots at home."

He looked me up and down, closed one eye as he studied me, and said, "Next time, *black* leather shoes or… " he pointed behind him towards the now-locked door.

"Okay!" I beamed at him. "Thanks *so* much!" and waggled my bum playfully at him as I wandered through to the club.

The first thing that hit me was the smell - a concoction of well-worn leather, a large helping of sweat, poppers and oodles of sex. Just what I'd hoped for! The lighting was poor to non-existent, so one became slowly aware of people milling and prowling around in the shadows, eyeing each other up. There were guys groping each other, in the midst of deep snogging, and even the occasional full-on fuck going on noisily against a wall.

As I stood for a few minutes, looking for the bar, I became aware of a chap to my right, looking down at another chap in a leather studded collar giving him a blow job. This went on for a few minutes until, with a little shudder of satisfaction, the 'master' lifted up his slave's head with a small whip-like thing in his gloved hand and ordered him to stand up. Without speaking, the slave did as he was told, standing stock still with his hands behind his back.

"Get me a beer!" the master ordered him.

With a sharp nod, the slave marched off. I took his lead, so to speak, and followed him in search of a much-needed drink.

I was quickly served by a hunky shirtless chap, who winked at me as he gave me the bottle. I smiled back and turned to scan the rather large room. Mini-scenarios of various levels of S & M were playing out before me, like a holographic porn video with split screen effects.

Finally, I saw a chap standing on his own, beer in hand, across the room from me. I gave him the eye and smiled and, as far as I could see, he did the same. He was a bit too slim for my usual taste but, myopia allowing, from a distance he looked quite cute and definitely interested. So, I began walking towards him, and to my surprise he also moved off in my direction. We both stared fixedly at each other and, as we got closer, I gave him my best sexy smile. Hallelujah, he did the same! Result! I moved in then – *Bang!!* I crashed into a mirror!

Like an embarrassed cat, I quickly schuszed my hair, turning my head this way and that as though checking for a blemish. It was hardly Mr Butch '86 but it gave me time to recover from the credibility disaster. Then, with a deep breath, not looking around me, I walked as nonchalantly as I could back to my original spot. I took a long manly glug from my bottle and glanced around. I could have wept with relief. Everybody was far too absorbed in their own evening of sexual humiliation to bother about mine.

I decided to have a wander and see if there was anyone similarly solo who I fancied. I made sure to only pick blokes who looked nothing like me, just in case there were more mirrors dotted around. In one corner of the room stood a fair-haired, German-looking guy in full leather gear: peak cap, biker's jacket, rubber T-shirt, chaps over jeans and knee length motorcycle boots. He looked to be about the same age as me – a nice change from the sixteen-year difference between Bayliss and me. He saw me, smiled a rather lovely smile and we sidled up to each other, beginning the mating dance of grope, snog, snog deeper, manhandle and get stuck in.

This went on for about five minutes but I soon realised that it didn't appear to be going anywhere beyond initial interest. Finally, he pulled away and looked at me, shook his head and murmured into my ear,

"Bread and bread, dear."

He patted me on the bum and walked away.

'Fuck you,' I thought, noting his posh English accent. Not German at all.

As I once again recovered my dignity, I noticed a seated bearded guy smiling at me from along the wall. He continued to leer at me as I wandered up to him, then, without warning, he jumped up, grabbed hold of me and pulled my face towards his.

"Let's have some fun, eh?" he growled, and thrust his disturbingly long tongue down my throat.

We must have been snogging and groping for about twenty minutes, when he said, "D'you have a car?"

I nodded.

He chuckled dirtily, "I wanna suck your cock in the back of your car!"

It seemed an acceptable suggestion and nothing else was in the offing, so I excused myself to go to the loo and promised to be back in a couple of minutes.

On my way out of the Gents (where the sound of slapped arses from inside the cubicles had ricocheted around me like rapturous applause for having a pee) I saw my pseudo German chap wandering towards me.

He smiled the dimply smile which had first attracted me, and, in his deliciously upper-class accent, said, "I was just on my way home. How do you fancy coming back with me for the night?"

"But I thought you said... ?"

He moved closer, "We'll work out something to our mutual satisfaction, I'm sure. Yes?"

"Yes!"

I left the club with him, wondering how long my potential knee-trembler would wait for my return before realising he'd been stood up. After all, I thought, brushing away any feelings of guilt, he only wanted a five-minute quickie. I'd hardly turned down the chance of a lifetime of happiness.

Once in the car, I put my glasses back on and started the engine.

"I *love* your spectacles" my beau for the night said. "*Very* sexy!"

"Thank you," I replied, wishing I'd not taken them off. "My name's John."

"Mine's Neil. My house is ten minutes from here."

He stroked my leg and off we sped.

* * *

The smashed window and ripped-out radio, which I discovered on returning to my car the following morning, was of little consequence as I drove away reflecting on a night of great passion with a really lovely, interesting man.

Over breakfast in Neil's spacious Edwardian terrace in Bow, he'd chatted easily and enthusiastically, making sure I had enough coffee and toast and occasionally kissing me for no reason.

As we munched away, he told me he was an actor and had trained at the Bristol Old Vic Theatre School. I was fascinated to hear that his fellow actors at Bristol had been Jeremy Irons and Pete Postlethwaite.

"I usually tell people I'm a chartered surveyor," he told me, "to stop them asking if I've been in anything on TV like *Coronation Street*, or if I've worked with anyone famous!"

"Well, have you?" I asked, his reluctance to talk about himself attracting me even more.

My quip cajoled out of him more snippets of information. He'd worked with the likes of Kenneth Williams, Roy Hudd, Helen Shapiro, Paul Eddington, Dora Bryan, Timothy West and Peggy Mount in various productions.

He'd been in Cameron Mackintosh's production of *Oliver!* at the Albery Theatre and told me, chuckling at the memory, "After the first night performance, when I'd gone on as understudy for Brownlow, Lionel Bart came around to the dressing room. He seemed a bit out of it and whispered in my ear, 'Not wicked enough, dear.' Apparently he thought I was playing Sowerberry."

During his two-years in the production, Neil had fostered the rescued dog they'd used for Bill Sikes' Bull Terrier.

"Bonnie was a beautiful dog," he said, and smiled. "I once claimed holiday pay for her from Cameron and he gave it to me in pennies!"

"What happened to Bonnie?" I asked, feeling very comfortable with this gorgeous man.

"After I left, she was adopted by Valentine Palmer who was playing Bill Sykes. Each year he sent me a Christmas card from Bonnie."

He looked out of the window, tilting his head on one side.

"I didn't get one last year… "

Neil was now playing the lead in No Sex, Please, We're British, which had originally starred Michael Crawford as Runnicles, the later inspiration for Frank Spencer.

"Would you like to come along one night and see it?" he asked me, beaming away. "I can arrange a comp for you."

All the way back to Terry's, the wind whistling through the smashed window which Neil had covered with some cardboard, I kept thinking, 'What if I hate it? What will I say?'.

I needn't have worried. Neil was absolutely brilliant. The audience, mainly American tourists, had laughed and hollered at Neil's astonishing business, which often defied gravity. It had us all rolling around in our seats, and was one of the funniest, most impressive things I'd seen on stage.

As I made my way out to the foyer, listening to the buzz of praise around me for Neil's performance, I was met by David Fleming, the company manager. He whisked me to the bar where Neil was waiting for me.

No Sex, Please, We're British poster outside Garrick Theatre

"I can't understand why you're not a star in a TV sitcom!," I told him, burbling away like a gushing fan. "You were amazing! Everybody loved you!"

Neil looked suitably abashed and gave me a peck on the cheek.

We'd arranged that I'd bring my car around to the front of the Garrick in Charing Cross Road and wait for Neil to emerge. As I parked the car, I noticed a group of ladies hovering by the door, autograph books in hand. When he appeared and walked into the street, he smiled politely as they surrounded him with words of praise, signed their autograph books, made his way to the car and quickly got in.

"Drive!," he said, as they rushed forward, banging on the window and pointing at him.

"I feel like a rock star's roadie!," I laughed, as we soared away down Charing Cross Road, across the bridge and back to Terry's flat in Balham.

* * *

In late July, with Neil's help, I moved into my flat in King's Court, a 1930's block of apartments which straddled Chiswick and Hammersmith. I'd bought it from my friends Stan and Larry after I'd walked out on Bayliss at the end of April. Apart from an art deco armchair Stan had left behind and a recently acquired Japanese lacquered cabinet, it was empty. But it was mine. My new home. The first property I'd ever owned. I was in heaven.

Later that evening, I sat in the chair with a cup of Earl Grey tea and watched the sun slowly go down over London. I looked around my little flat and saw a mansion. I'd finally flown the Bayliss coop. The only way was up.

I wasn't entirely free of Bayliss, however. A couple of times I was aware of being followed as I left the YMCA, certain it was him. And once as I drove off, I noticed his little bubble car Fiat parked along the road.

On Sunday evenings, Neil joined me at the Y and on one occasion as we left the gym I turned around after hearing footsteps following us. I saw what was clearly Bayliss shooting into a doorway and hiding.

We went on towards the car and, as I drove away, I saw in my rear-view mirror his Fiat pulling out into the road, staying close behind. He followed us for about a quarter of an hour until I finally lost him when a truck edged in between us.

Then the phone calls at work started. At first he begged me to come back, telling me he missed me, but when that didn't work his tone became more threatening.

"I've been seeing a psychiatrist," he told me darkly one morning.

"Oh? Is that helping?" I asked, as sympathetically as I could.

"I still haven't got over you leaving me," he said.

I replied with silence.

"You broke my heart you know," he continued.

"Well, I never meant to do that," I said.

"At first, I was blaming myself. You know, wondering what I'd done wrong. But my psychiatrist has told me I must direct all my self-hatred back at you. He told me that I must blame *you* for everything. That will cleanse me of this feeling of failure I've been having since you went."

My stomach muscles clenched.

"Er – would you mind giving me the name and number of your psychiatrist?" I asked him.

"Are you feeling bad too, babykins?" he cooed.

"No, not at all," I replied briskly. "I just want to tell your psychiatrist he's a *fucking idiot!* I will also tell him that if anything happens to me, if you so much as lay a finger on me, he will have the full force of the law on his head like a ton of bricks!"

Bayliss laughed nastily, "Oh yeah? How're you going to prove anything?"

"Because you silly man, I am *recording this call!!*"

The line went dead.

I looked up and there was Stevie's smiling face in the doorway, a cup of tea in her hand, "I thought you might need this," she said, putting the tea and a plate of chocolate biscuits on my desk. I could have hugged her.

"You weren't recording the call, were you?" she said, smiling wryly.

"Of course not," I chuckled, gratefully munching on a biscuit. "But as long as he thinks I was…"

"I like a man who doesn't take shit!" she said, blinking at me. "Enjoy the biscuits – they're Monty's favourites."

"*Monty's?*"

"For you right now, he's Monty. But only for you. And only right now. Okay?"

***

The following Saturday afternoon, Neil and I were enjoying a thoroughly camp time at Aston's, a friend of ours in Tooting, playing 'guess the record intro'. Neil was pretty useless at it, not being a pop music fan, but the rest of us were shouting the answers around the room like over-excited TV quiz competitors.

In the midst of me guessing 'Layla!' after the first note, to a roomful of screeching laughter, the doorbell rang.

"Whoever that is, they're *extremely* late!" Aston said archly as he went to answer it.

"Ooh! Smacked bottom!" one of the other guys, Neville, said, slapping the back of his hand with a thwack.

"You wish!" his boyfriend Martin said.

As the laughter subsided, we could hear Aston's deep booming voice coming from the hallway, obviously having a serious conversation with somebody. After a couple of minutes, the sitting-room door opened and he walked in, looking at me with widening eyes.

Stan followed him in, limping and obviously in great pain. He also had a nasty cut on his forehead. We all rushed up to him, helping him to a chair.

"What happened to you?" I asked.

"Queer-bashers!" Neville said, nodding at us all.

"Tooting's getting very dangerous for pooftahs lately!" said Martin, which got a reprimanding glare from Aston.

"No dears!" Stan shouted through the chatter, "John's fucking ex-boyfriend has just beaten me up!"

Everyone was suddenly staring at me.

"Bayliss?" I said. "*Bayliss* did this to you?"

"Yes! He did!" Stan replied, rubbing his leg and wincing. "I was having a drink at The Markham Arms when Bayliss suddenly appeared and started shouting in my face, yelling, 'How *dare* you sell your flat to John?!'"

Everyone was still staring at me.

"He then launched into me," Stan continued, almost in tears, "pushing me to the ground, kicking and punching me and saying I'd ruined his life!"

He looked up at Aston, who had brought in wet tissues and antiseptic cream.

"I thought he was going to kill me... Ouch!" Stan shrieked as Aston wiped his forehead with a tissue.

"So how did you get him off you?" Neville asked, revelling in the drama.

"Well, thank goodness for the landlord!" Stan replied as Aston rubbed the cream on his wound. "He rushed over and grabbed hold of Bayliss, pushed him out of the bar and into the street."

"How wonderfully butch!" Neville cried, getting a glare from Stan.

"King's Road has never *seen* such thuggery!" Martin shouted from the back of the melée. "Those poor rich Chelsea residents must be in *shock!*"

"It's not *funny!*" Stan howled.

Putting a plaster on Stan's cut, Aston stood up.

"You'll have to speak to him, John," he said sagely.

"If he doesn't kill *me*," Stan shouted, "he's going to damage someone else. I mean, does he *know* you stayed at Terry's before you moved into King's Court?"

I had a sudden vision of Bayliss knocking on Terry's door and barging in.

Aston closed his medical kit, "I'll call Terry to warn him," he said crisply.

Then he looked at me.

"For someone who treated you like *shit* when you were together, he's remarkably upset now you're gone!"

"How did you put up with him for so long, John?" Stan said, rubbing the plaster on his head and flinching.

Aston went to make tea, though Neville demanded a strong gin.

"Oddly enough," I said, settling on a sofa with Neil, "he never hit or hurt me the whole time we were together. I guess that shows he kind of cared for me in his way."

"*No!!*" Aston shouted from the kitchen above the noise of the boiling kettle. "Do *not* start defending him, John!"

He walked back in and stood in the doorway, tea towel in hand.

"He treated you like a piece of *trash*! He was *ghastly* to you. Don't go all soft on him now!"

"I'm not," I insisted. "But he does have problems, deep-rooted ones."

"Oh *Lord!*" Neville cried, quaffing his gin. "Not another queen who can't admit they're gay?"

"Will you speak to him, John?" Stan said, gratefully taking his cup from Aston.

"Of course," I replied. "I'll ring him tomorrow and give him a right bollocking."

"If he touches you, I'll kill him!" Neil said.

Neville mugged at me and mouthed, "Fabulous!"

"He won't," I replied. "I can guarantee that."

"Meanwhile, the rest of us are in for a good thrashing!" Aston said.

"Be still my beating heart!" Neville cried.

***

On the Monday, I arrived at my office early and closed the door. I picked up the phone and rang Bayliss. He answered after a couple of rings.

"What the *hell* do you think you're playing at?" I yelled at him.

I heard him sniggering and sounding rather pleased with himself.

"Oh, so you've spoken to Stan then?"

"I saw him at the weekend, after you'd *beaten him up*! What is *wrong* with you? You have to be a sick bastard to do that, Bayliss.

You need help!"

"I'm getting help, I told you," he replied like a scolded child.

"I thought your psychiatrist had told you to direct your hatred at me?!"

"Not anymore. He's now said that, instead of blaming you, I should direct all my anger and resentment towards anyone who has created our break-up."

I laughed out loud at that. "Then you should be knocking seven shades of shit out of yourself, you fucking idiot!"

He didn't reply but I could hear him breathing heavily. Then, sounding suddenly concerned he said, "Is he very badly hurt?"

"He was in a great deal of pain, with cuts and bruises all over him."

"Yeah, I did have a right go!" He giggled very oddly.

"Why attack Stan?" I asked him, trying to sound reasonable.

"'cause he sold you his flat, that's why! It's his fault you didn't come back to me."

"Oh, come on!" I shouted. "*You're* the reason I didn't come back. I had no intention of *ever* coming back as soon as I'd walked out that night. You're a fucking nightmare, Bayliss. So many of your friends warned me but I wouldn't listen."

"Who? What friends?"

"Oh no!" I said, "I'm not giving you someone else to go beating up."

I took a deep breath.

"Now heed this, Bayliss, and do please tell this to your *cretin* of a psychiatrist, if you ever hurt *any* of my friends again, I'll report you – and your psychiatrist – to the police."

He began to splutter a reply but I stopped him in his tracks. "I'm warning you. I mean it! Once more and you're in a police station, alongside your idiot sofa-confessor. This ends now, Bayliss. Or *else*!"

"Or else what?!" he yelled.

"Are you deaf as well as psychotic?!" I hollered back.

Then, on cue, the sobs began.

"I *love* you, babykins," he whined, turning my stomach.

"I don't want your love, I just want you to leave me and my friends alone."

"Okay," he blubbed. "I'll try."

"Look," I said, softening my tone, "here's *my* bit of advice. For free. How about directing your now unrequited love to someone else?" I attempted a matey laugh. "There has to be somebody daft enough to take you on!"

"So it's really over?" he whined.

"Yes, Bayliss, it's really over. Now, go and live your life, find someone new to love. He's out there somewhere."

Through sniffles and a choked 'Thank you,' he put the phone down.

A gentle tap on the door meant tea and chocolate biscuits. Stevie was fast becoming a friend.

The calls stopped after that and no more pals were attacked. A couple of months later, a friend told me that Bayliss had indeed met someone, 'who looks remarkably like you,' and that he'd begun doing voluntary work for the Terence Higgins Trust. He'd become their handyman-on-call, doing odd-jobs for people with AIDS who were no longer strong enough to tackle such things.

Life had finally moved on for us both.

Chapter Three

Change (Who Changed?)

In 1987, I met Elaine Saffer, who produced Pickwick's Ladybird Audiobooks, one of the best-selling children's cassette ranges in the UK at that time. I was finishing a meeting in Gary Le Count's office when she popped her head in. Gary introduced us and, as we nattered away, she asked me what I'd done before Pickwick. As soon as I mentioned that I used to be a recording artist I saw her eyes light up. I bade my goodbyes, went back to my office and left her to chat with Gary.

About half an hour later, she tapped on my open door and sat down.

"Hello, John," she said. "I hope you don't mind my asking you this – and please say 'No' if it doesn't appeal but... would you like to do some recording for me?"

I put down my pen as she caught me in her stare. Elaine was a wiry, rather intense person who glued her eyes to yours as she spoke.

"I need a good male singer for my Ladybird albums," she continued, still staring at me. "How are you with character voices?"

My first session for Elaine was with an excellent female singer called Jodie Wilson. She was Australian by birth but had lived in the UK for several years, pursuing a musical career in pop and also appearing in occasional TV commercials. We hit it off immediately.

There was something Hollywood-esque about her, with long blonde hair bouncing around her shoulders rather like an ad for Silvikrin shampoo. She was reassuringly confident with a languid infectious giggle and a dazzling smile.

I felt rather like a novice at this kind of character-driven recording, and Jodie, sensing my unease, told me how she approached these kinds of sessions.

"I tell myself, 'Imagine the character you're doing and just sing!'".

The more I tried, which often had Jodie giggling behind her hand, the happier I felt.

Her favourite – and Elaine's – was my 'Henry's Cat'. Not looking at Jodie for fear of cracking up, I began purr-singing and 'getting into character'. It was all great fun.

The following session was with Jodie's older sister, Tracey. She was appearing at the time in the West End production of *Les Miserables,*and had a more hyper personality than Jodie, always chatting about 'possibilities!'. Everything which presented itself as a career step, no matter how small, was 'a positive!'. She had dark wiry hair tied back in a tight ponytail, which added to her excited little girlish quality.

The third session involved all three of us, and, in between takes, we chatted among and about ourselves. Jodie especially loved to hear my stories of recording at Abbey Road and Apple Studios in 1974, and about my sessions with Trevor Horn and Steve Levine in the late '70s and early '80s.

"Frankie Goes to Hollywood!" Tracey cried. "John! How exciting!!"

"Culture Club!" Jodie shouted, joining in. "I *loved* Boy George!"

I'd never felt like a sage old timer before, but I did with Jodie and Tracey. They'd hang on my every word, leaning forward and going "Wow!" when I told them something impressive.

"Don't you miss all that?" Jodie asked me.

"I enjoyed some of it," I told her, "but I found a lot of it confusing and disappointing. Some of it *was* fabulous, like recording the theme song I'd written for a Peter Fonda movie in Rome… "

"*What?*!!" Tracey screamed. "*John*!! That's *incredible*!"

The two sisters stared at each other, wonder in their eyes. I'd never had such amazed reactions to what I'd done in my recording past. It made me giggle, which made them giggle even more. Soon, we were all laughing like three daft kids in the playground.

"Children!" Elaine said in the doorway. "We're ready to carry on now. Playtime over!"

At the end of the afternoon, Tracey held my hand and led me through to the control room, telling me she wanted me to meet her fiancée.

"Keff!" she cried, at the chunky guy who I'd noticed through the studio window sitting at the mixing desk. "Isn't John *amazing*?!"

As I shook Keff's hand, Elaine told me that he was not only the producer of all her children's recordings, he also played everything on the backing tracks.

"My one-man band-genius!" she declared.

Tracey rushed forward and hugged him.

"Keff," she said, snuggling into his broad shoulder. "I want to invite John to our flat. I want him to be our friend!"

Keff looked at me and smiled.

"Hello friend!" he said. "When can you come over?"

"How utterly lovely!" Elaine cried, beaming at us like a mother hen.

"Seestah!" Tracey cried at Jodie. "We have a new friend!"

She dashed up to me and hugged me, making purring noises in my ear. Then Jodie moved forward and joined in the hugging. Keff looked on like a benign Disney bear.

"Oh John!" Tracey suddenly shouted, laughing her head off.

"Oh Jo-o-o-hn!" Jodie said, stroking my shoulder like her favourite pet.

They both began nuzzling my neck, making baby animal noises and mumbling 'Bunny Wabbits!' to each other. It was both heart-warming and immensely unsettling at the same time.

* * *

One afternoon in late '87, I received a call from guitar legend Bert Weedon. He told me he'd been sent a copy of *The Best of Bert Weedon*, which I'd compiled from Polygram's catalogue. It had become one of Pickwick's best sellers and had prompted him to ring me.

"I'd like to come and have a talk with you, John," he said, "about a project I think may interest you."

Bert had been one of those British pop stars of the 1950s and early '60s who were never teen pin-ups but sold thousands of records. Roy Orbison, Frankie Laine and Karl Denver were in a similar mould, in that their ability to make extremely good singles, which sounded great on the radio, was what appealed to record buyers rather than their looks.

The Shadows were the attractive young teen-appeal instrumental stars of the day, while Bert's hits appealed to mums and dads and burgeoning guitarists. Appearing in various children's variety TV shows, he resembled a favourite uncle performing at a family party.

His single, 'Guitar Boogie Shuffle', was the first UK hit by a British guitarist, entering the charts in May 1959 five days after his 39th birthday – ancient to most pop fans. He went on to have several more Top 50 hits, albeit only peaking in the twenties and thirties.

His potentially biggest smash was 'Apache' which, he told me during our first meeting, was cruelly snatched away from him when The Shadows released their own version within a week of Bert's. While his record languished at No.24, Cliff Richard's backing group shot to No.1.

As he sat in my office, his huge BW gold ring twinkling in my overhead lights, he beamed benignly at me and, in unselfconsciously great detail, gave me a resumé of his career.

"I played on several hits by the big names, John," he told me proudly, "Tommy Steele, Adam Faith and Billy Fury, I played on many of their records."

He´d also accompanied some of the great American legends such as Frank Sinatra, Judy Garland and Nat King Cole whenever they performed in the UK.

"My guitar tutorial book, *Play In A Day*, sold a million copies!" he said, waiting for my gobsmacked reaction, with which I duly rewarded him. "I've been named by the likes of Paul McCartney, Eric Clapton, Brian May, Keith Richards, Pete Townsend and George Harrison as a major influence on their guitar playing! Just through that one little book!"

He sat back and smiled at me, as I shook my head with the amazement he expected. It was actually quite cosy listening to this satisfied man, listing his achievements like a thrilled teenager who'd won the end-of-year Best Prefect's Cup.

"So, John," he continued, sipping the cup of tea Stevie had made for him at her own behest, happy to shake hands with a legend. "I've seen the royalty statements Polygram have been sending me every quarter, for the *wonderful* sales of your *Best of Bert Weedon* compilation. Remarkable! Well done!"

This guy knew how to charm.

"And I've had an idea which I hope will appeal to you… " he waited to see if I leaned forward a little, so I did. "What if we, *you and I*, recorded a *brand new album* of today's greatest love songs?"

At first, rather stupidly, I thought he was asking me to sing on it, but then realised, as he explained his idea and listed on his fingers some of the songs he'd love to record, that he wanted me to *produce* it.

"'Three Times A Lady', 'Always On My Mind', 'I Just Called To Say I Love You', 'The Greatest Love of All', there are so many beautiful songs around! We could make a terrific guitar album together, John!"

In fact, it was a great idea. Bert's 22 *Golden Guitar Greats* had achieved platinum status for Warwick Records a few years earlier, keeping Stevie Wonder's *Songs In The Key of Life* at No.2 and becoming the first No.1 album by a solo guitarist.

In addition, Pickwick would own the tracks, rather than us having to license them in from a third party. My only unspoken concern was, 'Am I a record producer?'

* * *

As it turned out, I found Bert extremely easy to work with. The album more or less produced itself, his small combo of musicians being entirely in tune with what he wanted. The sessions were a lesson in efficient musicianship and unruffled professionalism. The guys waited for Bert's count-in and off they'd go, playing perfectly in one take. They'd watch for Bert's occasional nods and glances as his lead to slow down or get a bit pacier, while the studio engineer, Alan McKaskill, handled all the technical stuff. I just sat back and enjoyed listening to some very pleasant interpretations of beautiful songs, Alan occasionally turning to me and asking if I was happy with the balance. I always was.

The album, *Once More With Feeling*, was released in September that year. Bert, at his suggestion, attended the Pickwick sales conference to present the release to our salesforce and chief buyers of all the big retail stores. Bless him, he even gave me a namecheck, which created a bit of a murmur in the room. Nobody there had been aware that I was anything more than 'the guy who compiles all our big sellers.'

The Monday morning following the conference, Gary called me on the building intercom – 'John Howard on Two!'. It was a system which I'd always loathed. It was wholly intrusive, publicly announcing to everyone in the building that you'd been summoned by one of the directors, probably for a bollocking.

"Nice to see Bert presenting his new album at the conference, John!" Gary said, as I sat down opposite him, readying myself for a chat about the impressive first orders coming in for it.

He picked up the CD from his desk, opened it, studied the booklet and looked up at me.

"It says here 'Produced by John Howard'!"

He sniggered rather unpleasantly.

"That's right," I replied.

He put the CD, or rather tossed it, back on his desk.

"John, a word of advice. We don't *ever* give ourselves personal credit at Pickwick for *anything*. M.L. views such egotism *very* poorly. We are a team. Everything we do, every release we create, is for – and by - the *whole* company. *Everyone here* produced this album, John, because we, *Pickwick*, made its release possible."

I stared at him, fascinated by the pettiness and resentment emanating from his eyes.

"M.L. nearly had a *heart attack* when he saw this today."

He stared at me, clearly loving every moment.

"He has instructed me to talk to you and put you right. In other words, John, *don't* do this again."

Words fell out of my mouth. "What? You mean *don't* produce another album which has had one of the biggest Woolworth pre-orders of anything from our Autumn release schedule? Is that what you mean, Gary?"

He licked his lips like a lizard about to pounce on a bug.

"What I'm saying, John, is do *not* give yourself *personal printed credit* for *anything* you put together for Pickwick! We do *not* do that here! Is that clear, young man?"

"Fine," I replied, already fed up with the conversation.

"Understood?"

"Understood."

I stood up and went to the door.

"You're doing a great job, John," Gary told my retreating back. "Just don't screw it up by letting your ego get in the way. Okay?"

I went back to my office, trying to calm myself down, when Al, the company's sales manager popped his head in.

"Everything okay, my son?" he asked in his perky Manchester brogue.

"I suppose," I replied.

"I saw you coming out of Theo's office just now and wondered why your face looked like thunder."

He wandered in and sat down, smiling at me with raised eyebrows above twinkling blue eyes.

"Theo?" I asked mystified.

"You don't know?" he asked, beginning to chuckle.

"I don't know anyone called Theo."

"Oh, but you do, my son. It's our nickname for Gary."

He waited for me to twig, in vain.

"Gary Le *Count*?" he persisted.

I shook my head.

He smiled at me and said, "The 'O' is silent?"

Still nothing twigged then...

"Theo! The 'O' is silent!"

I burst out laughing.

"That's *brilliant*!"

"Came up with that meself!" he said, mock polishing his nails. "We all think of it when he's giving us one of his bollockings. A bit like imagining your headmaster naked."

* * *

A couple of weeks later, I received a call from a lady called Jan. She told me she was Acker Bilk's manager.

"Hi, John," she began. "Acker rang me today, first of all to say how thrilled he was by the royalty cheque from sales of your *Best of Acker Bilk* compilation!"

"Oh yes, it's sold really well," I replied, thinking how nice of an artist's manager to ring and acknowledge it.

"It's fantastic!" she enthused. "But he *also* told me that he'd seen your new Bert Weedon album in Woolworth's at the weekend. He bought a copy and rather liked it... and he wondered if you would consider recording a new album with him?"

"With his jazz combo?" I asked her.

"No, more like Bert's album, a romantic instrumentals collection. You would provide the musicians, Acker would bring his clarinet and play!"

I told her it sounded a great idea and that I'd put it to 'the A & R committee' and call her back. In truth, I needed to find someone who could produce it, deciding I didn't want any more hassle from Theo.

After a coffee and a mull, I rang Keff. Elaine Saffer had said he was 'a one man-band genius'; he seemed like the perfect guy. Happily, he jumped at it.

"It'll make a change from doing Elaine's nursery rhymes!" he joked.

I rang Jan and said her idea was perfect for Pickwick, and that I had a great producer for the album.

"Excellent!" she said. "Why not bring your producer to my office to meet Acker?"

Acker had found pop fame in the early 1960s, striking gold with 'Stranger On the Shore'. With his trademark bowler hat, striped waistcoat and goatee beard he was a constant staple of TV viewing. While 'Stranger' became the biggest selling single of 1962, it also topped the American charts. Since then his albums regularly charted, both as a solo artist and with Chris Barber and Kenny Ball – 'The Three Bs' filling concert halls across the UK. In more recent times, he'd had big hits with romantic instrumentals like 'Aria' and a series of laid-back easy listening LPs.

Keff and Acker hit it off immediately. There was an immediate musicians' empathy between them. I suggested that I compile a list of songs and send it to him for his approval before recording sessions began.

"Great, lad!," he said as Keff and I stood to leave. "If it worked for Bert then... "

I visited the studios over the next two weeks, sitting in on sessions while Keff and Acker got on with making what became *The Love Album*. It was the first of three hugely successful albums Acker and Keff recorded for Pickwick. Slowly but surely, a catalogue of owned recordings by name artists was being created. Soon we were being wooed by third-party catalogue exploitation companies who wanted to represent our growing portfolio. The way forward had been signposted.

* * *

In the Autumn of 1988, I put together a Barry Manilow compilation, *Reflections*. Coordinated with his manager Gary Kief, who joined me for lunch to discuss the project, and with Barry himself by regular faxes, the album featured many of his greatest hits as well as some lesser-known recordings which Barry wanted on there, such as the brutally beautiful 'Sandra' which Dusty Springfield had also recorded in 1978.

Needless to say, *Reflections* sold extremely well, leading to an invite from Gary to see Barry performing at the Alexandra Palace. I took my stepmother, Sybil, along as she was a huge Manilow fan, and during the interval Gary came up to us and asked if we'd like to meet Barry after the show.

"We'll come and get you as soon as the lights go up," he told me.

Sure enough, as Sybil was swooning about the thought of meeting her idol, and raving about what a great show it had been – and it was - Gary appeared and whisked us up to the Green Room, where we were told to sit at one of the tables and await the arrival of the great man.

"Here he comes," I murmured to Sybil, as he made his way through the invited guests, chatting briefly to them, having his photo taken and moving on with his minder, Chris, to the next eager group.

Sybil looked fit to wet herself as her hero approached us, Chris walking alongside Barry saying, "John Howard, Pickwick Records, the *Reflections* album, 180,000 units sold," into his ear.

I stood up to meet Barry and, as he reached us, hand outstretched, he cried, "John! *Great* to meet you! One-hundred-and-eighty thousand CDs sold! Wow! *Amazing!*"

He glanced at Sybil who cowered on her chair behind me.

"And who is this lovely lady with you?"

Sybil stood and did a kind of curtsy as he took her hand.

"This is my stepmother, Sybil," I said, readying myself to catch her.

"Would you like a photo with me?" he asked her.

"Ooh, Barry!" she moaned, "that would be wonderful! Thank you!"

She fumbled nervously in her bag, muttering several more thank you's, finally extricating a little camera, which she handed to me.

Putting his arm around her waist, Manilow gently pulled her into shot like the pro he was as I took the photo which, enlarged by Boots in Rochdale, stared down at my father and his wife from their bedroom wall every morning for the rest of their marriage.

* * *

I'd always loved Madness and had bought several of their singles. I especially liked the later ones like 'Wings of a Dove', 'One Better Day' and 'The Sun and The Rain', fantastic records incorporating great songs, wonderful arrangements and inventive production touches.

When Pickwick did a licensing deal with Virgin Records in 1989, I suggested several album ideas to Virgin's Head of Special Concepts, including a Madness compilation. To my delight, he not only agreed but arranged for band members Lee Thompson and Chris Foreman to visit Pickwick and discuss the concept with me. It was a fan's idea of heaven.

Sitting with these charming guys talking about their music and the band's history, I was enchanted. They'd always seemed slightly anarchistic on Top of The Pops, but in person they were the epitome of polite.

A couple of weeks later, at Lee and Chris's invitation, I took Gray, Pickwick's chief sleeve designer, to the band's recording studio, *The Liquidator*, in Caledonian Road to discuss the artwork for the CD booklet for *It's Madness*.

Chris showed us around the studio and then, over cups of tea, Suggs, Lee, Chris, Mike and Mark sat down with us and went through their ideas for the sleeve. Gray made a note of everything they suggested and promised to have something for them to look at within the week.

As we were finishing up, Woody turned up on his bike.

"Sorry I'm late!" he said, taking off his bicycle clips. "I've been signing on!"

I was amazed, and rather saddened, that someone from such a hugely successful band was having to claim dole money. The difference between what the public sees and the harsh reality of life in a charting pop group was depressingly marked.

"People think we're rolling in it," Suggs remarked, as Woody got himself a cuppa and came to join us on the sofa.

"We would've been," Lee added, not a little ruefully, "if Virgin hadn't taken the costs of our videos out of our royalties!"

"We hadn't realised that," Suggs explained. "As my dad used to say, always read the small print, sonny!"

"But they were great videos!" Woody said.

"Yeah, but dropping that mini out of the plane in the 'Wings of a Dove' video turned out to be a financial step too far!" Chris said, creating a ripple of laughter amongst the boys.

"It looked great though!" Woody laughed.

I really liked these guys.

* * *

One of our biggest sellers in 1989 was *The Andrew Lloyd Webber Collection*, which producer Gordon Lorenz recorded for me. It featured a selection of West End musical stars including Stephanie Lawrence, Paul Jones and Carl Wayne.

"This one's gonna be fucking massive, John!" Al told me over coffee one morning when I was chatting to him about the album. "And you're the man to present it to my sales team!"

"Doesn't Gary usually present the new releases?" I asked him.

"Yeah, and it'll piss him off no end when you turn up," he said, his eyes glistening, "but if you don't care, neither do I!"

"Fucking fantastic!" Al said to me after the sales meeting. "You know so much about music, John. *Really* interesting stuff! The guys loved you, and you were really funny too. Fan-bloody-tastic, my son! I'm going to tell Theo he should book *you* to present our Autumn releases at the Sales Conference this year!"

"But that's Gary's domain," I said, knowing the Annual Sales Conference was Theo's cherished chance of glory and praise from the chainstores' chief buyers.

My turning up to present one album had already created an unattractive twitch on Gary's face, handing over the whole conference presentation to me would surely be a step too far.

"Gary presents the Autumn releases every year, Al," I said. "It's his moment."

"Yeah, and everybody sits there falling a-fucking-sleep while he drones on, thinking he's the bee's knees! You'll knock all the buyers dead with your delivery, John, and that's what we need! Leave it with me, son! I'll sort Theo out."

Chapter Four

Deadly Nightshade

As the '80s was coming to a close, several of our friends, having been diagnosed as HIV Positive, were becoming increasingly poorly. There didn't seem to be any rules or formula regarding how this disease affected people. Everybody reacted differently to the virus, going down with various untreatable ailments, some of which had not been seen for over a hundred years.

The end, however, was nearly always the same: the loss of dear friends long before 'their time'. I remember commenting to Stevie that I now understood how it must have felt during the two world wars, when young men in their thousands were lost, years before their expected demise, swathes of lives ended before they achieved their potential and dreams.

Stan's now-former boyfriend Larry had fallen ill a couple of times with unspecified but debilitating illnesses. Each time he came home from a short stay in hospital he looked weaker. Over time, he became increasingly housebound.

My lovely friend Henners, who'd been manager at Covent Garden's Blitz Club where I'd played in the mid-'70s, remained surprisingly healthy-looking after being diagnosed. But he told me, "I always feel like shit, I have a pounding head like a road drill and my limbs ache all the time. Which makes everyone telling me I look great even more annoying!"

My old South London flatmate, Daniel, who had lost his American partner, Barry, to AIDS the previous Summer, came to see Neil and me in the Spring of '89. He looked well, extremely suntanned from his decade of living in Florida, but told us that he knew his time was limited.

"I eat all the right things now," he said, "I never touch alcohol and only drink fruit juices and tea, but it's just holding off the inevitable."

My Scottish long-time pal, Bill Gee, quickly went from a man with a few Kaposi Sarcoma scars on his neck, legs and arms to suffering a hacking cough, losing six stone in weight and gradually aging well beyond his years, needing a walking stick to get about.

Bill's mum, worried about how he had sounded on the phone, had come down from her home in Dundee to check he was okay. He had never come out to her, so this lady in her late sixties sat quietly horrified at her son's skeletal appearance while he told her that not only was he gay, but that he was also dying from AIDS.

"She wasn't in the least bit phased," Bill told me. "All those years I spent terrified she'd be disgusted that I'm a pooftah! I so underestimated her."

"Mothers always know," I told him.

"She said she's going to stay and look after me," he said, "until the end. Mums, eh?"

As a special thank you to her, and a 70th birthday treat, Bill asked me to book tickets for us to see the musical Me & My Girl, starring Gary Wilmot. Once there, he ordered champagne and sat in the theatre bar regaling Neil, me and his unshockable mum with tales of his misbegotten youth. I watched people glancing over nervously as my brave friend, looking twice his forty-one years, hobbled about on a stick in a great deal of pain, sweating profusely. But the thing I remember most from that evening is his deep joy at seeing his mum loving her birthday treat.

In his latter months, I used to visit Bill at least once a week after work. Initially, he'd be sitting in an armchair sipping the tea his mum had brought him, but as the months went by he would more usually be upstairs, exhausted, propped up by several pillows to ease his bed sores and various scabs.

He now had a daily carer, his mum not having the strength to lift him in and out of bed and take him to the loo. Very often, I'd arrive just as Mo was drying his groin with a hairdryer – 'Perfect timing as always, dear!' he'd shout down at me as his mum opened the front door. It was a basic but effective way to relieve the pain and itching from the pus-oozing sores, and as I sipped the tea his mum had made for me, I'd sit in the bedroom chair watching Mo waving the hairdryer around his nether regions. Bill would laugh throughout 'my beauty treatment', joking that it was the first hot stuff he'd had near his crutch for years.

When Mo had left us alone, we'd natter about what I was up to at work, and reminisce about all the great album sleeves he'd designed for me.

"My favourite was the T.Rex Best Of," I told him.

"Oh, I was really proud of the Punk One… "

"Viva La Revolution!" I reminded him as he searched his fading memory for its title.

"You giving me that design work really cheered me up, you know," he said, smiling fondly at me. "It was around then that I'd started to suspect I had AIDS. Those album sleeve commissions were like a lifeline out of growing despair."

"I wouldn't have asked you if I didn't think you were up to it," I said.

"But the fact you knew I was up to it, that meant so much, my dear."

"And Julian the printer rather cheered you up too, as I recall."

"I only looked from afar, dear, but my, what an eyeful of manhood he was!"

We both giggled salaciously and for a moment we were back in our days at The Coleherne in the '70s, where we'd stand by the bar and discuss the cutest guys on offer and betting which one of us was going to make the first move.

Sadly, though, Bill's once-stocky lithe body and attractively handsome face was now reduced to skin and bone. His eyes looked huge in his skull, which seemed to have actually shrunk.

But, thankfully, he hadn't lost his wicked sense of humour. "I was telling Mo the other day – 'Whenever John leaves I always feel better!'"

We both laughed at his double-handed compliment, though it was quickly followed by, "But you know what I mean, John. You always lift me, you always make me laugh, you always help make the day feel good."

The last time I saw him, I sat on the edge of his bed as he told me what he had planned for his funeral and the memorial service he wanted. He'd thought of every detail, describing it as though it was for a friend's last farewell rather than his own.

"I want 'Bridge Over Troubled Water' when people walk in and Bette Midler's 'Hello In There' as they're leaving. If they're not all sobbing their hearts out by then, I'll be extremely pissed off!" He chuckled then said, "And after the service is over, we'll all come back here for sandwiches and tea!"

Then he stopped and stared at me, "Oh no!" he said, looking shocked, "I won't be here, will I?"

Although he giggled, I could see that it had pulled him up. His eyes filled with a kind of panic.

"You must be sure it's done as I ask!" he said, grabbing my hand. "It has to be a day for mum, for her, to see how much her son was loved."

I held back tears and said, "Your mum will be very proud of you, darling. She already is."

We were both saved from blubbing like babies by Mo returning with creams and ointments for Bill's 'tender regions'. She made it clear it was my cue to leave.

"Jeez!" Bill laughed. "He's seen you drying my bollocks with a hairdryer, for God's sake! I don't think him watching you slap some cream on my arse would embarrass the lad!"

Mo looked at me and I nodded. I kissed Bill's forehead and left.

"Bye, John!" he shouted as I reached the landing. "See you next week!"

However, my planned next visit to Bill's became weighed down with preparation work for the upcoming MIDEM Music Festival in Cannes.

The evening I was due to go and see Bill, I was still copying catalogues and checking CDs so I had to ring him and explain that I wouldn't be able to see him until I got back.

"That's fine, darling," he laughed, "I'm really pleased you're so busy. It means you're doing well. Come and see me when you get back and tell me all about it! Cannes! How grand! Have a great time!"

A few days later, Neil rang me on the Pickwick stand to tell me Bill had passed away that morning.

On my return, I visited Bill's mum at the house and asked if I could go upstairs to his bedroom one last time.

"Of course, John, you need to say your goodbyes," she replied.

Alone in his empty room, I sat on the bed and stroked his pillow, apologising for not being there when he'd passed. I imagined his smiling face looking up at me as I stroked his forehead, telling me he understood.

At that point, his tabby cat, Tigger, ran in, jumped on his pillow and started kneading it before settling down for a nap. I stroked him and told him how much Bill had loved him.

When I went back downstairs, I told Mrs Gee about Tigger's grand entrance.

She smiled sadly and said, "Bill's last words were, 'Where's Tigger?'"

"Well, right now, " I replied, "he's fast asleep with his dad."

The service went without a hitch. Many of Bill's friends, including me, got up and chatted about our pal and the hilarious tales of his scrapes and adventures. It would have amused Bill greatly that the only person who broke down as he was talking about 'the great man', was straight. I could hear Bill in my head screeching with laughter.

'Typical!' he'd've said, 'A roomful of queens and one straight guy, and who loses it and blubs like a baby?! We ladies are made of much sterner stuff, darling!'

The cassette I'd put together of Bill's selected songs played perfectly, Bette Midler singing us out beautifully as we emerged into the winter sunshine, tears in everyone's eyes. The day could not have been a more fitting goodbye to an amazingly resilient man and someone I will always remember with love and affection.

We lost Larry in the Spring of 1991, as well as Bayliss's old friend, Alistair, and dear Henners finally gave in and passed away in the October. More funerals, more friends gone before their time.

Sitting in Henners' memorial service, I remembered a wonderful story he'd told me after one of his stays in a local hospice, recuperating from a bout of pneumonia.

He'd been reading Armistead Maupin's Tales of The City when a minor hullabaloo began outside the door. He'd looked up to see Elizabeth Taylor standing in the doorway smiling at him.

"Hello there, honey!" she'd said, walking towards his bed. "I LOVE that book!"

"You could've knocked me down with a feather!" Henners told

me. "She sat on the edge of my bed, held my hand and nattered away with me for at least ten minutes!"

Finally, she'd taken his face in her hands, kissed him on both cheeks and tickled his nose.

"You take care, honey," she'd said, "and be sure to read that whole series of darling Armistead's books. I'll be asking questions about them next time I see ya!"

"Elizabeth Taylor called me honey!" Henners said, roaring with delighted laughter.

"And tickled your nose!" I said.

"AND tickled my nose!"

I also remembered a rather sadder tale of when his partner, Frank, had died a few months earlier and his family had called at their Fulham flat.

Marching through the door with no announcement, nor any acknowledgment that Henners was having lunch in the sitting-room, they'd gone into every room and stripped them of Frank's belongings. Even things he'd bought for Henners during their five years together had been thrown into large bin bags and carried out.

"What did you do?" I asked him.

"Nothing," Henners had replied. "What was the point? I had no legal right to any of it."

This was fifteen years before Civil Partnerships made same-sex couples secure in the eyes of the law. It would have prevented many similar situations happening to bereaved friends of ours who, having just buried the love of their life, were powerless to do anything about their memories being stripped away before their eyes by people who they'd thought were family.

Daniel died in 1992. He'd finally returned for good from America, his mum wanting him back home where she could care for him as his health worsened.

On New Year's Day, he'd rung to wish me a Happy New Year and to tell me he loved me. He had never, would never have used such affectionate terms of endearment before. But, now, knowing that he was dying, he wanted to make sure he saw or spoke to all his friends before he went, to thank them for their friendship.

I went to see him in hospital a few weeks before he died. Again, he was a skeletal remnant of the man I'd known. I tried to engage him in chatting about our times living in his house in Norbury back in 1975, the pick-ups we'd dragged back from various West End clubs, and the deliciously lurid stories of our nights of passion across the landing of his suburban semi, which had filled our mornings after the nights before.

But dementia had overtaken him by then. He seemed to recognise me at first but it soon became obvious he was in his own hallucinatory world, constantly looking over my shoulder and smiling at his dressing-gown hanging on the back of the door and telling me to 'invite him in!'.

Treatments have, of course, improved vastly since then. People we know with AIDS are now living relatively 'normal lives', though taking a variety of medications to keep them healthy and active. They are managing to work, live, socialise, enjoy partnerships, living almost as though, day-to-day, nothing is wrong. We have friends who were diagnosed in the late '80s who are still alive, many of them now drawing their pensions.

What had been 'Dying from AIDS' has become 'Living with AIDS'. But there was a time when my friends and I all wondered if we were, every one of us, bound for an early grave. No-one felt safe. AIDS became the talking point of every social occasion; who had died recently, who had been diagnosed recently, who was worrying about a lump, a bruise, a bad chest; every ailment, no matter how small, became a talking point, a possible beginning of the end.

Every gay man who survived, who remained free of the disease, at some point must have thought, 'There but for the grace of God.' Even unbelievers must have muttered it to themselves, having walked away from yet another funeral, another memorial service, another hospital bed. I certainly did more than once.

Chapter Five

Becoming

Neil and I left London at the end of the '80s, moving to the market town of Wantage in Oxfordshire. We'd grown out of living in London and felt that it was time we bought a house instead of being flat-dwellers forever. Although it would make our journeys into the capital longer, the new M40 extension was in the process of being extended to Birmingham so going back and forth – me to Pickwick each day and Neil for auditions, since he'd left 'No Sex, Please, We're British' - wouldn't be too much of a problem. I had my company car and he had recently bought a new motorbike.

Our Victorian terraced cottage was one of just twelve plonked in a field opposite a convent. The terrace even had its own name, Naldertown, apparently after a local factory owner who had built the cottages for his employees. We amassed six cats (my rescued cat from Dawes Road in 1977, Pudsy, having left this feline coil when he was ten), which patrolled our garden full of hollyhocks, delphiniums, lupins and foxgloves, and settled quickly into our new 'village life'.

I eventually got used to people in the street bidding me a cheery good morning, rather than the eyes-down-don't-make-eye-contact behaviour of Londoners. During my fifteen years living in the capital, I'd got to know an awful lot of people's shoes, travelling to and fro on the Underground. It was the safest place to let your eyes rest. So this new neighbourly friendliness was a surprise, but a pleasant one.

There were plenty of great treks into the hills and outlying villages, ending up with lunch at an old country pub, the perfect end to an excursion when friends and family visited.

It was the first house I'd ever (co-)owned, and for quite a few weeks after we'd moved in I'd stand at the end of the terrace when I got home from work and just look at our new home, 'Honeysuckle

Cottage', quaint but reassuring to this 15-year-long city boy.

My job at Pickwick remained fun and productive, and I rarely thought about my years as a recording artist. That roller-coaster time was part of a past which only occasionally entered my mind. It felt like a lifetime ago, inhabited by someone else with a different plan, different dreams.

However, one afternoon, I was wandering along the corridor towards the photocopier when I noticed the Commercial Director, Dick Speller, coming up the stairs from reception with Maurice Oberstein, Chairman of CBS Records. I hadn't seen Obie since 1980 when I was signed to the label.

As Obie chatted to Dick about something to do with sales forecasts, and Dick was muttering back everso respectfully - "Yes, Mr Oberstein, that's absolutely right Mr. Oberstein, of course Mr Oberstein," - I stopped and waited.

As he got to the landing, Obie looked up and saw me. Throwing his arms out, he shouted "John!" at the top of his voice and ran towards me. Laughing his head off, he picked me up and hugged me, swinging me around and kissing my neck. Dick stood aghast, speechless.

"How are you *doing*?!" Obie cried, gently putting me back on the floor and studying me from head to foot.

"I'm great, Obie!" I replied.

"You look *fantastic*!" He turned to Dick. "Why didn't you *tell* me John Howard worked here? One of my *favourite* people!"

Dick stepped forward, almost bowing said, "Er- well, I'm - er- sorry Mr Oberstein, I-I-I-I had no idea you and John were -"

"Jeez!" Obie cried again, still looking at me and beaming. "This *guy*! You're a very lucky man, Dick! John is *amazing*! Oh man! It's great to see you, John!"

"Well, yes, of course, Mr Oberstein," Dick stammered on. "John is very good at his job but..."

"He is *fantastic*, Dick!" Obie almost yelled at him. "John, it is so good to see you. Please! Come and see me, we can have lunch and catch up on things!"

Dick's mouth actually fell open, he was clearly in shock. Then, giggling nervously and not looking at me, he ushered Obie along the corridor to his office. All the while Obie kept turning around, giving me the thumbs-up and saying,

"John Howard! Jesus, how great!"

About half-an-hour later there was a knock at my door. It was Dick.

"John!" he cried, almost as loudly as Obie had done. "I had no idea you knew Maurice Oberstein!"

"Obie? Yeah. We go back a long way, Dick."

"Obviously! He just told me about your recording career at CBS!"

He pulled up a chair like a reporter about to get a scoop. "Tell me more!"

I laughed at his eager face and recounted my story about being signed to CBS in 1974 to record my debut LP, Kid In A Big World, at Abbey Road, my launch concert at The Purcell Rooms, in fact the whole shebang of my life as an aspiring star. Dick listened, fascinated, shaking his head as my tale unfolded.

When I'd finished, he stood up, exhaled loudly and looked askance at me, "I didn't know about *any* of that, John. I'm *so* sorry!"

"Why would you?"

"But I should have asked!" he replied.

"Why would you?"

With a long glance and another shake of the head, he laughed and said, "Obie -er - Mr Oberstein sends you his love, by the way." He grinned at me like a proud father. "Jesus, John! What a dark horse you are!"

Finally, he left me alone to privately reminisce about years gone, years lost – and to smile about my delightfully unexpected coup.

* * *

One Sunday afternoon, Neil and I were having a few friends around for lunch, when Angus, a successful solicitor we'd known since the early '80s, told us he was considering writing a revue featuring a series of songs and sketches.

"But where would you stage it?" Aston asked, chomping on a crispy piece of radish.

"I've spoken to Roy's Restaurant, and they're happy to put it on!" Angus replied.

Roy's was a popular gay eaterie in Fulham, its mirrored walls very useful for vada'ing potential trade on the tables opposite if you had your back to them. The food was okay, but it was the camp ambience and available men which people went there for.

"But who would be in it?" Aston asked again, choosing a stick of celery to munch on from the cold collation I'd put out as hors d'ouevres.

"We would!" Angus replied, looking around the table.

Neil and I glanced at each other, wondering what we were going to say.

Angus saw the look between us, taking it as his prompt, "Neil! You could help us in the direction side of things!"

"I'll be happy to advise on technique," he replied, "but amateur revues are not something I usually get involved with."

Undaunted by Neil's less than enthusiastic response, Angus strode on, "John! You could play the piano and perform a couple of songs!"

"It *could* be fun!" Aston said, tucking enthusiastically into the Roquefort dip with a bread stick.

"I want to give the proceeds for the show to St Stephen's AIDS ward," Angus told us. "We'll charge, say, ten pounds a head on top of the cost for a meal."

"Will people pay ten pounds to come and see *us*?" Aston asked.

"If they know where the money's going, then yes, they probably will," Neil replied. "I'll help all I can."

Angus's script arrived in the post a couple of weeks later. It actually was very funny with some inventive sketches, the climax of the show being a mime-drag ensemble performance of 'I'm In Love With A Wonderful Guy' from *South Pacific*.

With the kind permission of my former manager's old partner Frank Coachworth, we all got together at his Denmark Street office two evenings a week to rehearse. It was never going to win any awards, but over about a month we honed it into as much of a passable shape as we could.

Neil advised us on timing and delivery of lines, emphasising how things had to be much pacier.

"Untrained actors tend to do everything extremely slowly," he told me over dinner one evening, "in their heads they think it's really snappy and quick, but in fact they're moving and speaking at a snail's pace."

His advice certainly helped. The rest was up to fate and the day.

As it was, the event went very well. It sold out, in fact, much to Roy's delight. I opened the show, sitting at an upright piano dressed in nothing but a pair of torn jeans and a leather waistcoat, performing Cilla Black's 'Love's Just A Broken Heart' and Pet Clark's 'Don't Sleep In The Subway'; the sketches ran as smoothly as could be expected, our many fluffs getting huge laughs from a crowd there to have a good time and give money to a charity dear to everyone's heart.

However, the grand finale was a triumph. It brought the house down. A superbly coquettish Angus, surrounded by five preening, pouting drag queens trilling merrily, "He's in love, he's in love, he's in love, he's in love, he's in love with a wonderful guy!" ended the afternoon with cries for 'More!' and an emotional Angus presenting a sizeable cheque to our guest of honour, St Stephen's Dr Charles Farthing. It was also nice for me to know that our show had benefitted the hospital which had nursed me through my broken back injury so brilliantly over ten years earlier.

Over the next few months, we did a couple more shows at Roy's, each one something of a flawed triumph, each one raising money for St Stephen's. I had to admit, it had been fun being back on stage again, having the chance to perform some of my favourite pop songs at the piano to an enthusiastic audience. It reminded me a little of the years when I'd play to packed crowds in April Ashley's Knightsbridge restaurant in the mid '70s. The difference was that then, restaurant work was my only source of income. Now, it was done purely for enjoyment with friends and a good cause.

* * *

In the Summer of 1989, marketed alongside his latest album, *Flowers In the Dirt* (which had been produced by my old friend Trevor Horn), Pickwick licensed Paul McCartney's latest video, *Put It There*. As a result, several of the Pickwick directors and managers received invitations to Paul's Wembley gig, the culmination of a hugely successful UK tour, his first for ten years.

I hadn't seen Macca on stage since 1975 when he was in the midst of a record-breaking Wings tour. He'd sung hardly any Beatles songs that night except for an acoustic version of 'I've Just Seen A Face' and, for an encore, sitting alone on a stool, he gave a beautiful performance of 'Yesterday' which had everyone in floods of nostalgic tears.

The concert had been a personal triumph for Paul; for what he'd achieved, through dogged hard work against many naysayers' criticisms and sheer persistence since The Beatles had split up. By the mid-'70s, Wings had become one of the biggest concert acts in the world, selling out stadia across America, Paul becoming once again the adored and million-selling pop star he'd been as one of The Beatles.

In complete contrast, McCartney's 1989 concert was as near to a Beatles tribute show as was possible for an actual ex-Beatle. Only a smattering of his solo and Wings material was interwoven with stunningly near-perfect renditions of 'Penny Lane', 'Lady Madonna', 'Can't Buy Me Love', 'Hey Jude', 'I'm Down' and 'Fool On The Hill'.

'The Long and Winding Road' gave us collective goosebumps while a rollicking 'Get Back' had us dancing in the aisles. Other Fabs favourites thrilled the packed stadium; 'Let It Be', 'Back In The USSR', 'Birthday', 'Good Day Sunshine', and 'Drive My Car', all played to Beatles-esque perfection by a fantastic band.

At one point, as they were performing the famous jam session from the closing moments of *Abbey Road*, I closed my eyes; it could have been John, Paul, George and Ringo up there on stage. When they went flawlessly into 'The End', as it had on the original L.P., I actually cried.

Paul was finally acknowledging his distant past, after virtually denying it for the first ten years after The Beatles split. It showed a man at peace with his legacy, loving once more playing the songs which had made him one-half of the most successful songwriting partnership in pop music and a member of the greatest pop group in history.

While I still wished he'd have given us more stuff from *Ram*, *McCartney*, *Band On The Run*, *Red Rose Speedway* and *Venus & Mars*, as he had that night in '75, I silently congratulated him on successfully negotiating what must have been a difficult career transition over twenty years.

* * *

A few weeks later, as Al had insisted, I presented Pickwick's Autumn

Releases at the company's annual conference for the first time. The day before, I'd returned from a holiday in Cyprus where, on a whim, I'd had something of a makeover. I'd shaved off my moustache, had my hair cut and styled into a spiky mass of gel and replaced my Marge Proops glasses with round tortoiseshell jobbies. I looked like an extremely tanned Pet Shop Boy.

My 'audience' was made up of the chief buyers from all the major music stores, Woolworth's, HMV, W.H. Smith's, Our Price, Menzies, Virgin. The company's sales team and staff were also there, as were several of my record company contacts to see the albums they'd licensed to us being given their springboard to success.

This was Pickwick's strongest release to date. It featured new compilations I'd put together by Elton John, Culture Club (with input from my old friend and the band's former producer, Steve Levine), a *Best of Lindisfarne* and a personal favourite of mine, *Diary - The Best of China Crisis*. There was also a second Madness collection, *It's Madness Too*, helmed once again by the group themselves, and a reissue of The RPO's *Orchestral Tubular Bells*.

For the older market we had Elaine Paige, Connie Francis, *Monty Python Live at Drury Lane* and the always big-seller, James Last. There were two wonderful new Pickwick-owned albums I'd commissioned from the RPO of specially-written arrangements of Les Miserables and Miss Saigon, arranged and conducted by an old friend of Neil's, Tony Britten, plus the second Andrew Lloyd Webber Collection, *The Magic Of ...* , featuring Phantom of The Opera star, David Willetts and Stephanie Lawrence making her second appearance on a Pickwick new recording.

As I walked on stage to begin my presentation, I heard a slight murmur spreading around the room. Very few people had seen my new spiky-haired clean-shaven look. Even more shocking, I was wearing a very sharp dress suit, topped off by a red bow tie and a bright pink hankie cascading out of my top pocket. I'd never worn a suit to work. Ever.

In the front row were our new Chairman and Managing Director Ivor Schlosberg, who'd taken over from Monty Lewis after his recent retirement, and next to him, Gary Le Count, no doubt already wondering if he'd made a huge mistake agreeing to Al's suggestion of handing over his treasured baton to this 'newbie'.

I took a deep breath. I felt many in the audience doing the same.

"Good afternoon," I said, then looked down at Gary and smiled. "This is the first time I've presented the Autumn releases at one of our conferences so, last night, I decided to ask Gary Le Count, who's done lots of these, for some advice."

Gary shuffled in his seat and tried a friendly grin. I smiled back at him, "'Be yourself, John,' he'd replied, 'Just be yourself'. So, for the run-through this morning I arrived in… drop earrings, a little low-cut black sequinned number and sling-backs."

The place *erupted*. A storm of laughter burst around the room. I even heard screams from somewhere. I stood smiling out into the darkness and let the applause subside.

"But you'll have to use your imaginations," I continued, waving my hand over my gorgeous suit. "I decided to dress down for you after all."

After that, I could do no wrong. There are times when an audience wants you to succeed and you are carried along on their wave of sheer pleasure, even of love. This was one of them. When I finished forty-five minutes later, a roar went up and filled the room, people were stamping their feet. The front row of directors were standing and cheering. Gary actually whistled.

"You were fucking amazing!" Al shouted at me during the buffet lunch afterwards. "I knew you'd be good, but bloody hell, John!"

"Thanks for the opportunity, Al. I enjoyed it."

"We fucking loved it, John! The chief buyer of Woolworth's was gobsmacked!"

"In a good way, I hope!"

"Fuck, yeah! He's doubled his order!"

Several more people came up to congratulate me, one of them "amazed that you performed up there like a *professional*!".

I smiled wryly and gracefully accepted the compliment. The thought, 'If you only knew... ' did slip into my mind for a moment.

As I was thanking my new admirers for their kind words, an expensively-suited chap I didn't recognise approached me, beaming away.

"Hello, John, I'm Richard Rowe, Director of Business Affairs at CBS Records," he said, shaking my hand. "That was fantastic!"

"Thank you, Richard!"

"You should be on the stage, my friend!"

"I used to be – when I was signed to CBS Records."

He grinned.

"Ah! It *is* you! I did wonder. The spiky hair and suntan threw me! You've changed a little since your days as the label's Next Big Thing!"

I thoroughly enjoyed the burst of murmurs and awed whispers from my Pickwick colleagues who were clearly aghast. It was yet another Dick Speller/Maurice Oberstein moment. I almost purred.

The name Rowe was swimming around my head, then the penny dropped, "Richard Rowe! Are you any relation to Dick Rowe?"

"You knew my dad?"

"I met Dick in the early '80s. Lovely man. He introduced himself as 'I'm the man who turned down The Beatles'!"

Richard laughed.

"Yeah, dad always used to get that in first, before anyone else mentioned it! But he did sign The Stones, The Zombies, Van Morrison, The Moody Blues and The Small Faces!"

"So he's forgiven!"

Richard laughed.

"I would imagine so!"

He shook my hand again. "Well, congratulations, John. You made today a lot more fun than I was expecting! I wish my dad could have been here, he'd've loved it."

After that, my reputation at Pickwick seemed to go up several gears. I was no longer 'the backroom boy' who quietly got on with compiling and clearing monthly releases. I had become a personality recognised by everyone at the company. For quite a few weeks, people I'd only seen walking past me in the corridor now stopped, shook my hand and congratulated me.

I even got a new office – with a window! That was indeed a coup. Only the directors had offices with windows. In 1990, when the company was floated on the stock exchange, I was given a large gift of shares, 'in recognition of what you do here, John!', Ivor told me. For the first time in my life, my bank balance went above £20,000.

* * *

One afternoon in late '91, Tracey rang me to ask if I could give her a lift into London. She was auditioning for a part in the recasting of the musical *Buddy*, but Keff was stuck at the studio working on a children's album for Elaine Saffer.

Based on the life of Buddy Holly, the musical had been playing to packed houses at London's Victoria Palace Theatre for two years and Tracey was going for the part of Buddy's wife's best friend.

Happily, her call came when I was taking a couple of days off work, preparing the house for a visit from my sister, Sue, who was due for her annual stay at Chez Howard-France. I'd had enough of cleaning and hoovering the place and needed a break from housework so was pleased to oblige.

As we sat in the car singing Holly songs, Tracey suddenly said, "John! You'd be great as Buddy!"

I laughed and carried on belting out 'Peggy Sue'.

"I'm serious, John! Why don't you crash the auditions?"

I had no idea what she meant.

"Anyone can audition, John!" she said.

"But I don't have an agent!"

"Use Neil's!" she countered.

"You're crazy!" I said, parked the car and walked her to the stage door.

"Come in with me, John," Tracey begged. "I want you to be there when I do my audition!"

She dragged me through the door and, giggling like ingénues, we ran down the stairs to a small basement room where auditionees were nervously awaiting their call.

As we sat with all these young, wide-eyed kids, all going over their lines and occasionally breaking into a Buddy song, complete with perfectly rendered harmonies, I was reminded of the famous old Hollywood line, "Let's do the show right here!". It all felt very young and starry-eyed, a mass of ambitions were bouncing off the walls.

As Tracey and I sat and enjoyed the atmosphere, she suddenly told them, her voice rising with excitement, "John's thinking of crashing the audition!"

Their faces turned to me in wonder, lighting up as they gathered around me.

"Oh wow! That's so *brave*!" one of the guys said.

"Fabulous! You look a bit like Buddy too!" said one of the girls, dressed in a '50s dirndl skirt and bobbysox.

"Can you sing?" a blonde, crewcut guy asked.

"Sing?!" Tracey said, bursting into laughter. "This guy can sing *anyone* off any stage *anywhere*!"

Her eyes burned into me. She bit her nails furiously, willing me to say, "Okay!"

"Okay!" I said.

Tracey grabbed my arm and shrieked.

"You'll *do* it?!"

"Yeah. I'll do it."

I was instantly surrounded by a roomful of yelling kids. I felt (and was) twenty years older than them, but, at the same time, that youthful tingle of expectation began stirring once more. Damn it.

Ten minutes later, I was standing on stage with just one spotlight on me, and a dimmer one lighting up the pianist sitting behind me.

"So, what do you want to sing?" a chap asked me from the back of the stalls.

"'Raining In My Heart'," I replied and nodded at the pianist who began the intro.

As I trilled one of Buddy's loveliest songs, I was aware of three people standing up together and walking slowly down the aisle towards the stage. They stood and watched me, occasionally nodding at one another.

'Bloody hell!' I thought.

When I'd finished, I received a rather joyous ripple of applause from them.

"That was *great*, John!" one of them, who introduced himself as Paul said. "Will you read something for us?"

"Sure!" I replied, knowing this would be my end.

And, as I knew I would, I read terribly, trying an American accent and failing miserably. I felt their interest wane with each dreadfully delivered line.

"Okay!" Paul said brightly when I'd ground to a halt. "Do you play an instrument, John?"

"The piano!" I replied.

He signalled to the accompanist who got up and vacated his seat for me. "Play and sing whatever you fancy, John."

As they all settled in the front row, I gave them a rendition of

'Star Through My Window', a song I'd written in 1976 which I'd not performed for fifteen years. It's a hackneyed phrase, but you could have heard a pin drop.

When I'd finished, all four of them stood and applauded. I even heard a 'Bravo!'.

"Well, John," Paul said, still clapping, "you may not be able to act, but you can certainly hold an audience with your music. Well done, and thank for coming along today. I really enjoyed it. Now, don't let that talent go to waste!"

On the way home, Tracey told me that 'Paul' had been Paul Elliott, the producer of 'Buddy' and that one of the other chaps in his group had been Rob Bettinson, the show's director.

"Oh *John*!" she cried out, "They *loved* you! You have to make another record! You *have* to!"

The following day, Neil's agent, Barrie Stacey rang me. "Daughter!" he cried, "I'm told you wowed Mr Elliott himself at your audition for 'Buddy'!"

He left a gentle pause before adding, "You didn't get the job, dear, but I've booked you for an evening with my photographer, Tony. He's great! Let's get a portfolio done for you. You never know what may come up! Tomorrow at 8 p.m."

He gave me the address of the photographer's studio in the West End and rang off with his usual, "'Bye, daughter!"

The photo session went well. Tony took lots of pics of me in various outfits and he had a great way of relaxing his models, chatting and joking as I struck various poses. It felt like the old days posing for Dezo Hoffman shortly after I'd arrived in London and secured a management deal with Stuart Reid.

"You're good at this!" Tony said as he snapped away. "You've done this before, yes?"

"Oh yes," I replied, "a long time ago though."

"Like riding a bike, though isn't it? The knack for loving a camera never leaves you. It's inbuilt. Some have it, some don't."

A couple of days later, as I was studying Tony's photos and choosing a couple to send to Barrie, Keff rang me, "Tracey said you were fab in your 'Buddy' audition! I think it's about time you and I recorded a couple of tracks together! Don't you?"

* * *

As I had very little new material written, I decided to do new versions of 'Kid In A Big World' and 'Family Man' and a song I'd almost finished in the early '80s, 'Blue Days', which I completed one evening at home the day before the sessions began.

Using Pickwick's studio, Keff created three fabulous backing tracks for me, Tracey sang great backing vocals and we had my lead vocals done and the tracks mixed in a couple of evenings. 'Kid In A Big World' had been given a very '90s trance vibe and 'Family Man' had turned into a Calypso-style reggae number, with a middle section featuring me and Tracey rapping a conversation together. But I was particularly taken with 'Blue Days', which now had a kind of Phil Collins feel. It actually sounded like a hit to me, something I hadn't felt since I'd recorded 'Nothing More To Say' with Pete Bite in 1984, which had turned out to be my final 45.

Although I'd retired from recording shortly after its release to concentrate on a new, much more rewarding career in the music business, that old devil called thrill of being in a studio again, recording my own songs, listening to the mixes with my producer and imagining them on the radio, had returned. No matter how much I told myself 'those days are over,' they kept coming back to reclaim my soul.

As Keff and I left the studio and bid each other a satisfied good evening, he asked me, "What are you going to do with the tracks?"

"I have no idea," I replied, "My A & R contacts these days are zilch. But I really enjoyed the session. Thanks, Keff!"

"Let me have a think," he said, getting into his car. "I may have a couple of people I can play them to. I think they'd be impressed."

As he drove away, I had no idea just who 'they' might be. I put the cassette on in the car as I made my way home and knew we'd done a good job. But was that enough? Probably not. It didn't matter, I'd had a great time anyway. I didn't think about it again...not for several months.

* * *

One of Pickwick's more important licensors was Disney, with whom the company had an exclusive deal to release all their soundtrack albums. Disney constantly wanted their older soundtracks repackaged and repromoted on the back of a movie's re-release, or if they had a new film on the way, Pickwick was expected to pull out all the stops to get the accompanying soundtrack album in every major retail outlet. This meant that I liaised regularly with Disney's product manager, Johnson Pierre. While Disney had a reputation amongst the public for being adorable and cuddly, I very quickly learnt that as a licensor it was a strict stickler for tradition.

First of all, Disney had extremely set ideas as to how its characters were presented. Any deviation from these was met with stern rebukes and slapped hands. I was given a set of instructions and diagrams as to how the various Disney characters *must* be portrayed on record sleeves and promotional material which I passed onto Pickwick's album design and marketing departments.

Mickey Mouse, for example, had to always be drawn with ears which were perfect circles, never at an angle, never sideways on, no matter where his face was directed. If any of our designers strayed just a tad from the instruction book, their beautifully illustrated sleeves were sent back with a stern "No!" scribbled over them, the offending bits of the drawings circled in red felt pen.

Meetings at the Disney offices in Soho Square were even more surreal. Several blow-up Disney characters, which smiled at you in that creepily unyielding, wide-eyed way and smelt of beach balls, sat at the boardroom table. I was often tempted to turn to Mickey in mid-discussion and ask him what he thought. There were also rumours – gossiped about but never proven - that every room was bugged and conversations reported back to senior management.

In the Spring of '92, Neil and I were invited to the opening of the EuroDisney theme park in Paris. We arrived on a very cold and rainy April night, falling asleep covered by Mickey Mouse bedlinen in the Disney-themed hotel room. I woke up during the night to go to the bathroom, spooked by Mickey's staring eyes following me from the wallpaper.

The next morning, while we ate breakfast in the vast dining-room, we were constantly interrupted by the arrival of various Disney characters, Mickey, Minnie, Goofy and pals, who would nod silently and stare at us from unmoving huge eyes, insisting on shaking our hands. Their tiny fingers inside huge spongey gloves gave me the creeps.

"Oh no!" I'd moan, whenever I spotted these creatures from Disney Hell approaching our table, "It's the monsters with the glovey-hands again!"

During the VIP opening day, Snow White's float broke down, bringing the whole parade to a standstill. It meant that she and the seven dwarves, along with the rest of the Disney creatures behind them, had to dance in zero temperatures and biting winds for over half an hour. Opening a theme park in freezing cold Paris was beginning to look like a very bad idea.

Frantic men in bright yellow boilersuits, carrying Mickey Mouse walkie-talkies, nattered manically to each other as to what they could do to fix it. I heard at least one of them mumble "Merde!" as he passed us by looking anything but wide-eyed and smiling.

Snow White looked more like Snow Blue by the time the float finally, with a jolt, sprang into action, sending the dwarves and various woodland animals almost crashing off it into the street.

Later in the afternoon, we were almost lost forever in Peter Pan's underground cavern. Hundreds of us had traipsed down endless corridors to what felt like miles below ground, and patiently waited for our gondolas to appear out of a cave at the banks of a twinkly-lit river. However, half an hour later, nothing had arrived. As patience grew thin and the air grew thick with worry, we were finally told to "Leave the area! Leave Immediately!" by the walkie-talkie men, who led us back through the corridors, rushing around shouting at us and each other.

Daylight never looked so good as we finally emerged into the pouring rain. Peter Pan may have never aged, but I'd certainly put on a couple of years down there.

"Did you see all the emergency exits as we walked back up the slope?" Neil said. "Why couldn't they let us out through one of those?"

"Apparently, no-one knew how to open them," a chap next to us said. "Talk about Chaos in Disneyland!"

Chapter Six

A Quiet Success

"John?!"

It was an early Summer evening in 1992 and Tracey was on the phone, sounding a little overwrought.

"John?!!" she shouted even louder, on the verge of hysterical.

"Yes, Tracey," I replied, wondering what had happened but trying to radiate calmness in a potential crisis. "Are you okay?"

"I can't believe what I'm about to tell you!"

The words poured out of her mouth in a torrent, as though she'd had them locked up in there for weeks. "Des O'Connor's just spoken to Keff and he's going to call you in ten minutes!"

"Why?"

"He wants to record 'Blue Days'! Oh, *John*!"

She was screaming now.

"Blue Days? How did he hear it?"

"Keff played it to him! He *really* loved it, John! Des played it to his producer, Nigel Wright, and he loves it too!!"

"Right!" was all I could manage. It sounded too good to be true.

"Oh *John*! I can't be*lieve* it!" Tracey bounded on. "I *knew* that song was a hit! Okay! Des is going to call you as soon as I get off the phone!"

Then the line went dead.

"Was that Tracey?" Neil asked, as he came down from packing for his trip to Jersey. (He was appearing in Summer Season in the comedy farce, Don't Dress For Dinner, having worked with John Inman there the year before in Bedside Manners).

"Yes, it was. She said Des O'Connor's going to call me."

"THE Des O'Connor?"

"Yeah. Apparently, he wants to record 'Blue Days'."

Five minutes later, the phone rang. Sure enough, British TV's most successful chat show host was on the line. His familiar easy-going voice was telling me how much he loved 'Blue Days', and that he wanted to record it for his new album.

Now I yelled, albeit internally.

"Keff played me the song, John," Des continued, "and I flipped. It's beautiful! It made my producer cry!"

"Wow, Des!." I said and, realising that now I was gushing but what the hell, told Des I would be delighted if he recorded it.

"Excellent! Thank you, John! Look, come to the recording of my next show. You can sit with Jodie and Tracey and then we can have a chat in the Green Room afterwards. We've got Diana Ross, Cilla Black and Robin Williams this week; it's going to be a great evening!"

* * *

Des was Mr Professional. He came out on set before the show and chatted to the audience like they were old friends. Some of his stories were very funny and I was impressed by how relaxed he seemed, giving us a run-down of who was on the show and warning us that, "it's going to be a long evening, folks, so get your loo breaks in now or forever hold your 'peace'!"

Over the next three and half hours, we watched Des head towards his chat show sofa several times in various outfits, natter to the audience about who was coming up, each time with a different list of guests. Then, after another longer break and yet another outfit, with touch-up powdering by the always-on-hand make-up artist, he introduced Robin Williams.

For the next twenty minutes Des didn't so much interview Robin, it was more a case of him sitting smiling and laughing as Williams performed an utterly breathless and brilliant one-man show.

As Des finally thanked Williams and they left the set, the warm-up guy, Ted Robbins, took over and did his own stand-up act, while crew and technicians wandered around him, getting everything ready for the next guest. I was amazed at how seamless it all was.

Des then joined Ted and indulged in some 'unrehearsed' banter before the floor manager signalled that everything was ready. Ted left the set, Des turned to his autocue, smiled 'for the audience at home' and introduced Diana Ross. With unnecessary encouragement from the floor manager who lifted his arms and clapped, we all cheered to the rafters.

Diana looked sublime. Tiny and glamorous in a sequinned tight-fitting purple gown, she mimed perfectly to her latest single, 'One Shining Moment'. As we all applauded like mad, an over-enthusiastic fan who'd been standing behind the barrier holding out his arms in supplication to his goddess all through the song, broke through and, crying his eyes out, rushed towards his idol.

"I love you Diana!," he shouted, arms outstretched, running towards the tiny star.

"I love you too, darlin'!" she replied, neatly backing away as two burly bodyguards pulled the weeping boy into the wings.

Undaunted, she beamed at the audience, received a loud cheer from us all and went straight into her very first hit with The Supremes, 'Where Did Our Love Go'.

Then, with a final wave, she wandered over to the sofa where Des was waiting. This time, the interview went to plan, she answered every question with charm and insight, making us laugh a few times at her memories of the early days of Motown. She told us, with no self-conscious modesty, that 'One Shining Moment' was her forty-eighth British hit.

"Here's to Number Fifty!" Des said, getting a huge round of applause from a studio-full of Diana's adoring fans.

One final beaming smile, and it was over.

"Fantastic!" I said to Jodie. "Des is so good!"

"I love him to bits," she replied, squeezing my arm.

After another warm-up set by Ted Robbins, Des appeared once again in a different suit and introduced Cilla Black.

She was my pop hero as a child but I hadn't taken to her more recent variety TV role as queen of game shows, such as Blind Date. However, the audience clearly loved her and applauded enthusiastically as she sat down on the sofa and beamed at Des. For the next fifteen minutes, they chatted like old pals about their concurrent careers as pop hitmakers in the '60s and TV show hosts in the '80s and '90s. Cilla was her usual witty and warm self, talking about The Cavern, Brian Epstein and The Beatles, stories she must have told hundreds of times but managing to make them still sound fresh and amusing.

I was struck by how much stronger her Liverpudlian accent was compared to how she'd spoken when interviewed on pop shows like Ready, Steady, Go! in the '60s. Back then, she'd sounded more 'posh Northern', but for her new career as leading lady of light entertainment she'd clearly discovered how an exaggerated Scouse accent appealed to her fans.

Des then told us that they were going to sing a duet, and thanked Cilla for being his guest. The floor manager appeared, once more raising his arms to encourage us to applaud, while Des and Cilla stood and kissed cheeks.

Cilla's husband Bobby came on set, chatting briefly to Des before leading Cilla off into the wings. Des went off in the opposite direction with one of the technicians, deep in conversation about something.

I turned to Jodie.

"When are they doing the duet?" I asked her.

"They filmed it this afternoon," she replied.

I must have looked very disappointed as Jodie squeezed my hand and smiled apologetically.

"Ah John! Bless you! Nothing is ever filmed in sequence," she told me. "That's why Des has to change suits so much, he's actually filming about four shows tonight, into which musical numbers filmed on different days will be slotted and his introductions edited in to fit the guests appearing on that show."

"But Diana did her chat *and* the songs tonight."

"Yes, that's unusual. It obviously fitted in with her schedule, but most artists like to perform their songs in the afternoon before the audience has arrived, then they can re-do the number if something goes wrong."

"God! Doesn't Des ever get confused and wear the wrong suit?"

Jodie laughed, "He has a brilliant team of floor managers and assistants who keep him up to date with who he's 'introducing' next and what to change into. I think he's wonderful. Such a pro!"

As the theatre emptied, Jodie grabbed hold of my hand and led Tracey and me along various corridors towards the Green Room.

"How long have you known Des?" I asked her as we walked along, trying not to pry but dying to know the answer.

Jodie and Tracey flashed a look at each other and giggled.

"Oh John, you're very sweet," Jodie said, cuddling up to me. "It's still not public knowledge but... I met Des last Christmas when I played Cinderella in his panto. I knew we'd clicked as soon as we were introduced. You just know, right?"

"When are you making it official?"

"The press are already sniffing around, so we're going to have to 'come out' soon. Especially now we're living together."

She searched my face for a reaction but, before I could respond, said, "I know there's a big age difference between us, but, John, he's so young at heart! We're even writing songs together!"

"A partnership made in heaven!" Tracey chipped in, beaming at us both. "And now he's recording *your* song, John!"

She and Jodie grabbed each other's arms and shouted "Seestah!" in unison.

"Oh John, I am so pleased for you!" Jodie said as we reached the door to the Green Room.

Des was standing in the middle of a small group of guests telling them a story which had clearly amused them. He looked smaller and thinner than he had on set, and I remembered how Stuart once told me that a successful performer always looked younger and physically bigger on stage, good lighting and the sense they're stars in our midst affecting how we see them.

When he spotted us, Des waved and hurried over, hugging Jodie and greeting Tracey with a blown kiss.

"I am so excited about recording your song, John!" he told me, shaking my hand. "I think it could be a hit! Don't you think so, Nigel?"

A burly, bearded chap stepped forward and shook my hand. "Nigel Wright, John. Good to meet you. Lovely song!"

"Thanks Nigel, " I replied. "You also produce Andrew Lloyd-Webber's albums, don't you?" I asked him.

Nigel cocked his head on one side, "Ah! Not only a great songwriter but knows his music stuff too!"

"John works in the music business!" Jodie said, bigging me up like an agent. "He knows so much about... !" She laughed, "so much!"

"Then we should talk," Nigel said, nodded to us all and moved off to chat to some other guests.

A couple of months later, Des rang to invite me to his house in Buckinghamshire, saying he wanted to play me his new album, *Portrait*, which featured his recording of 'Blue Days'.

It was only a twenty minute drive from Wantage and, as I pulled up in the lane outside Des's lovely home, a large automatic gate opened and Jodie's voice on the intercom said, "Drive in and park next to my car, John!"

As I stepped out of the car, I took in what was a truly beautiful house. Surrounded by a large flourishing garden and hilly woodland it was completely private, more like a country estate than a house five minutes off the M40. Jodie came out of the front door, beaming at me and hugging me.

"What a beautiful house!" I said, looking around me.

"Yeah, it is," Jodie replied, totally at ease in such grand surroundings, a sense that she'd finally found her place emanating from her like a calm aura.

She offered to show me around the grounds and led me through the gorgeous garden, past a 1920s style conservatory packed with hanging plants and exquisite furniture, finally to an invitingly spotless swimming pool to the side of the house where, Jodie told me, guests regularly gathered for family barbecues and parties.

"We have great parties here, John," she told me. "Lots of fun people, music and showbusiness friends of Des's and mine come along. We eat fabulous food and then always end the evening with a singalong in the music room. You and Neil will have to come over."

We made our way back to the house and into the music room, where a white baby grand piano sat on a raised platform. As I was admiring it, Des suddenly appeared through the door.

"You'll have to come over and play for us, John!" he cried, rushing over to shake my hand. "Maybe you could play us a couple of your new numbers – I'm always looking for great songs!"

He winked at me and went over to the hi-fi, picking up a CD and putting it into the machine. Above his head was a beautiful 1950s red guitar hanging on the wall, shining in the spotlight directed at it. Des saw me looking at it.

"That was Buddy Holly's guitar, John!" he said. "Buddy gave it to me after we'd done a UK tour together in 1958."

Also on the wall were several cartoons of Des, Bruce Forsyth and Jimmy Tarbuck playing golf, and a framed photo of Des with Morecambe and Wise. I remembered how Eric used to send Des up on the duo's popular '70s TV show each week. As if reading my mind, Des laughed. "Deaf O'Connor, Eric used to call me. 'Des For Desperate'. He loved sending me up!"

"Didn't you mind?" I asked him.

"Mind? Of course not. Every time I appeared on Morecambe & Wise my record sales went up the following week!"

He pressed play on the hi-fi and sat opposite me and Jodie, smiling at me as the first track on his album, 'Portrait of My Love' began. I recognised it as the song Matt Monro had had a big hit with it in the '60s, but Nigel Wright had given it a completely modern feel. Synths and drum machines created a perfectly produced '90s digital expanse. For all the world it could have been the intro to a Whitney Houston record. Only Des's warm crooning style kept it firmly where his fans would still appreciate it and buy the record. This guy knew his market well, and tailored his delivery accordingly.

When 'Blue Days' came on, Des beamed at me and watched for my reaction. I could also feel Jodie's eyes on me. The two of them glanced at each other and blinked affectionately.

I loved what Des and Nigel had done with my song, it rang around the room and actually sent shivers down my spine. It was my first cover by a big name! I kept my emotions in check – just. When it had finished, Des pressed pause on the remote, his face eager for my response.

"What do you think, John?"

"I love it, Des!" I replied. "It sounds like a hit to me!"

"Me too, John," Des replied. "And Sony agree with us. 'Blue Days' is the first single!"

"This could be the break you've always needed, John," Jodie said to me.

"Everybody needs a break," Des said, and we continued to listen to the rest of what was a truly lovely album.

'Blue Days' and *Portrait* were released in November. Des performed the single on his chat show and during his interview with

Neil Diamond when he'd presented the American superstar with a gold disc for his latest album, Diamond returned the favour by giving Des his own gold disc, "for sales of over 100,000 copies of *Portrait!*".

Des promoted 'Blue Days' like mad, appearing on several TV and radio programmes, always giving me a namecheck as he chatted about the song. It entered the Top 100 at No.95 while *Portrait* came in at No.62 the same week.

"Christ!" I thought, as I watched it slowly but steadily climbing the chart. "This might just be it!"

The single rested at No.76 for two weeks, then, just as I was hoping it might possibly be my first Top 75 song… it fell to No.80. Within a couple of weeks it had dropped out of the charts. It was the nearest I came to a hit single, albeit as the songwriter. However, I did have a song on a Gold Selling hit album!

* * *

Around the time 'Blue Days' was threatening to break into the Top 75, Gordon Lorenz asked me to write the title songs for the new Dave Willetts and Stephanie Lawrence albums, which he was producing for Pickwick.

On condition that Gordon didn't tell either artist who had written the song until they'd heard it – not wanting to lay any pressure on them to 'like' a song written by their A & R manager - I wrote 'Stages of Love' for Dave, and for Stephanie, 'Footlights'.

Happily, a couple of weeks later, Gordon told me they both loved the songs, so I gave him permission to reveal the songwriter's identity.

Dave invited me to the opening night of his *Stages of Love* tour at the Birmingham Symphony Hall. He put on a great show, the audience being mainly female fans of his successful lead roles in *Les Miserables* and *Phantom of The Opera* who happily waved Dave Willetts memorabilia above their heads throughout the two-hour concert.

Of course, the highlight of the show for me had been when Dave sang 'Stages of Love'. Not knowing the song as well as his usual repertoire, he'd had the lyrics taped on the floor at the foot of his stool, something which Elvis had done during his later Las Vegas shows. It didn't spoil Dave's performance, which was exquisite, and I allowed myself a tiny gulp-back of tears as the audience stood and cheered when he'd finished the song.

At the after-show party, Dave took me aside and said, "You're a little tinker, Mr Howard!"

I laughed innocently and looked faux-puzzled.

"I didn't know you wrote great songs as well!" he continued, twinkling at me and patting me on the back. "Well done, my son!"

"I really enjoyed hearing you sing it tonight, Dave," I replied.

"And I enjoyed singing it! Thank you, John! And judging from the audience's reaction tonight, it's going to stay in my setlist for some time!"

* * *

In August '92, the annual Pickwick Sales Conference once again took place. Each year, since my first – and now infamous - presentation in 1989, I'd tried to better the previous one, incorporating humour *and* product knowledge into the proceedings. There was always a tinge of camp, of course, gently sending up guys from the sales team with naughty innuendo or, during one year's presentation, doing a drag version of a Holistics Exercise expert, whose own presentation of her video the day before in a skimpy black leotard had caused several male collars – and no doubt other bits of clothing - to need adjusting.

I knew that as well as showing off innate knowledge of your product, if you could make your audience laugh they would remember the new album releases that much better.

Presenting Autumn Releases at Pickwick Conference

For the latest one, I had an idea which I thought might possibly backfire. So, for guidance *and* security, I explained to Ivor Schlosberg that it would be a skit on Julian Clary's current TV series *Sticky Moments*, a mock game show where Julian, dressed in ever more outrageous costumes, sent up the contestants mercilessly, much to the delight of the studio audience – and the contestants.

"Go for it, John!" Ivor told me without hesitation. "There are no barriers, no boundaries. I want you to bring the house down! You've given us some tremendous releases this year, but we've paid big advances for them. We *have* to sell a lot of albums this Autumn! Knock 'em dead!"

So, there I was, standing on stage before a full house of the chief buyers of the biggest music chain stores in the UK, made-up to the nines with glitter and rouge on my cheeks, wearing a pink bikini top, very tight-fitting lycra pants and a yellow sequinned jacket with black feather collar and cuffs. Knee-length leather boots finished off the ensemble as I paraded about with clipboard in hand as, one by one, various hapless sales guys were called on stage to take part in my question and answer session.

The questions, while based on the albums we were releasing that Autumn, also included salacious nudges of rumours and gossip about the 'guest' sales guys. They stood blushing up as tales of past drunken encounters with female colleagues, which the girls had delightedly told me about, were bandied around the room to cheers and laughter from their peers and colleagues. It verged on the cruel but the guys all took it in good humour.

I doled out 'Naughty Slaps' when a panel member got an album fact wrong, or a kiss on the cheek for those who got the right answer. While seemingly just camp fun, it rammed home important information for the gathered salesforce and chief buyers, helping minds to be made up about the size of orders for their stores.

I finished the afternoon with a singalong of Abba's 'So Long', instructing everyone in the room to stand back-to-back with their neighbour, a la Agnetha and Frida, and "Do The Abba!". It ensured that our anticipated top-seller that Autumn, *Abba – The Love Songs*, would be the last thing the chief buyers would remember.

As the room applauded my risky but successful presentation, a voice in my head said,

"This will be the last one."

***

In January 1993, I was informed by Ivor that I had a new boss. After I'd been more or less in charge of the music department for the past four years, out of the blue Malcolm Simpkins, the company's Marketing Manager, was made Head of Music.

The decision caused several raised eyebrows, not only from my Pickwick colleagues but also amongst our licensors.

"What does Malcolm know about licensing?" my contact at Sony asked me over lunch.

"*That* is the 50,000 dollar question," I replied as diplomatically as I could.

However, we both knew the answer.

To add insult to injury, I was told that Malcolm would be taking my place at MIDEM at the end of the month, Ivor apparently needing someone 'more suited to business meetings this time'.

"Ivor and I expect you to furnish me with all the information I'll need while I'm there," Malcolm told me in our now-daily music meeting. "To ensure a successful MIDEM."

"Successful for whom?" I asked him.

"I could give you a written warning for that!" he said, flushing up.

"But you won't, Malcolm," I replied. "You need me too much."

The day Ivor and Malcolm left for Cannes, I got a phone call from Judy Legg. She ran a successful third-party licensing consultancy, representing independent repertoire owners, which, since I'd been commissioning several new recordings to add to our growing catalogue, now included Pickwick.

"Did you know that MCA's looking for a new Head of Special Projects?" she asked me.

I didn't.

"Steve's moving on to Polygram," she explained, "so MCA needs a good guy to take his place – someone like *you*! I've put your name forward for the job. I hope you don't mind?"

"Not at all, Judy!" I replied. "Thank you! The timing couldn't be better!"

"Thought that may be the case," she said, chuckling. "I'd heard Malcolm was going to MIDEM instead of you. How ridiculous is that?! Anyway, Jeff Golembo, MCA's Deputy Managing Director, is interviewing all this week; can you get to him by four o'clock tomorrow?"

MCA was situated at 100 Piccadilly, the Hyde Park end. It was a beautiful white Georgian building with stories that the ghost of Nelson's lover, Lady Hamilton, who had lived there, was often seen walking up and down the grand sweeping staircases.

It had also apparently inspired Bram Stoker, the author of *Dracula*, who, as he'd strolled by each morning, imagined that the grand four-storey building was the vampire's residence.

Jeff Golembo was an extremely easy-going and genial South African guy. With his feet up on his desk, a cricket match silently progressing on TV, he listened as I told him about my life and career in a nutshell.

"Well, John!" he said. "You're obviously very knowledgeable. But I need someone who's going to exploit our catalogue. It needs to be out there and it isn't!"

"I'd *love* to get my hands on your catalogue!" I told him. "MCA owns some amazing stuff which isn't being used at all."

"I *know!*"

Jeff suddenly took his feet of the desk and sat up.

"Licensing our catalogue to third parties is great," he said, "it brings in revenue, but... "

"But," I politely interrupted, "you should be releasing your *own* albums, exploiting the catalogue with great MCA compilations. I'd be very happy to put them together, getting your fabulous legacy out there!"

"Absolutely, John!" Jeff laughed out loud and clapped his hands. "Christ! You're like a breath of fresh air!"

When I got home that evening, Jeff rang to tell me I had the job if I wanted it. I couldn't wait to give Malcolm the good news when he returned from MIDEM a few days later.

The next morning, Malcolm rang me. At first I thought he must have heard my news on the grapevine, but he was obviously in the dark about that. As he chatted happily about being in Cannes, about the fabulous weather they were having and what a great hotel Ivor had booked them into, he sounded extremely pleased with himself. I was tempted to burst his balloon with my news but decided to keep that moment for his return.

"It's really fantastic here, John! I've been to several meetings with Ivor already!"

He sounded like a little boy thrilled at meeting Santa.

"He introduced me to various CEO's of international companies," he breathlessly went on, "and I think I went down *very* well with them. *But*, he's made it clear that *I* have to now initiate some meetings myself for the rest of the week."

I didn't reply, imagining him waiting for my reaction.

"I *really* want to impress Ivor, John!" he persisted through my silence. "So! What I need from you is a list of your contacts, *all* the people you know who I should be going to see while I'm here."

Once again, I left him hanging.

"I *need* that list, John," he insisted, his voice shaking. "*Today* please!"

I sighed happily.

"I'm sorry, Malcolm," I said, as casually as I could. "I can't help you, I'm afraid. I'm not there, you see. How can I tell you who to go and meet if I don't know who's there?"

That completely stumped him. "But-but… surely you know who's *probably* here?"

I found myself shaking my head, as if he could see me.

"No, Malcolm, I don't. The same people don't go every year, some only visit MIDEM every couple of years. If I'd been invited to go there *with* you and Ivor, then I'd've happily taken you around the Palais and introduced you to my contacts who *are* there. But, as it is – I'm here and… you're there… without me… so… "

"But surely you can give me *some* names?"

"Sorry, no, I can't."

"Ivor won't be happy about this, John!"

"No, probably not, Malcolm," I replied. "I would imagine he'll be extremely pissed off with you. I mean, you're my boss, you're there in *my* place, so he'd've expected you to know my contacts already. Wouldn't he?"

"So! You won't help me then?"

"I'm afraid I simply can't, Malcolm. As I say… "

"Yeah, yeah, if you'd been here… "

"Exactly. Never mind. Enjoy the rest of your time in sunny Cannes!"

* * *

On his first morning back, Malcolm summoned me to his office on the public intercom. I'd seen him arrive a few minutes earlier from my office window in his brand new company car. He was a tiny, skinny guy and looked almost child-like as he emerged from the massive four-by-four.

When I sat down opposite him, I noticed that he looked a little flushed. I asked him very pleasantly how his first MIDEM had gone, and he stiffly told me about the few people he'd managed to see.

"I could have got to meet many more though, John, if *you'd* been more helpful!"

He stared at me. I found myself smiling back.

"That seems to amuse you, John!" he said.

"No, not really. I'm just sorry I'm such a disappointment to you," I replied. "But don't worry, Malcolm, I won't be here much longer."

I savoured the moment. Malcolm flushed up some more.

"Why?" he asked. "Where are you going?"

"I've been offered the position of Head of Special Projects at MCA."

He gulped, took a swig of his filter coffee and failed a smile.

"Well! This is a surprise!"

"To you, perhaps, but not to many of my music business colleagues."

"You've told them?!" he shouted. "Before you informed me?!"

"I didn't have to, Malcolm. I've already had three phone calls this morning, congratulating me on the move."

His shoulders seemed to sag a little.

"I guess I should be congratulating you as well then!"

"Thank you. I am hereby giving you my one month's notice."

He flinched slightly then, gathering himself, said, "I have to say, I am *very* surprised that you didn't discuss this with me before accepting the job!"

He jutted out his jaw, probably something he'd learned from his *How To Be A Senior Manager And Deal With Your Staff* manual, which he often had his face buried in whenever I came to his office unannounced.

"Jeff needed a yes or no there and then," I told him.

"Jeff?"

"Jeff Golembo. *The Deputy Managing Director of MCA.* I don't think you know him. He'll be my boss."

He leaned forward and ground his teeth, making the bones in his jaw protrude rather unattractively. "You do know that Ivor won't be happy about this, John?"

"Can't please all the people all the time, Malcolm. But I do hope *you're* pleased for me."

Without warning, he stood up, excused himself and hurried out of the office. A few minutes later he returned, his face now an odd shade of grey.

"Ivor wants to see you!" he said.

It was obvious he'd been royally bollocked by his new patron.

"Excellent!" I replied, "I'll pop along there now."

I walked down the corridor and knocked on Ivor's always closed door. He was also a tiny little man, but unlike Malcolm he would have been rather a dish if he'd been a couple of feet taller. He'd apparently ordered all the handles on the doors to be lowered, and there were rumours that he had lifts in his shoes and wore a wig to give him a couple of inches extra height.

"Come in!" he called out.

I found him staring out of the window with his back to me. I sat down and waited. Finally, he turned around.

"I am so disappointed, John," he said, fiddling with some papers on his desk.

"Yes, I know, Ivor, but *I* am extremely excited." That got a glance from him. "Working for a major record company is a great step up for me, Ivor," I continued, "and you, of all people, should understand ambition."

"But you have a great future here!"

"What? Like being passed over for a man who hasn't a clue what he's doing, you mean?"

He couldn't help a private smile.

"I really respect you, John. I thought you knew that."

"Odd way of showing it, Ivor, if I may say so."

"I understand you're not happy having Malcolm as your boss. I do. But things are changing, John. Everything is becoming much more... corporate and...," he smiled at me, "you are not – and have no desire to be – a corporate guy! It's one of the things I admire about you."

"Well, that's as may be, but there is no future for me here now. I've done a great job the last few years -"

"And you have been rewarded for that!" he said firmly.

"Yes, thank you for the share options. But, one needs professional respect too, Ivor, and frankly, I haven't felt too much of that lately."

"What if Malcolm was no longer your boss?"

Ah, the loyalty of the work place! I shook my head. "I've already accepted the position at MCA. I've given Malcolm my contractual one month's notice."

He suddenly thumped the desk, stamped his foot and pointed his finger at me.

"*You* will *not leave!*" he yelled. "I will *not* allow it! I will *sue* MCA if they take you away!"

As calmly as I could, my heart beating like a drum, I said, "Ivor. Please don't screw this up for me. I am going to MCA, and that's that. And, don't forget, as the guy in charge of licensing, I will be a *very* useful contact for Pickwick."

He seemed to briefly consider that, then, nodding to himself, said, with disturbing calm, "I am calling Jeff Golembo *now.*"

He checked for my reaction and smirked.

"I will tell him that you are *not* leaving Pickwick. I *will* sue him. I will *sue* MCA."

He chewed his thumb and stared at the floor.

"Now *go,*" he said, without looking at me.

I went to the door and, bending a little to get hold of the handle, said, "Ivor, this is very silly."

"I said *go!*"

He turned back to the window and I left.

Back in my office, I closed the door and rang Jeff. When I told him about Ivor's tantrum, he burst out laughing.

"He *can't* sue MCA! What's the man talking about?"

He laughed again.

"Leave it with me, John. I'll call him. He and I go back a long way, I knew him in Jo'burg. Don't worry, John! I've got this."

* * *

Amongst the many calls I made with my news to music business colleagues over the next four weeks, the one to Gordon Lorenz, with whom I'd put together the successful *Shows Collection* range of West End musical recordings, was the most intriguing.

"John?" he said, after sounding suspiciously unsurprised. "How do you fancy coming into the studio tomorrow to record a few tracks for me? They'll be for our *Shows Collection* range."

"Me, Gordon?"

"Yes, young man, you! First of all, you'll enjoy it. I know for a fact you miss your days as an artist, it's in your blood, my friend... but also, it would mark your farewell to Pickwick, and to the albums we've done together, rather perfectly. It would be a very nice sign-off! 11 o'clock? See you then!"

The following morning, I was standing at the mike singing the hippy-nonsensical 'Glibby gloop glooby, nibby nabby nooby, la-la-la-lo" chorus of 'Good Morning Starshine' from *Hair* followed by 'Aquarius/Let The Sunshine In'. I felt that its youthful sunny optimism perfectly represented this period of great change in my life.

I also loved singing 'Family Solicitor' from *Me & My Girl*. After I'd camped it up like mad, which the number called for, I went into the control room to have a listen.

"Fantastic, John!" Gordon yelled at me. "You're a natural, my son. In another life, I'd loved to have produced an album with you."

My friends at Pickwick organised a leaving 'do' for me at a nearby pub. They gave me a huge, signed farewell card and a purple felt gift box containing some of the albums I'd compiled and commissioned during my time at the company. About halfway through the evening, Malcolm walked in followed closely by Ivor.

To my surprise, Malcolm walked into the middle of the room, clapped his hands and made a very gracious speech, thanking me for all my 'wonderful work' at Pickwick.

"And of course," he said, smiling at me, "John will be giving us the *best* repertoire *and* the best deals when he's in charge of licensing at MCA!"

'On your bike,' I thought, smiling back.

Neil and I stayed for a couple more drinks then, after hugs for the people who I would definitely miss, we made our way out. As we passed the bar, I saw Ivor standing there alone, looking quite disconsolate, seemingly ignored by his staff. Feeling rather sorry for him, I went over and offered my hand.

"Thanks for coming, Ivor," I said. "It means a lot."

He blushed up a little, shook my hand and nodded, though still not able to completely look me in the eye.

"You'll be great, John," he said. "I always knew you'd go places."

"Just not to MCA, eh, Ivor?"

He couldn't help chuckling at that and finally looked at me.

"Malcolm will be coming to see you within the week, John. We expect only the best from you."

"Depends on the deal you're offering, Ivor."

"That's my boy," he said, and tapped me on the shoulder.

Chapter Seven

Outward

Within a couple of months of joining MCA, I got a call from the company's Head Office in L.A., inviting me to attend their annual New Release Meeting.

"We like the stuff you're putting together, John," Bruce Reznikoff, Head of Special Markets in America told me. "Your Buddy Holly comps are ace! We'd like you to do a presentation of what you're planning, for our guys to see and maybe to release over here."

After being upgraded to Virgin Upper Class - arranged via a quick phone call by Lynn, the MD's secretary - I arrived at LA-X feeling relaxed and refreshed. Free Virgin-monogrammed track suit outfits handed out to us by the stewardess as soon as we sat down, foot massages, excellent food and Bucks Fizz on tap made the journey extremely palatable.

I was met by a uniformed hunk, who led me to a stretch limo and whisked me off to the Four Seasons Hotel in Santa Barbara, where the music meeting was to be held. 'Old Spanish' in style, it was made up of a rather grand main building, with marble floors and a huge semi-circular reception desk, which led out to lots of well-maintained chalets on the edge of exotically planted-out grounds wrapping around them.

The porter manfully carried my bags while telling me, "The hotel is *very* old, sir, it was built *sixty-seven* years ago!".

It had been, he explained, "the hotel of choice for Golden-Age Hollywood stars. Judy Garland, Errol Flynn, Clark Gable, Joan Crawford, Shirley Temple, Gregory Peck, they *all* stayed here, sir!"

As star-struck as my good-looking companion, once ensconced in my extremely pretty chalet I happily proffered him a ten-dollar tip.

"If you need anything, sir, just holler!" he cried, rushing off across the lawn. "I'm James!"

"Oh, I will, James!" I cried back, waving at his rather lovely retreating arse.

I ordered a light dinner in my room and slept off the approaching jet-lag.

The following morning, I met the team over a buffet breakfast on the lawn, then we settled in the light and airy meeting room where Bruce's people went through their presentations. After I'd done mine, going through all my upcoming releases, I sat down to light applause and positive murmurings. One of the product managers, Pam, mouthed "Fabulous!" at me across the table. Bruce was nodding at me and smiling.

Bruce then decided we should have a couple of hours break 'off piste' and took us to a lovely café-cum-health resort, just a short walk from the hotel. It was dotted with fit-looking Californians, some of them lying on sunbeds, others sitting together in white dressing gowns, chatting easily over fruit juices, while others dined in small groups around the bamboo tables by the pool.

As I munched with the team on a tasty pasta salad and wholemeal bread, nattering about this and that, I spotted Bruce Johnston from The Beach Boys coming out of one of the sauna rooms. In a spotless white dressing gown and smiling in that amiable, non-connective way stars do when strolling by members of the public, he flip-flopped his way towards his friends who were lying on loungers a little distance from us.

I have no idea why I did it, or how I plucked up the courage, but just as Bruce walked past our table, I piped up. "Hi Bruce! Steve Levine says hello!"

He literally stopped in his tracks, beamed at me and sat down.

"You know *Steve*?" he asked, his eyes searing into mine.

Thrilled and a little taken aback, I said, "Yeah! Steve produced some of my records back in the '80s!"

"No *way*!" Bruce shouted, laughing and slapping his leg. "How *is* he? My *God*! I haven't seen Steve for ages! *Such* an excellent guy!"

My colleagues had all shut up as one and just stared.

"He's great!" I replied. "He speaks very fondly of working with you and the rest of the band."

I introduced him to the MCA team and he greeted each one of them by name, finally making a quip about there being "two Bruces here!".

"There can never be enough Bruces!" Reznikoff joked.

Bruce laughed and nodded.

"We're in great company, my friend!" he cried. "We salute you Mr Springsteen!"

"Amen to that!" Reznikoff said.

Glasses were lifted, everyone had relaxed and you could feel the atmosphere had changed around the table. We were now a group of music business friends enjoying a chat and some banter.

Seamlessly, Bruce carried on talking about Steve and the album he'd produced for The Beach Boys in 1984 – "it gave us our first US hit for a while!".

"'Getcha Back'," Pam murmured.

"'Getcha Back'!" Bruce said, beaming at Pam. "That's right!"

"I loved that record," Pam replied.

Everyone nodded and murmured agreement.

"So are you making a new album, Bruce?" Reznikoff asked him.

"I'm actually recording a new solo album at the moment with George Martin!" he replied. "Another excellent – well legendary! - British producer. I've known George since the '60s, of course, when I used to hang out with The Beatles during my London trips."

It could have sounded boastful, but somehow Bruce's easy charm and clear enjoyment of who he was, his legacy amongst pop's greatest legends, completely avoided that.

As he chatted, I remembered that I had a cassette copy of some unreleased tracks he'd recorded with Doris Day and Terry Melcher in the early '80s. When I mentioned it his eyes lit up. He actually grabbed my shoulder.

"Wow! You've *heard* those? So few people have! I really loved working with Doris, such a fine lady!"

I told him how much I loved her version of 'Disney Girls'.

"Thank you, John!" he said, and for a moment it felt like we'd known each other for years. Then he leaned forward, "How come you have a cassette of the tracks?"

I explained that it had been sent to me by a UK representative of Terry Melcher's when I was working at Pickwick.

"I lobbied hard for us to do a deal," I told him, "but sadly, senior management wouldn't agree to the advance."

He nodded sadly.

"Yeah, it's always the money which lets us down. So many great projects get screwed up by the money."

He laughed at a memory then nodded at us all.

"Okay! Well, it's been so great meeting and talking to you guys, but I have to get back to my friends."

He stood and shook my hand warmly.

"John! Excellent seeing you! Give my love to Steve!"

He waved 'Bye!' to everyone at the table and sauntered off, an aura of deep contentment surrounding him.

As I watched him joining his friends and obviously telling them about our conversation, I realised there was an odd silence at the table until, finally, Bruce Reznikoff whistled to the sky.

"Jesus, John!" he said. "I have lived in L.A. *all my life* and I have never – *ever* - met a Beach Boy!"

He laughed and stared around the table. "But you're here for just *one day* and look at you! Shooting the breeze like old buddies with Bruce *fucking* Johnston!"

He shook his head, everyone started laughing and I felt like the luckiest man alive.

* * *

However, my inner flame of achievement was utterly extinguished just a few days after I returned to the UK office. I'd received an invitation from MPL Music, Paul McCartney's publishing company, to a Buddy Holly Day luncheon that he was hosting at a wine bar just a ten minute walk from MCA. McCartney owned the copyrights to Buddy's songs, and, as MCA owned all his recordings which I was currently promoting with a series of new compilations, I won the lottery.

I arrived planning to introduce myself to Paul and tell him about my new Holly projects. 'I'll offer to drop them by his office,' I thought, as I wandered into the packed bar.

I found myself a table, ordered a beer and a small snack, and watched various people of varying fame milling about and chatting in little groups, their alert faces expectantly waiting for the Great Man to arrive.

When Paul eventually walked in, accompanied by Linda and a couple of friends, he settled himself at a table in the middle of the room and immediately immersed his group in that instant animated chat only stars can create. We all tried not to stare and so became even more obviously in awe of one of the most famous men in the world.

I waited for a few minutes then, knocking back my beer, got up and wandered towards Paul's table, not looking at him but trying to ready myself for an introduction. Heart beating like a drum, opening line rehearsed, I was within touching distance when something awful happened. I suddenly got cold feet and carried on walking past his table.

I was shocked. This had never happened to me before. Ever.

'What is *wrong* with you?' my head yelled.

Feeling like an utter fool, I stood in the doorway and glanced surreptitiously across the room. Paul was still chatting and laughing, clearly unaware of my failed attempt at self-promotion. I almost turned and left but instead I steeled myself for another go.

I wandered slowly back, staying calm and pasting on a light, affable smile. However, the closer I got, the more I felt any confidence I'd mustered sapping away from me like blood from a wound. Feeling absolutely pathetic, I carried on to the bar and ordered myself another beer.

Minutes ticked by as I inwardly kicked myself. Then, with a final 'Now or Never' surge of determination, I took a deep breath and set off once more, rehearsing again what I was going to say, 'Hi Paul! May I introduce myself, I'm -'

Then, just as I got to his table, Paul stood up and walked towards the stage.

"Okay!" he said, bounding towards the mike and beaming at a full house. "We're here to honour one of the greatest songwriters ever. Mr Buddy Holly!"

Little cheer from the room.

"I'm gonna sing a few of his songs for you now, hope that's okay!".

Everyone cheered very loudly this time, as Paul and his four-man combo blasted into a great rendition of 'That'll Be The Day'.

I stayed to watch the half-hour show which was full of great performances and amusing anecdotes, but it passed in an instant. At the end of the final number, 'Brown Eyed Handsome Man', Paul thanked everyone for coming, waved and, putting his arm around Linda who'd been watching from the side of the stage, quickly disappeared into a room at the back of the restaurant.

I guessed it was the VIP area as several mildly famous people appeared out of the crowd and swanned in, looking affably important.

I checked my invitation but there was no 'VIP' on it anywhere. My best chance at meeting one of my all-time heroes had gone. I berated myself all the way back to the office, throwing my invitation in the bin in disgust at my ineptitude.

I've never quite forgiven myself.

* * *

One of the most successful MCA projects I worked on, which the company's former Managing Director, Stuart Watson, brought to me, was a Joint Venture with Polygram TV, *I Know Them So Well - The Best of Tim Rice*. Stuart was a great friend of Tim's and, seeing how well Lloyd Webber had done with his compilation albums, he decided to do the same for the other half of that songwriting team, and asked me to handle the track clearances and licensing agreements in tandem with Polygram TV's head honcho Brian Berg.

The album was made up of not only hit songs Tim had written with Lloyd Webber, there were also the *Chess* co-writes with Abba's Benny and Bjorn, 'I Know Him So Well' and 'One Night In Bangkok', and his massive Christmas hit with David Essex, 'A Winter's Tale'.

One of Rice-Lloyd Webber's earliest musicals, *Joseph & the Amazing Technicolour Dreamcoat* had recently enjoyed a successful West End revival starring Jason Donovan, which had given the former *Neighbours* star his first Number One hit for quite a while, 'Any Dream Will Do'. That track was obviously included as was 'Close Every Door, which had been a moderate hit for Phillip Schofield who had taken over from Donovan in the lead role.

I Know Them So Well – The Best of Tim Rice reached No.2 in the UK albums chart, selling in excess of 100,000 units, garnering me a Gold Disc for my involvement in its creation.

As a result of the album's success, I was invited to attend an afternoon at Tim Rice's beautiful house in Barnes where we presented him and David Essex with their Gold Discs. I hadn't seen David since the mid-'70s, when we were both signed to CBS and he was the biggest teen idol in Britain.

I'd often bump into him at CBS functions and, although he'd clearly aged since then, he was still as charming as ever, with the same goofy grin which had sent thousands of girls – and boys - into paroxysms of ecstasy twenty years earlier.

John and Tim Rice celebrating 100,000 sales of I Know Them So Well

As we chatted on Tim's enormous lawn, quaffing champagne and enjoying the sunshine which glinted on the disc under his arm, I wondered if I should remind David of when we'd first met. Happily, such thoughts were interrupted by Brian Berg coming to join us just as a Polygram photographer began weaving around us snapping away. We all duly grouped together and gave our best 'success smiles'.

Finally, the afternoon over and everyone making their farewells, I was walking towards the front door when I noticed a cassette on a table in the hall. Tim saw me glance at it and picked it up, smiling fondly at it.

"These are the songs for a musical John Farrar and I are writing for Cliff," he told me. "It's based on *Wuthering Heights*."

"Is Cliff playing Heathcliff?" I asked, trying - and failing – to imagine it.

"Yes, he is," Tim replied without a flicker, "and I think he'll surprise a lot of people. It's going to do well."

Sure enough, the musical defied all the critics. *Heathcliff* became one of the UK's most profitable musicals, breaking box office records everywhere it played, taking 8.5 million pounds in advance takings alone, a record in itself.

Clearly, Sir Tim had not lost his touch.

* * *

One thing I have never been is 'a team player', a phrase that makes my stomach sink whenever anyone says it. It reeks of all that false camaraderie large companies instil in employees to make them think they're part of 'the family' – until they're no longer needed, that is. In my experience, big company managements expect absolute loyalty from their employees while giving none back.

As far as I have always been concerned, if you do your job well and get results, then that's all that should be expected of anyone, and due reward comes from a good competitive salary, not pally pats on the back and fine empty words of praise.

After I'd been with MCA for a year or so, the company got a new Managing Director, Nick Ainsley who was coming in from EMI. I naively commented to Lynn, who had been kept on to work for Nick, that the former MD, Tom Harker, would be okay.

"He no doubt had a huge salary," I said, sitting down for our daily gossip, "and probably got a fabulous pay-off, so why should he worry?"

"Because," Lynn told me, putting down the memo she was glancing at and staring across her desk at me, "that great salary coming in every month meant his daughters were both sent to private schools and given horses as birthday presents, which are stabled at an expensive top-of-the-range place nearby. His wife has got used to two glamorous holidays every year and a clothes allowance which would make your eyes pop out. Suddenly that regular monthly cheque is no longer coming in and his pay-off will only cover about one month of his expenses. Along with his family's expectations of continuing to live the high life he also has a huge mortgage on a vast house his wife refuses to leave. So, yes, John, he has plenty to worry about!"

I felt suitably put in my place and apologised.

Lynn smiled. "Oh, you're not alone, John, everyone has said the same to me in the last few days. You're unfortunate that it was you I finally let off steam to. I'm sorry for that!"

We decided to get out for a bit and go for lunch – "I'll charge it to Nick's new expense account!" Lynn told me with a smile - and enjoyed an hour's good old gossiping over a gorgeous smoked salmon salad at Fortnum & Mason in Piccadilly.

We were pals again, and stayed so for several years.

Nick was an attractive suave-looking guy, one of those chaps who have been born into money and command any room they enter. He was only thirty-two but already a self-made entrepreneur from a music business family background.

He clearly wanted to shake things up when he arrived and, as he told me in our first meeting that he wanted to "create a new team spirit at MCA", my heart sank. His eager eyes burned into me across his vast polished desk.

"I've decided to organise an 'Awayday Weekend'," he told me, explaining that it would entail the whole MCA staff staying at a hotel "which specialises in fun and team-building events."

'Oh God!' I thought, as he smiled away enthusiastically. 'My idea of Hell.'

While there we would "enjoy bonding and taking part in a series of wacky sports activities", in which departmental teams would compete with each other. As I had a department of three including myself, we were on a loser straight away.

"Er – do you mind if I pass? It's not really my thing, Nick."

His face fell like a little boy who had been refused a bag of sweets.

"I hate sport," I ploughed on, "and my small department is bonding perfectly well already. We don't need an Awayday Weekend to help us work any harder."

Nick sat up in his chair and glared at me.

"John," he said, "this is an opportunity for *all* departments to get to know each other better and have fun while they're at it. Why is that such a bad idea?"

"For those who'll enjoy it, it's a great idea," I replied, "But I think we should be given a choice, let those who don't fancy it stay behind."

"What about Keren and Jess? Do they not want to go?"

"Oh, I'm sure they'll have a ball, but they won't need me there. I'll be absolutely no use at all, in fact I'll probably be the reason my department does extremely badly."

"It's not about winning, John!" he told me, looking exasperated. "You are their boss! You *have* to be there. Show leadership, man! There will be no drop-outs, everyone is going! *You* and your team *will* be there."

He stood up, the meeting was clearly over.

"The games start at ten o'clock sharp on Saturday at the Medway Hotel," he informed me, glancing through some papers on his desk. "I've memo'd all department heads with the address."

Then he smiled at me like a football coach egging on a reluctant wimp.

"It'll be *fun*, John! What's wrong with having fun?"

I could have replied, 'It depends what your idea of fun is,', but instead I shrugged my shoulders, nodded and left his office, memories of my P.E teacher yelling, "Run, Jones, *run*!" flooding back like a bad dream.

So, on a rainy Saturday morning, with heavy heart I drove to Letchmore Heath in Hertfordshire, arrived at the hotel just before nine o'clock and checked into my room. It overlooked the 'games area' where I saw a line of go-karts waiting in the downpour for the 'Fun-Time 10 a.m. Race!'. I also spotted a strange collection of giant fluffy hammers propped up near some sort of rope bridge which stretched across a pool of distinctly unpleasant-looking water.

I decided to lie on the bed and read for a while, hoping I'd be forgotten about. No such luck. At five-to-ten there was a heavy rapping on my door, followed by Lynn shouting,

"The games start in five minutes, John!".

I opened the door and tried to look pathetic. Lynn burst out laughing. "Oh, John! Come on! It'll be fun. You'll end up loving it!"

"It won't and I won't, Lynn. I can guarantee that."

"Nick's determined I get you down there, John. There's no escape! See you at the Go-Karts!"

After downing one of the mini-bar's whiskies and getting my brolly from my suitcase, I trudged downstairs and, following the arrows on the soaked ground, arrived at the Go-Kart track.

"You taking part, John?" Jeff Golembo shouted at me, shielding his face from the torrential rain.

I shook my head, "No way!"

"Don't blame you!" he shouted back and laughed. "I see you came prepared for our lovely English weather!"

"I was in the Scouts, Jeff!"

He patted me on the back and wandered off in search of shelter.

I moved to a fairly inconspicuous spot and watched several mud-splattered go-karters, including my assistant Keren, tearing past us having a marvellous time. My brolly only partially protected me from the rain and, finally, my legs wet through, I made my way back to the hotel, determined to get in the dry and have a cup of tea.

As I approached the hotel foyer, Nick appeared, beaming at me.

"John!" he cried. "I've been looking for you! The jousting competition is in fifteen minutes."

He waved his sodden Awayday Weekend Guide Book at me.

"I look forward to seeing you battle it out with Julie from Production!"

I proffered a withering smile and hurried back to reception to check the 'event guide', which was pinned to a brightly illustrated noticeboard, all smiley faces and crayoned yellow stars. Sure enough, there it was, '10.45 – John Howard and Julie Green in jousting combat over the medieval moat!'.

I checked my watch, it was 10.35.

'Fuck!' I thought. 'There really is no escape from this nightmare!'

I trudged back towards the signposted jousting area, thankful that at least the rain had eased to a mild drizzle.

One of the Promotions Department girls waved when she saw me, marched over with a giant drenched fluffy hammer in her hand and told me to "take this and cross the rope bridge over there to the middle – then when you and Julie are in position… joust!".

All my childhood fears and insecurities poured back as I walked across the filthy, wobbly contraption and faced the clearly eager Julie who seemed ready for battle. Determined not to fall into the muddy pool below – what happened to the 'medieval moat?' I asked myself - I whacked her as hard as I could, the weight of the rain-soaked hammer knocking her off balance. She teetered slightly so I whacked her again and down she fell. Thankfully, she seemed delighted and thrashed around in the mud shouting, "You beat me, John! Well done!"

With a quick arms-up celebration, I threw the hammer onto the ground, struggled back across the rope bridge and, ignoring everyone, strode towards the hotel and ordered scrambled eggs and garlic mushrooms at reception. It arrived at my room ten minutes later, I tucked in, downed a couple more whiskies and lay on the bed, falling fast asleep.

At about one o'clock the phone rang. It was Jeff.

"John! Why aren't you down here enjoying the fun?"

"It's my asthma, Jeff," I lied. "I had an attack and had to come back for my inhaler. I'm lying down at the moment, hoping it'll pass but… "

"Well, just to let you know, we're having lunch in the Veranda Bar. You should come down to that, John."

"Are there more fun and games after lunch?"

"Yes! It's the three-legged race at three-thirty! You're tied in with Jamie and Dan from Promotions!"

I let out a hacking cough and pretended to gasp for air.

"If I can, I'll be there," I said, as pathetically as possible.

I put down the phone, ran a hot bath, checked the room service menu and ordered lunch for two o'clock. It arrived just as I was emerging from the steam-filled bathroom, wrapping myself in a lovely thick hotel bathrobe. After a delicious and rather enormous pasta cheese bake, I relaxed on the bed with a book before falling asleep again until six o'clock.

It was getting dark when I looked out the window and saw no activity at all. The rain was teeming down again so I got dressed and wended my way downstairs.

"John!"

It was Nick, who was beginning to feel like a stalker.

"Are you okay?" he asked. "Jeff said you were unwell?"

I produced my inhaler. "It's my asthma, Nick. It comes on badly when I'm stressed."

He looked either pitying or disbelieving, I wasn't sure which.

"Dinner's at seven-thirty, John, in the main banqueting suite down the hall. Do try to come along!"

I ordered a gin and tonic from the bar and sat down, thankful Nick had gone off in search of Jeff. A few minutes later, Lynn's smiling face was hovering over me.

"I assume your asthma attack is over?" she said, raising her eyebrows.

"Yes, thank you," I replied as she sat down next to me, smiling wryly.

"Jeff made a bet with me that you'd find a way to escape eventually. He thinks it's funny. He likes your refusal to fall in with the rest of us. 'Our delightful rebel', he calls you."

"I didn't do it to rebel, Lynn. I just can't stand these kinds of things, all this bonding crap. I hate it. I do a good job -"

"- a great job!" she interrupted. "Why do you think Jeff lets you get away with being late in every day?"

The dinner began well. We were all seated around a large oak banqueting table in an impressive wood-panelled room on the second floor. Hors d'oeuvres were served and we chatted amongst ourselves, mainly about "the fun" everyone but me had had earlier in the day. I even enjoyed the affectionate joshing at my 'no-show'.

After we'd started on our main courses, I was having an interesting chat about one of the company's biggest current bands, Nirvana, with one of the marketing girls, when Damien, Head of Promotions, stood up and threw a bread roll at Justin, Head of A & R. He promptly threw one back. Within minutes, the place was a bombsite of bread rolls. They flew past our heads like gunshots, one of them hitting me painfully on the ear.

Then food from the plates was tossed across the room, landing in laps, on faces and, to uproarious laughter, down the front of one of the girls' dresses. But the piece de resistance was when several heads of department stood as one and overturned the dining table. Plates, dishes and cutlery fell with a crash to the floor, while our three waitresses ran out terrified.

Minutes later, two sturdy blokes arrived, watching proceedings for a few minutes as bedlam raged. Then one of them walked up to Nick, grabbed him by the shoulder and whispered something in his ear.

Nick nodded then cupped his hands, "Folks!" he yelled. "Guys! We have to stop this now! Or we'll be turfed out on our ears."

Slowly the mayhem subsided, as a roomful of people covered in food and goo stood giggling at each other.

"And!" Nick announced grandly. "I have informed our friend here that MCA will pay for any damage caused!"

A cheer went up from his staff, though the sturdy chap at his side, looking decidedly unimpressed, glared at everyone with contempt.

A voice behind me said, "Come on, John, bring your drink, let's get out of here."

It was Lynn. She grabbed my hand and led me down the corridor to a small, divinely quiet bar.

"Welcome to sanity!" she said, sitting down with her white wine.

"I'm disgusted," I told her. "They're all acting like yobs!"

"Rich yobs, John. It's the music industry. Overpaid executives, free to act like cretins because they bring in the cash for the American head office. 'twas ever thus."

'Hm', I thought. 'Not sure about that.'

* * *

In the Summer of '94, I had lunch with a music business friend of mine, Don Reedman. He'd recently set up his own label, Vision Music, and had a concept he was keen to tell me about, knowing what a fan of the artist I was.

"I'm going to visit Doris Day at her home in Carmel and ask her if she'll record a new album for me!" he told me, eyes sparkling in the candlelight on our table.

Don was one of those people who emanated energy. He wasn't a big chap, more 'little and cuddly', but his enthusiasm for what he did was enormous, and filled any space he inhabited. I don't think I ever saw Don not smiling.

He was not only full of ideas, he made them happen. He'd created *Hooked On Classics* with The Royal Philharmonic Orchestra in the '80s, and more recently had signed Michael Crawford to record four platinum-selling albums with him.

"Well, if anyone can persuade Doris to come out of retirement and record a new album, it's you, Don," I told him.

"Gee, thanks, John," he said, blushing up.

"Can I ask you a favour?"

"Sure, John, and I think I know what it is!"

"Would you ask Doris to sign a photo for me?"

"Sure will!" he replied, laughing at my teen-fan's stare of wonder.

A few weeks later, Don called me, "Just got back from meeting Doris and her son, Terry, at their beautiful home, John!"

"Wow! What was she like? Divine I assume?"

"Completely adorable! And I brought back a little something for you, my friend!"

Lunch a few days later was on me!

As it turned out, Doris didn't want to record again, but she did have a lovely surprise alternative for Don.

"Terry?" she'd said. "Get the tapes of the unreleased album from the music room would you?"

A few minutes later, Don was holding in his hands the reel-to-reels of an album Doris had recorded for Columbia in 1968, which had never been released. It contained beautiful renditions of 'For All We Know', 'Are You Lonesome Tonight', 'Street of Dreams' and Irving Berlin's 'All Alone'.

"My heart was in my mouth, John," Don told me over our lunch at The Ivy. "I couldn't believe these gorgeous recordings had never seen the light of day. She wants me to release it! A previously unknown album by Doris Day, for fuck's sake!"

The Love Album went on to become, remarkably, Doris's first UK hit album featuring previously unreleased recordings, everything which had charted before had been Greatest Hits compilations.

It - and my signed photo – '*To John, with love, Doris Day*' - remain treasured possessions.

* * *

Something which I kept forgetting during the '90s, whenever meeting people I hadn't seen for years, was that I had become something of a Muscle Mary, making me unrecognisable to those who'd always known me as a skinny eight-stone weakling. I was not only regularly going to the gym, I'd also installed a weights machine at home and, three times a day, was imbibing a 'bulk-builder' drink.

The 'non-steroidal anabolic supplement' had produced the desired effect in just a couple of months. I quickly almost doubled my weight to an impressive fifteen-stone. I was impressed anyway, and clearly I wasn't alone. For the first time in my life I began to get admiring looks from skinny gay guys. They stared at my huge arms and chest and gawped at my hefty thighs.

The 'Muscle Mary' period

Even Neil hadn't recognised me when he'd been playing Summer Season in Jersey in the September of 1992.

There were no understudies in the company, so none of the actors were allowed to leave the island for the four months the play was on, and as I hadn't been able to get over to the island since the play had begun in early June, it had been months since we'd seen each other. During which time my appearance had radically changed.

So there I was, standing on my own in the pub next to the theatre, waiting for Neil to arrive after I'd watched the play, when he wandered in. He looked around the room for me and even briefly glanced at me, but as I was about to wave he walked right past me to the bar.

"Has John arrived yet?" I heard him ask the barman.

"Er… a chap called John came in about fifteen minutes ago and said he was waiting for you… " He looked at the now packed room and saw me. "Yeah, there he is!" he said, pointing in my direction.

Neil bobbed his head up and down, following the guy's finger, finally seeing me as I waved at him. His mouth literally fell open, his eyes like saucers. He got his beer and rushed over to me.

"I didn't recognise you!" he said, his hand clasping his face in shock. "You're *huge*!! What have you *done*?!"

At which point, one of the other actors in the play, John Blackman, wandered over, looking me up and down admiringly.

"Well, who is *this*?" he asked, offering his hand like a Jane Austen maiden. "A new beau methinks!"

"It's *John*!" Neil almost yelled. "It's *my* John! I didn't recognise him!"

"Good God!" John shouted. "Is it really you? What an improvement! Last year there was nothing of you, dear, and now... well! You're at least three feet wider!"

He smiled salaciously at Neil and then eyed me up and down again like a fine piece of furniture.

"Doesn't he look delicious?!"

"No!" Neil cried. "I want *my* John back!"

"Well," John said, "All I can say, dear, is if *you* don't want him anymore, I'm more than ready to take over!"

Half-an-hour later, as Neil and I walked back to where he'd parked his motorbike, he lectured me about how "your heart isn't any bigger, your lungs aren't any bigger, all this extra weight could be very harmful, John!" He was clearly concerned.

"You were never meant to *be* this big!" he continued as I tried to explain that I felt great, better than I ever had.

"I actually feel that, physically at least, I finally exist in people's eyes," I told him.

"Don't be ridiculous!" he replied.

"It's true!" I protested. "When I walk down the street now, people actually see me, they even move out of the way to let me through. I've never had that kind of physical presence before. I'd got so used all my life to being the stick insect everyone ignored, the one who got out of *their* way. I love the feeling my new body gives me."

"People looked at you before, darling. I certainly always felt proud to walk down any street with you."

"Yes, but you've never had kids coming up to you shouting 'AIDS Victim!' in your face. You never overhead people muttering 'Don't die of AIDS' as they walked past."

"Did they?"

"Many times. But not anymore."

"It's still not good for your health, John," Neil persisted as we reached the bike and he gave me the spare safety helmet. "I hope it still fits," he joked.

"My head hasn't got any bigger!" I laughed as I sat behind him.

"Sure about that?" he said, winked at me and off we roared out of St Helier.

His case wasn't helped once we got back to the farmhouse, which he was sharing with Sue the costume designer and her husband Dave who was the musical director at The Fort leisure centre. I hadn't seen them since Neil was in Jersey the previous Summer and Sue shrieked when she saw me.

"Oh my God! You look absolutely *gorgeous!*" she yelled, and hugged me tightly. "Ooh! Wonderful! Muscles on muscles! How divine!"

She stood back and admired me. "Isn't he fabulous, Neil?" she said, then realising how unhappy Neil looked, said, "Don't you like the new look?"

"He does look great," Neil finally conceded, "if you like that kind of thing. But he doesn't look like the John I know and love, and I'm worried all this extra weight is going to harm his health."

Sue laughed. "Oh, don't be so dramatic, dear! He looks the picture of health – and then some!"

At which point Dave walked in. "Bloody hell!" he said, "Is that really John? You look amazing, my son!"

Neil shook his head and went to pour us two very large gin and tonics.

Later that evening, Neil made us all scream with laughter when he imitated my walk, going seamlessly from my previously schuszy camp wander into an Incredible Hulk stomp.

"I *don't* walk like that!" I insisted.

"You do, love," he said. "It's a complete transformation!"

"Well I heartily approve!" Sue exclaimed. "You'll just have to get used to it, Neil."

The look he gave me wasn't too convincing.

One afternoon in 1993, while wandering down Bond Street after a lunch with a licensing colleague, I spotted Lynsey De Paul coming out of a jeweller's shop, walking towards her limo which waited for her at the kerb.

I'd not seen her since we shared the bill on the Musical Time Machine TV show in 1975. Perhaps in view of my pathetic inability to introduce myself to Paul McCartney a few months earlier, I briskly approached Lynsey, ready to share happy memories of sitting in her dressing-room at Broadcasting House, drinking champagne and discussing whether she should wear her hair "flicked in, or flicked out?"

"Hello, Lynsey!" I bellowed down at her tiny frame.

Looking utterly terrified, she kind of gasped and stepped back, leaning for support on the car. Her huge, frightened eyes glared up at me from her porcelain doll face.

"Er-hello!" she said, as brightly as she could, obviously thinking I was some nutter fan about to accost her.

"We did The Musical Time Machine together in 1975!" I happily carried on, garnering an even more petrified stare from the diminutive singer.

"Did we?" she replied uncertainly, her voice beginning to tremble.

Undaunted, I offered her my hand,

"John Howard!" I said, "You were so sweet to me on my first day in a TV studio!"

"Really? Was I?" She proffered a tiny shaking mitt. "That's nice to know!"

She tinkled out a laugh, though clearly unsure if I was about to start yelling obscenities at her.

"You stood in the wings as I sang my song," I ploughed on, "and were simply adorable! I just wanted to thank you, Lynsey, your kindness made the day very special."

Her driver, obviously concerned that his boss was being assaulted by this muscle-bound hunk with the beaming smile, got out of the car and walked between us, opening the door for Lynsey and glaring at me. She dashed in as though escaping from a bomb raid.

Her chauffeur closed the door, pulled himself up to his full height and nodded at me, as if to say, "Now back off, mate!".

My last glimpse of Lynsey as the car pulled away was of her little face, staring at me through the back window like a terror-stricken child.

In May of '96, my old friend, Terry, had a lunch party at Roy's Restaurant to celebrate his sixtieth birthday. When Neil and I walked in, some of the camper skinny queens gave me the once-over and while I was beginning to get used to this new admiration, it still felt odd. I had once been one of those skinny camp queens ogling a beefy number walking in.

I spotted Bob, who'd lived in Terry's Fulham house in 1975. I hadn't seen him for years and, ready for a lovely catch-up chat, I marched over to him, leaning in to give him a peck on the cheek. He stared at me as if I was an axe murderer.

"Who the *fuck* are you?" he said, backing away.

"Bob! It's me!" I cried. "It's John!"

His eyes nearly popped out of their sockets.

"Bloody hell!" he shrieked. "What the *fuck* have you done? You're *enormous*, you silly cow!"

I finally gave up weight-training in the early 2000s. Approaching fifty, I decided the time had come to cease trying to maintain a ripped Mr Universe look. I'd also become concerned at how obsessed I was getting at putting on increasingly more weight. It was I suppose the opposite of anorexia. I began to believe that if I hadn't lifted weights that day, I'd lose bulk and my shape would disappear. I'd then do a double routine the following day, studying myself in the mirror to make sure muscles were once more defined and massive.

Like a recovering addict, I gave up the anabolic drinks and sold the weights. Alarmingly quickly, the pounds, the *stones* in fact, fell off me within weeks.

"You see!" Neil said, delighted he had got his thinner man back. "I told you it was unnatural!"

Chapter Eight

It's Full of Stars

In the Spring of 1995, I got a phone call from a lady called Bobbie, secretary to Paul McGrane, who had recently become the new Chairman of Pickwick.

Following the company's purchase by Michael Green, Chairman and owner of Carlton Communications, I'd watched, from my new position at MCA, the old familiar senior management figures gradually dissolve and reappear in new bodies, housed in sharper suits and with a lot more money at their disposal.

Bobbie, an extremely chirpy-sounding lady, told me that Paul wanted to invite me for lunch.

"He's been told, by numerous former colleagues of yours, how great it would be if you would consider coming back!"

I was flattered, but told her, "I'm very happy here at MCA, Bobbie. I don't really want to come back to Pickwick. Seven years there was quite enough!"

I imagined her throwing her head back as she laughed a tinkly laugh.

"Oh, it's quite a different company now, John!" she bubbled. "Nothing like it was when you were last here. There are *so* many new departments now, new members of staff and *lots* of cash to spend on new projects!"

I paused, not sure how to respond to all this "new" stuff she was trying to impress me with.

"Can I at least book you in for a lunch with Paul?" she giggled persuasively, breaking my silence. "He's *dying* to meet you!"

* * *

Paul McGrane was an extremely tall, large-boned man with a big lugubrious face, framed by oversized glasses. He had a constant half-smile, as though expecting you to make him laugh at any minute. It was hard to tell if he was actually inwardly smiling or whether nature had shaped him that way.

As we settled into our pasta dishes and clinked glasses of chilled white wine, he told me he'd previously been Marketing Director of Guinness, during the period when they'd won several awards for their brilliant 'Horses in the ocean' advertising campaign. He had been hired by Michael Green to head up "the new Pickwick with a brief to make it one of his most profitable investments."

It soon became obvious as we chatted that the thing Paul lacked was any apparent knowledge of music or the music industry itself. Therefore, as he freely admitted, he needed a team of people to help grow the business for him and Green.

"We still have a good range of budget and sub-budget CDs," he told me, "utilising mainly public domain material, and we're continuing to build the Shows Collection range."

He stared meaningfully at me at that point, adding,

"Which you and Gordon Lorenz created of course."

He smiled that expectant smile.

"Which is why I want you back! We have to own a lot more of our own recordings, and sell them at full-price, if our business is to become more profitable."

Prompted by the handwritten note he'd unfolded and placed in front of him, he listed all the new recordings I'd brought to the company's owned portfolio in my seven years there. Even to me, it sounded impressive!

"What I need, John, is somebody – like you – indeed, you - to grow that side of things, to bring in more new material which we can then license out to third parties. It's clearly the way forward to building a profitable music company now."

He had, as he realised, ticked a box with me. I'd thoroughly enjoyed being at MCA for two years, watching my department's profits grow each year – from £900,000 when I'd joined in 1993 to the most recent figure of five-and-a half million pounds, much to Jeff Golembo's satisfaction. As he'd picked me for the job of Head of Special Projects from a wide range of applicants, Jeff would constantly sing my praises to Nick whenever I was attending a meeting with them.

In weekly A & R meetings, I was regularly lauded by Joe Cokell, the Marketing Director, for the difference I'd made in exploiting MCA's catalogue, creating new product ranges which sold in their thousands into Woolworth's and Smith's, thus giving the company more money to spend on new artist signings.

However, in truth I had missed the A & R side of things which I'd enjoyed while at Pickwick. I had once asked Jeff if he would be interested in me looking at signing older 'MOR' artists for the label and recording new albums with them. He had listened to my suggestion impassively then shaken his head, telling me to "carry on bringing in the money, John, not spending it needlessly."

While I had no feel for 'youth' pop music any longer, I knew there were many artists out there filling large concert halls, who had once sold hundreds of thousands of albums but were now without record deals because the major labels considered them 'yesterday's news'.

So, I knew that if I accepted Paul's offer to return to Pickwick, I would have the opportunity to achieve that goal of signing more artists with a ready-made audience. It was certainly tempting. My title would be A & R Director - the first time I'd been elevated to such a lofty height - and I was being offered a salary more than double what MCA was paying me, with added bonuses too.

"I'll pay you a bonus of £1,000 for every new album you bring in which Pickwick owns, John," Paul told me, his half smile increasing to a veritable beam.

But what convinced me in the end to make the move was Paul's assertion that "the company will soon be changing its name to Carlton Records," thereby instantly losing its long-standing budget-albums image, a change which I knew I needed if I was to convince sceptical big-name artists and their managers to sign with me.

"I know you don't need us, John," he said, sipping his coffee and looking over his glasses as we got to the end of the lunch, "but we certainly need you."

We shook hands and another step forward in my career had begun.

I left MCA in June. The company gave me a fabulous send-off party and presented me with a beautiful watch and a speech from Jeff which actually brought a lump to my throat. As I sat with Neil and watched so many friends cheering and clapping, one or two having a little weep, I momentarily wondered if I was doing the right thing.

I could have stayed at MCA for as long as I liked, trundling along in a job which wasn't difficult, the recipient of annual Christmas treats from licensees of champagne, smoked salmon and lavish lunches at the best restaurants, and with regular trips to LA to meet with the American Special Projects team. But I had recently reached the age of forty-two and felt that if I turned down the challenge Paul McGrane had set me – and the offer of a lot more money – I would always regret it.

My dad had recently told me that in his fifties he had actually requested a demotion at work as he was finding being in charge of a large department too much, the responsibility was causing him stress and sleepless nights. I was determined not to follow in his footsteps of uncertainty as my mum's genes came to the fore; she'd always embraced a challenge and often criticised Dad for his lack of ambition and drive.

So, on a sunny Summer morning, I joined 'the new Pickwick' at their Elstree-based offices. I'd driven there from our new home, a beautiful 17th century cottage in Lewknor, near Thame. We'd moved there the previous week so my drive would be shorter than the two-hour slog it would have been from Wantage.

My bottle-green company Audi 6, complete with plush white leather seating and wood finish, smelt wonderful as I sailed down the M40.

A few weeks earlier, Neil and I had gone on a very enjoyable search for our dream car, with a healthy budget of £25,000 to spend. As we perused various car showrooms, Neil, especially loving the adventure, asked one of the sales guys, "Is this the top of the range?"

The smart young well-groomed chap in a sharp mohair suit and polished shoes shot a glance at Neil who was dressed in his usual old denims, white T-shirt and scuffed leather boots.

"Company car, is it, sir?" the sales chap said, smiling wryly and as politely as he could.

Neil smiled back at him and replied, "How did you guess?"

Although the sales team at Pickwick welcomed me back with open arms, "because," as one of them told me, "you'll get this company back to where it was,", I had no intention of going backwards to the old Pickwick days. And in any case, that would have been impossible.

Although Pickwick had for years been the top budget record label in the UK, licensing from all the major record companies, in the time I'd been away a lot had changed. The majors, having learnt how we did it, had set up their own successful budget lines. They had a vast and varied catalogue of owned repertoire to choose from, which was why Jeff Golembo had wanted me to take the job at MCA and exploit their recordings more aggressively. It cut out 'the middle man' completely, i.e. the third-party licensees like Pickwick.

All the deals Pickwick had in the bag when I'd left in 1993, with Sony, Polygram, BMG, Virgin and MCA had expired, and there was no longer any desire by the labels to renew them. Why would they? Woolworth's and WH Smith were full of their own ranges of low-price CDs featuring top artists. Pickwick had become redundant, no longer necessary.

In my first few weeks back, I attended meetings, headed up by Paul McGrane, with all our previous licensors.

"The income from an Elton John or an Abba collection would instantly give you more money to expand our owned-repertoire catalogue even further," he'd told me, which while true became increasingly unlikely as the meetings progressed.

They were extremely pleasant and friendly, my old licensor chums chatting away to me about 'the good old days of Pickwick', but it soon became clear that they had nothing in common with Paul, and vice versa. When they'd reminisced with me about my time at MCA and the fantastic freebie days out we'd all had, drinking Pimms and eating smoked salmon at Ascot, Wimbledon and Lord's – 'The Special Projects Holiday Breaks' as we'd called them – Paul obviously felt left out of the picture, and looked increasingly bored.

He was even less happy when an old colleague of mine from Sony asked me why I'd turned my back on all that to return to Pickwick. It was obvious that Paul was out on a limb with people he'd never met before and who I'd known for several years – from both sides of the licensing desk.

I could tell straight away that none of them had any intention of licensing anything to us. I had a go at persuading my successor at MCA to let me have a Mamas & Papas compilation for our budget line, and while, again, he shot the breeze with me about how much he was enjoying his new job, I knew I'd never get the compilation cleared by him.

It was a whole new world indeed, and not one which anyone at Pickwick had seen coming.

"Now you understand why I need you here," Paul told me after one of the meetings had ended with pleasantries but no promises. "These guys are screwing us – we have to have a Plan B ready."

What I hadn't known before I re-joined was that a TV Albums Division had been set up by a chap called Tel, who I'd known from the old Monty Lewis days. He used to represent and license recordings to Pickwick, but he had since branched out to much bigger things. His new TV division enjoyed large spends and massive promotion budgets, signed off by Paul McGrane.

More worryingly, Tel had also been signing up several pop singles, readying them for release into an already jam-packed arena, and handled by a sales team which had no idea what was hot to trot in the pop charts. We chatted in the corridor on my first day and I wished him well with the new venture, but I knew from my time at MCA how difficult and expensive singles were to get away, even by established acts signed to major companies.

* * *

My own first signing was a lady Neil and I had watched on TV one evening, Maria Friedman. She had blown us both away when she'd performed Sondheim's 'Broadway Baby' at the Laurence Olivier Awards, having won an award earlier that evening for her one-woman West End show, *By Special Arrangement*.

The next morning, I made enquiries and found out who her manager was, ringing him as soon as I got to the office. To my surprise, when we sat over coffee in his kitchen that afternoon, Alan Field told me that I was "not only the first record company to call me, you are, in fact, the *only* record company to call me!". I had assumed, having been bowled over by Maria on TV the night before, that he must have been inundated with offers from the likes of EMI, Polygram and Sony. I was astonished that Maria's talent had gone so unnoticed by the majors.

Alan arranged for me to go and meet Maria, during rehearsals for her upcoming new show, *By Extra Special Arrangement,* but my first meeting with her began a little choppily. She seemed rather suspicious of "record company people", and, while not unfriendly, gave me the impression that I had to prove myself as someone she could trust, before she'd even consider making an album for me.

As I chatted to her over coffee, dropping in anecdotes about my own recording past, I felt her thaw a little, even enjoying a few shared giggles about the ups and downs of performing.

However, the thing which bothered her the most was the name of my company.

"Pickwick… " She pulled a face. "That's a kind of low-price outfit isn't it? I thought they only did cheap stuff for Woolworth's."

I explained that Carlton Communications had recently purchased Pickwick and plans were afoot to change its name to Carlton Records. I also assured her that I would be releasing exclusively full-price albums. That seemed to allay her worries somewhat.

"I like you, John," she said, smiling at me warmly for the first time, "but I still need time to decide if I trust you!"

"No problem!" I replied. "There is no rush, Maria. Have a think about it for as long as you like. Ask me anything, and come back to me when you're ready. I'm happy to discuss any matter which concerns you."

She looked across at Alan and her jaw firmed up.

"I definitely don't want to do one of those *Songs From The Shows* things I've seen Pickwick selling in Woolworth's!"

"Of course not," I replied, rather disingenuously.

Finally, we shook hands, she promised to have a think about my proposal and she went back to rehearsing with her director and partner, Jeremy Sams. As I was leaving, Maria called out, "What if we do an album of the songs I'm singing in my show – the album of the show?"

"Yeah!" Alan shouted. "We could record it live in the theatre!"

Maria pulled a face at him and glanced over at Jeremy as if to say, "No way!"

"Any ideas any of you come up with, just call me!" I replied diplomatically. "But do please keep in touch!"

The next day, I got a call from Alan. However, it was not to talk about furthering Maria's project – "She's still mulling it over" - but about one of the legends of pop music.

"I also manage Lonnie Donegan," he told me, "and next year will mark forty years since his first hit record, 'Rock Island Line'. He wants to make a new album in celebration, and, well, I was wondering, how about I bring him in to meet you at your office?"

Lonnie's arrival the next morning caused something of a minor commotion. Both Paul McGrane and Managing Director, Gerry Donohoe, bobbed and blushed around him like shy fans in the presence of their idol. Behaving like star-struck schoolboys, they even did a little bow as Lonnie shook their hands.

He amiably chatted with them for a few minutes, listening benignly to their stories of how their teenage years had been "enriched by your wonderful records."

"You made me want to be a musician," Gerry told him, trying to look relaxed, while the reddening of his neck betrayed his worshipful nervousness.

"I learnt the guitar because of you," Paul added.

"Yeah, a lot of people tell me that," replied Lonnie, hands in pockets, used to such fascination from long-time fans. "One of the reasons I want to talk to John here is because it's forty years next year since 'Rock Island Line' was a hit."

At that, both Paul and Gerry began playing air guitar and singing a couple of lines from the song. They were actually sharing their teenage memories with the very man who created them. Lonnie was utterly charming and professional, while Alan beamed at this display of adoration from the people who were likely to give his client a new record deal.

With some difficulty, I extricated Lonnie away from his fan club and offered him a seat in my office, while Paul and Gerry continued to smile through the window, giggling at each other. Finally, they waved and left us alone.

What I realised early on in our discussions was how focused Lonnie was. He knew what he wanted to record, why he wanted to record it, and who he wanted to record it with. I had naively, indeed ignorantly, assumed that this one-time huge pop star would be only too grateful to sign with me. How wrong I was!

"First off, I don't want this to be a nostalgia trip," Lonnie began. "If that's what you want, then we'll say goodbye now. Yes, I'll record a *couple* of my big hits, obviously 'Rock Island Line' and maybe one more from the old days. But I see this as a *new* album, not a re-tread. I'm still writing songs, I can still sing as well as I ever could, and I believe I would still have a market if I brought out a great album. *That's* the album I want to make for you. And *I* will produce it!"

"Excellent!" I replied, a little taken aback. "Sounds like a plan, Lonnie!"

"I'm great friends with Van Morrison," he told me, "and Van has said he'd love to record a couple of duets with me. That would help sales, wouldn't it?"

He sat back and smiled at me, waiting for me to look impressed. I was pleased but I didn't want to come over as a novice to this legendary guy.

"Great idea!" I said. "When could you start?"

"When you give me a contract to send to my solicitors! Which hopefully I'll be happy to sign!"

* * *

A couple of weeks later, I attended the music business UK forum, 'In The City', which was held every year in Manchester. The city itself had come on in leaps and bounds in the culture stakes since I'd last visited back in the '80s. As I got out of my taxi and walked towards the Midland Hotel in St Anne's Square, I could have been in Paris or Berlin, it felt so 'now' and new, really cosmopolitan and buzzing. The busy street cafés dotted about, with their waiters and waitresses rushing out with trays of food and drinks for chatting customers, gave it an air of multi-cultural confidence it had never even contemplated when I was growing up there.

The Midland was a large Edwardian, rather elegant hotel. Its wood-panelled halls and corridors were impregnated by decades of pipe-smoking besuited businessmen, whose hushed conversations on shiny leather chairs in quiet ante-rooms still whispered in the air of a grand long-gone past.

However, those whispers were now drowned out by noisy crowds of non-smoking T-shirted music business executives, all milling around or sitting in huddled meetings, discussing the various forums and seminars which were to take place over the weekend in specially constructed areas. It was like a mini-MIDEM.

I needed to freshen up after my journey on the train from Euston, so went straight to my room, poured a welcome G & T from the mini-bar and rang Neil to tell him I'd arrived safely. Then I had a long hot bath, looking through the many leaflets and invites I'd been given after checking in, helped myself to another G & T and got dressed. As I emerged from the lift, the buzz of conversation, music biz stories and gossip emanating from the bar area was even louder than when I'd arrived.

I ordered a drink and was casually looking around for a familiar face to have a chat to, when suddenly a hush descended over the room. We all looked at each other wondering what was wrong, when someone whispered very theatrically,

"Gary Glitter's here!".

It was as though royalty had arrived in our midst. As one, we moved like a glutinous liquid into the foyer, all craning our necks to see where he was. A scrum of journalists and photographers, who'd been nattering with each other just a few minutes earlier, were now cramming around the main door. In the middle of the melée, the top of a familiar mop of black lacquered hair bobbed up and down as the surrounding ocean of bodies slowly reached the bar. When they parted like the Red Sea, a diminutive Gary stood beaming at us all and bowed theatrically.

He looked rather perfect, dressed from head to foot in a silver silk suit with a purple satin shirt and pink sparkly leather boots. Camply sniffing the matching pink flower in his lapel, he twirled a silver-headed cane like a magician.

"Hello, Hello!" he chimed. "I'm back again!"

He was ushered rather briskly towards a seat in the bar, where he was once more submerged by journalists and cameramen who descended on him like ants, trying desperately to get a quote or a photo.

It was rather touching to see a once-enormous pop icon, who had fallen on much leaner times since his '70s Glam heyday, being given this fabulous accolade of acknowledged starriness. Many of those who were massing around him were probably only toddlers when he'd reigned at No.1 with 'I'm The Leader of The Gang' and 'I Love You Love Me Love'.

"He looks great!" one of my companions shouted above the furore.

"He's gigging again!" another said. "Packing 'em out at Universities around the country. It's like he's never been away!"

I waited for about half an hour until the scrum had thinned out to a few ardent admirers, and then went over and introduced myself to a small stocky chap who seemed to be in charge.

"I'm Jeff," he said, shaking my hand. "Gary's manager. Come and sit down."

I followed him to a seat by the bar and explained my mission at Carlton.

"I'm convinced that artists like Gary just need the right record to sell to the fans again," I told Jeff, and, utilising the snippet of info my acquaintance had given me earlier, "all the Uni kids would definitely buy something new by him."

Jeff nodded and got up.

"Okay, come with me," he said and took me over to meet Gary.

Giving his charge the relevant information about me and Carlton, he moved back as Gary stood and shook my hand.

"John!" Gary said, beaming at me and studying me head to foot. "Yeah! I like the sound of that! I really want to make a record again! Sit down with me and we'll talk!"

He was very easy to chat with, although he did most of the talking. He excitedly told me how he was "selling thousands of concert tickets around the country, doing all the old stuff, obviously", but that he'd been writing some new material as well.

"But as you and I know, John," he continued, leaning into me conspiratorially, "to get any new album off the ground, you need something the fans can recognise first. Right? So! How about this for an idea?" He sat even closer to me, lowering his voice as though worried someone might overhear. "Why don't we record a new version of 'Hello, Hello, I'm Back Again'?"

He jumped back in his seat and did his trademark manic stare which had always amused me when watching him on Top of The Pops. Then he nudged me, like an old mate.

"Oasis recently sampled that track for their new album. It's given it a whole new audience."

He chuckled to himself and nudged me again.

"I'd call the new version, 'Hello, Hello, I'm Back Again *(Again)*'! It could be a smash hit!"

While he'd clearly thought it up before our meeting, his enthusiasm, and boyish need to make you think he'd just come up with the idea, was rather infectious. He had a knack for making you believe in something simply because he recognised its potential. I was rather enthralled by this man who still possessed a huge dollop of star charisma.

"How'd you fancy coming to see my show at Wembley next Saturday?" he said. "Bring a special friend!" he added, twinkling away. "I'd *love* to meet him!"

* * *

An artist who I'd admired for decades was Elkie Brooks. Although she'd been around on the pop scene since the '60s, a contemporary of Cilla and Dusty and touring with The Beatles and The Animals, she'd never had a hit during that Swinging decade. Then, in 1977, seemingly out of the blue, she struck gold with 'Pearl's A Singer'.

A & M Records, who had signed Elkie in 1975, recruited Lieber and Stoller to produce her album *Two Days Away*, resulting in her first charting album and moving her immediately into the major league. She spent the rest of the '70s and a good deal of the 1980s in the singles and albums charts, particularly selling huge quantities of her *Pearls* and *Pearls 2* Greatest Hits albums.

I'd personally seen how big her fanbase was when I compiled a hits collection for Pickwick in the late '80s called *Priceless*. It sold bundles of CDs in Woolworth's and Smith's, becoming one of our autumn best-sellers that year. *Priceless 2* the following year did just as well.

By the mid-'90s, however, while she still sold out large venues, her records hadn't sold in the same large quantities. She had also changed labels several times, seemingly not as settled with things as she'd been at A & M.

However, I felt that with the right project she could hit it really big again and Gerry Donohoe agreed.

"If we can put together a fantastic TV campaign for an album by Elkie Brooks, John," he said to me after I'd told him about my plan to get in touch with her, "it could go Top Five! God, John! I can see it now! Fabulous, my son!"

I found out that she was managed by her husband, Trevor Jordan, and, after some research, rang him. He was very friendly on the phone and said he'd put my idea – *Elkie Brooks with The Royal Philharmonic Orchestra: The Abba Album* – to her, but laughed saying, "I don't think she'll be impressed with your *Elkie Sings Abba* concept, but I like the sound of you, John, so I'll get her to call you."

He was right. She deftly knocked my suggestion out into the ocean of lost million sellers.

"I wouldn't be *in any way* interested in singing *Abba songs!*" she told me, spitting out the words like a rebuke.

However, once past that hurdle, we had a really good chat and agreed to meet for lunch with Trevor the following week.

I took along one of the albums Tony Britten had arranged and produced for me, *The RPO Perform Les Miserables,* as a demonstration of the kind of thing he could do with wonderful songs backed by a massive orchestra.

"Great, John!" Elkie said, studying the CD booklet and sipping her coffee, after an enjoyable meal with lots of anecdotes about her extraordinary recording career. "It looks like a very nice album. But, my friend, as I told you on the phone, I am *not* recording any fucking Abba songs!"

I laughed out loud.

"Oh my god!" I shouted. "Elkie Brooks just swore at me. How *fabulous*!"

At that Elkie started to giggle, and Trevor took over as we fell about.

"What Elkie would love to do, John," he said, bringing us both back to serious discussion, "is to record an album of her greatest hit songs with the RPO."

"Try to imagine it, John," she added. "'Nights In White Satin' and 'Lilac Wine' with the RPO backing me. It would be amazing!"

"Fucking amazing!" I said.

"Exactly," Elkie said, breaking into a smile.

"*Amazing!*" Trevor jumped in. "*That's* the album title!"

The three of us stared into space and pictured the album sleeve.

* * *

1996 marked what would have been Buddy Holly's 60th birthday. To celebrate the event, I wanted to find an artist who could do an album of his songs. I was putting together some ideas when my secretary, Marion, brought in an invite from a chap called Alfie Shore. He was hosting a talent contest in Liverpool in aid of The Sunshine Club, and wanted me to be one of the judges. It sounded rather fun, with the chance of hearing burgeoning young talent from the city which had produced so many pop stars in the 1960s.

I told Marion to call Alfie and accept the invitation. Within a few minutes, she called through saying Alfie had "an exciting proposal!".

As soon as I heard him greet me with, "Mr. Howard! I have something you will definitely be interested in," it was clear that he was your typical smooth operator, telling me I was a "great sounding guy!" and "what an honour it will be to have you judging the event!".

"My secretary said you had something exciting to propose," I interrupted his smarm.

"Yeah, that's right John! How would you like to have Connie Francis make a record for Carlton?"

I'd compiled a couple of greatest hits of hers for Pickwick a few years earlier which had sold extremely well, but I was unaware that she was still recording , less than two years off her own sixtieth birthday.

"Oh! She's still performing *and* recording!" he told me. "In fact, John, I'd like to arrange a meeting between the two of you."

"Is she in the UK?" I said, already imagining her doing my Buddy Holly album.

"No! She's performing in Atlantic City next month. I've approached Stuart Colman already, and he loves the idea of producing an album by Connie for you. Why not fly over with me, meet Stuart and come see Connie perform and talk to her after the show?"

Stuart Colman had made his name mainly from producing big hits for Shakin' Stevens. He'd been voted top singles producer of 1982 by Music Week and had also worked with Kim Wilde, Phil Everly, Alvin Stardust and Little Richard. Stuart now lived in Nashville and so was well-placed to record an album with Connie.

He rang me from there a few days after my call from Alfie. When I mentioned my idea of Connie doing an album of Buddy songs for the 60th anniversary, he was very enthusiastic.

"What a great concept!" he said, the trace of an American accent already coming through. "Here's an extra great idea, John... why don't we get Connie in the studio with The Crickets?!"

"Can you make that happen?" I asked him.

"Of course! They're great mates of mine and knew Connie really well back in the day! Imagine it, John! Connie Francis singing Buddy Holly songs backed by *The Crickets*! How great would *that* be?!"

* * *

127

In the late Summer of 1995, I suggested to Paul McGrane that he do an interview with Music Week. We needed to raise our profile in the music media and make the big announcement that Pickwick had now officially changed its name to Carlton Records, specialising in releasing brand new full-price albums. Paul was up for it and asked me to set the wheels in motion.

I spoke to Sally who now ran the new Carlton Music Company press office and she duly contacted the magazine and set the interview up. It appeared a couple of weeks later, and set off a new round of phone calls from interested artists, managers and producers.

One of them came from a chap called Paul Mason who was managing Hazell Dean. She had been a big gay icon in the '80s, crossing over from disco sensation to mainstream pop star with 'Searchin' (Looking For Love)' and 'Whatever I Do', both of which hit the UK Top 10 in 1984.

When Paul told me he was looking for a new label for Hazell who was "very keen to record again", off the top of my head I suggested that *she* do *The Abba Album*. It was a concept I was unwilling to drop so I was extremely chuffed when, instead of turning down the idea, as Elkie had done, he was very interested.

He called me a couple of days later.

"Hazell adores Abba! She would *love* to do it!"

Another call came from a guy I hadn't heard of, John Wilson. Although his sister Mari had hit it big in the '80s, with 'Just What I Always Wanted' and her lovely cover of the Julie London classic, 'Cry Me A River', I was unsure about taking on a virtual unknown to the record-buying public. It was an unplanned deviation from my mission to sign up name artists with a legacy of hits or at least a growing prestige and acclaim in their particular fields, such as Maria Friedman.

I knew that our fledgling press and marketing departments would find it hard to build an artist from scratch - never easy for established record companies – but I agreed to meet with John, and I was very glad I did. When he brought me in his cassette, full of wonderful new material he'd written, I knew he was an artist I wanted on the label. Fabulous voice, good-looking guy with oodles of charm and self-belief, great original songs and an enthusiasm which was truly infectious. I thought – and convinced my colleagues - that it was worth a punt.

In the early autumn of '95, a lady called Grace Chalmers called. She told me she'd recently become Sonia's manager and, having read Paul McGrane's Music Week interview, said she believed that "Carlton Records sounds just the kind of company I'm looking for."

Sonia had been one of Stock, Aitken & Waterman's successes in the late '80s, a tiny Liverpool girl with a massive voice who'd hit No.1 with 'You'll Never Stop Me Loving You'. She'd kind of lost out thereafter to the increasingly huge Kylie Minogue, who seemed to get the better songs and a chain of chart-toppers. Sonia did have a few more hits, a couple of them even scraping the Top Ten, but nothing ever matched her debut success. In 1993, she'd come second in the Eurovision Song Contest with 'Better The Devil You Know' (cheekily named after Kylie's 1990 smash) but it had only reached No.15 in the charts.

On a whim, I called my old friend Steve Levine, with whom I'd recorded a couple of singles in the early '80s before he'd hit it massive with Culture Club. I asked him if he fancied producing an album with Sonia and, to my delight, he jumped at the idea. I suggested she record another concept which had been floating around my head for weeks – The Philly Album, made up of covers of hits by artists signed to the Philadelphia label in the '70s.

There were so many great songs written by Gamble and Huff to choose from, and Steve and I began running them off our fingers:

When Will I See You Again, Back Stabbers, If You Don't Know Me By Now, Love Train, Year of Decision, The Love I Lost, Show You The Way To Go, I'll Always Love My Mama, 992 Arguments, Wake Up Everybody. As we listed them one after the other we both became increasingly excited about the idea. I also believed that such a concept would take Sonia out of the middle-of-the-road disco market I felt she'd become trapped in and give her the credibility she deserved.

"Sonia - *The Philly Album*!" Steve said. "Love it!"

A few weeks later, Sonia and her manager visited Carlton, wandering around chatting to everyone with great ease and charm, winning over any doubting Thomases immediately. Sonia herself was over the moon about the project, and really excited about working with Steve.

"I loved Culture Club!" she bubbled as my colleagues joined her in a glass of champagne. "I bought all their records!"

"I'm certain Boy George is going to buy your album too!" I ventured, getting an enormous grin from Sonia.

"Yeah!" she cried, throwing back her head and laughing. "Wouldn't that be *fab*?!"

So, after a few months which had raced by, I had a healthy roster of artists which I hoped would produce some great albums and put the company on the map and in the charts. And, with the change from 'Pickwick' to 'Carlton Records', it meant that I would no longer have to reassure artists that they weren't signing to a budget label. Finally, we sounded like a full-price record company. Full steam ahead!

Chapter Nine

Oh Dad (Look What You Done)

For a few years after my mum died in 1974, I only occasionally saw my dad. It wasn't due to any falling out, simply that he very quickly found a new life for himself which didn't require his son to be closely involved.

Initially he was the 'widower about town', having fun as an available guy in his late 40s, playing in jazz bands, enjoying rounds of golf with friends at weekends and dating quite a few single ladies of a similar age.

After his various 'bachelor flings', he got married in 1976 to Sybil, who he'd met at Ames Crosta Mills when she worked in the accounts department. 'Ames Crosta', where Dad had worked as a draughtman from the age of fourteen, designed and manufactured sewage purification plants and between 1980 and 1982 the company sent him and a few of his colleagues to Singapore, working on designs for a new sewage system there. (As a child, whenever we went out in the car, he'd point out where a new sewage system he'd helped design had recently been installed. It made for fascinating day trips around the country).

Dad's Singapore jaunts were six month stints, home for three, then back again for six months and so on. He'd loved it there but could never persuade Sybil to join him.

"She hates the heat and won't like the food," he'd told me once.

After working in an air-conditioned office all day, he'd spend his evenings playing piano in the convivial heat of one of the most popular jazz clubs in the area. He was making quite a name for himself locally, drawing crowds whenever he performed.

"It was steaming hot in there," he told me once, "both the music and the temperature – but I had a ball!"

I guessed that, during his time in Singapore, he became the man I remembered from my childhood – fun-loving, relaxed, a bit reckless and enjoying a boozy night with his musician mates. He once showed me a photo album of his Singapore life and in every picture he's smiling, surrounded by friends, taking boat trips out to various islands and tucking into barbeques and beers at local restaurants.

Apparently, Sybil hated the photos, she even got upset if she caught him looking at them. Listening to him talking about his time in Singapore was a no-no too. During a visit to their home in the '80s, I'd asked him about his trips, but was met with an embarrassed glance across the room at his wife who sat on the edge of her chair glaring at him.

"It upsets her," he said, when she'd left the room, "so I stay off the subject."

He eventually gave me the photo album "to keep safe", and to look at whenever he visited me and Neil, without the disapproving stares and tutting from his wife.

Apart from me occasionally going up North to visit him and the rest of the family, usually for a funeral or to greet a new baby in the clan, through most of the '80s annual phone calls at Christmas kept me in touch with Dad along with a postcard from my twice-yearly holidays in Mykonos.

But in 1988, when Neil and I moved out of London to Oxfordshire, he suddenly seemed to want to establish closer contact with me. He began visiting us every year, and by the early '90s twice a year, staying for almost three weeks each time. Sybil never accompanied him. It became his little getaway treat to himself, while she was glad not to have him sitting around, getting in the way of her daily cleaning regime.

"It gives Sybil some time to herself," Dad would say, smiling benignly at the thought of his wife washing floors, scrubbing bathrooms, hoovering and polishing everything till it squeaked.

During his stays, on weekdays I'd take him into London, dropping him off near a tube station from where he would visit galleries, museums and various exhibitions, and then meet me in town at about six o'clock for dinner after I'd finished work. We'd sometimes go to see a play or enjoy an evening of Old Time Music Hall at The Players Theatre.

At weekends, Neil and I would take him out to various riverside pubs and restaurants for lunch. He loved hearing Neil's stories of plays and pantos he'd been in, and my updates of recording projects I was working on. He once told Neil that he had never felt closer to me than he did at that time.

The first sign that things were getting increasingly bizarre in the Jones homestead was when Des O'Connor had just recorded my song 'Blue Days' in 1992. Dad had come down for his usual second visit of the year, and we were enjoying a lunch out together. (Neil was away playing Ugly Sister to Christopher Biggins' Buttons in *Cinderella*).

I was chatting excitedly about Des's single of 'Blue Days' about to be released, as well as telling Dad what I thought were fun stories of the invites Neil and I had enjoyed to the recordings of Des's weekly chat show at Thames Studios in Teddington.

"Jodie always comes with us," I told him, "and after the show we join Des and his guests in the Green Room for cocktails."

He sat smiling rather oddly at his napkin as I nattered away, and then, just as I was expecting him to reply with his usual, "I'm so proud of you, son", he said, "Sybil's not pleased at all, you know."

I stopped eating and stared at him. "What do you mean?"

"Well, it's *that* woman you keep company with, and the way he left his wife for her."

I was gobsmacked.

"What *are* you talking about, Dad?"

"It's in all the papers!"

"What is?"

"Des and *your pal*, 'That tart', as Sybil calls her, cavorting in public together."

I put down my knife and fork and took a deep breath.

"Okay! First of all, I do *not* take kindly to your wife calling one of my best friends a tart!"

He started to reply but I held up my hand.

"I haven't finished, Dad, not by a long shot."

"Oh, here we go!" he said, doing his nodding into his shoulders routine, which I remembered from my childhood when he was being nagged by Mum.

"Yes! Here we go, Dad! Firstly, what right does Sybil think she has to say that about anyone? She has never *met* Jodie or Des. She's just taking in what she reads in her trashy papers as gospel."

"Now, now," he began, pointing his fatherly finger at me.

"Don't now, now me! For your information, though it's none of your business, Des had left his wife *before* he met Jodie. They fell in love while working together in a panto. They are a wonderful couple, full of affection for each other, and *great friends of ours*!"

"It's not what Syb -"

"I don't give a damn what Sybil says, Dad. I told you years ago she has psychological problems; the clean-aholic behaviour; her controlling of what you do and say; her resentment of anyone in the public eye finding success – unless they're called Barry Manilow. She's an emotional tyrant, Dad. And now, she's got you reporting, like a scared little messenger, what she thinks of my friends. I am so ashamed of you, Dad! What the hell has happened to you?"

"She's a very good woman!" he insisted, not actually replying to any of my points.

"Anyone who calls someone she has never met a tart, is not a good person, Dad." I was fuming, and getting stares from other diners. "You can report back to her from me, that I *do not* take kindly to her offensive views. She needs to keep them to herself, and inside the pages of the tabloid crap she reads."

Embarrassed that my rant was making him a person of interest in the restaurant, he tried to calm the waters.

"You know what she's like, son," he said in his best self-effacing Northern.

"I'm beginning to realise just how *damaged* she is, Dad! And just how much she has you under her thumb. Tell her to mind her own bloody business and keep her nasty little comments to herself – if you dare to, that is!"

Perhaps because my rant had finally cut a crack in his silent wall of tolerance of his wife's unbalanced behaviour, during Dad's next visits he started to let slip little tales about life with Sybil, drip-dripping the facts a bit more each time.

One afternoon, staring across the river as we lunched outside the Rose Revived Inn, he said, "I don't think I've ever told you this. On the first night of our honeymoon in London, Syb and I were walking along The Strand back to our hotel when two women with short skirts and low-cut blouses walked past us. When they'd gone, Sybil accused me of staring at them. I hadn't been but she never stopped going on about it the whole night, nagging me for the rest of the week about these two bloody women. She was convinced I was eyeing them up – 'Those tarts!', she called them."

"She seems to enjoy using that word rather a lot, doesn't she, Dad?" I replied.

"You know," he said, taking a long glug of his beer, "she cuts photos of women she disapproves of out of the newspaper before I've had a chance to read it."

Neil and I actually burst out laughing at that. The image of Dad picking up his tattered newspaper full of holes every morning was like something from a comedy series from the '60s. But he was looking anything but amused.

"Dad," I said, "why have you let this situation go on so long?"

He smiled darkly at me. "I thought she'd change, stop accusing me of those kinds of things." He looked coyly at me. "You know, sexual things, once she realised I wasn't like that."

"Why does she think you are 'like that', Bert?" Neil asked him, trying for a smile but getting a flinch instead.

"Her first husband knocked her about, you know, probably played around a lot and it damaged her. She's at heart a nice girl."

"And now you realise, she's not going to change, Bert?" Neil said, serious again.

"If anything, she's getting worse," he replied, playing with his food like a doleful little boy and shaking his head.

As I watched this lost, unhappy man staring at his plate, a thought popped into my head, 'If Mum were alive, she'd give you a good long talking to.'

But as Mum had always said, Dad never tackled anything head-on, he preferred to ignore problems and hope they'd go away.

"He's got his head so deep in the sand," Mum used to say, after they'd had words about something she wanted him to sort out, "he couldn't get it out of there if he tried."

During another visit, we took Dad to a play Tracey was performing in. Jodie was going to sit with us in the audience and I was hoping that, having met her in person, he'd realise how lovely she was.

We arrived at the packed theatre, the foyer buzzing with people and very soon Neil and I were deep in conversation with friends of Keff and Tracey's we'd met at one of their house parties. Dad seemed to be enjoying it all, smiling in his, "I can't hear what anyone's saying so I'll just look interested" kind of way. Then, from behind me I heard

Jodie's voice.

"Hi John! Hi Neil!" she said, hugging us.

I introduced her to Dad and as she proffered her hand he shook it like a frightened little boy. She asked him how long he was staying with us, and saying how nice it was to meet him at last, which garnered one-word replies followed by embarrassed silence. Finally, giving up on the one-sided conversation, Jodie turned to tell me about some new songs she'd been writing. After a few minutes of us chatting away, I suddenly realised Dad had disappeared.

"Oh, John!" Jodie said, looking worried. "Where's your dad gone?"

We both looked into the crowd until, pointing to the far end of the room, Jodie said,

"Er, John... your dad's over there. Is he okay?"

I looked where she was pointing and there he was, sidling backwards, letting the melée carry him along and engulf him like a willing flood victim. We both watched fascinated as he eventually came to a standstill right at the back of the room, only his head visible above the sea of people, benignly staring into space with the disconnected smile he'd come to perfect in recent years.

Shaking my head and chuckling, as though to say, "Dads, eh?" I excused myself and pushed through the crowd towards him.

"Are you okay, Dad?" I said, worried he might be having a senior moment.

"I didn't want to, you know... "

"You didn't want to what?"

He jutted out his chin at me.

"Well, I didn't want to spend any more time with... with *her*. If Sybil asks me what I did this evening, she'll get it out of me that Jodie was here and that I shook her hand. I thought if I at least got away from her, I wouldn't get too much of a bollocking when I get home!"

I stared at this pathetic little man who was my father. Just as I was about to start haranguing him, the five-minute bell rang and the crowd began to move out of the bar into the theatre.

"They're going in now," I said, pushing him forward, "come on!"

"Don't sit me with her!" he said, fear widening his eyes.

"I'm tempted to, just to make you squirm all evening!" I said.

"Then I'll walk out!" he said, like a little lad having a tantrum.

"Don't be so stupid!" I replied and ushered him into the auditorium.

"You don't know what it's like for me!" he protested in the car on the way home, after I'd had another go at him as we'd left the theatre. "Sybil interrogates me every time I get home, as soon as I walk in the door."

"Then it's your own fault, Dad," I told him in the rear view mirror. "You should bloody well stand up to her!"

"I can't!"

He seemed near to tears, Neil squeezing my thigh as though to say, 'Ease off.'

I sighed, trying to control my exasperation and left a few minutes silence to clear the air. Then as gently as I could, I said, "You really should have nipped it in the bud years ago, Dad, as soon as she gave you a bollocking for looking at those women in The Strand!"

"I *wasn't* looking at them!"

"So what if you were, Bert?" Neil said. "It's what straight blokes do, look at women! What world does your wife live in? Disney World?"

"She wishes she did live in Disney World, where everything is… "

"Not real!" I said. "Lordy, Dad, you really picked one this time!"

The rest of the journey home was decidedly quiet.

* * *

The following year, when Dad came for his Summer break, we resolutely avoided the subject of Sybil. I didn't ask and he didn't tell. I assumed his silence on the subject meant nothing had changed, and, after all, he was visiting us to get away from her. So, we gave him the respite he needed and took him out and about, to Stately Homes, of which there are lots in Oxfordshire, beautiful public gardens and parks and the usual round of restaurants and riverside pubs for Sunday lunch, which he especially loved.

However, the evening before he was due to go home, I was hosing the garden at the back of the cottage when Dad appeared through the French windows. He came out onto the lawn and followed me around, occasionally commenting on a particularly lovely set of hollyhocks and how good everything was looking, when, out of the blue, he said, "My life is hell, you know."

I wasn't sure I'd heard him right, so I turned off the hose and asked him to repeat what he'd said.

"My life with Sybil. It's a living hell."

"Come and sit down," I said and led him to the stone bench by the back wall, bathed that evening in the beautiful smell of honeysuckle.

"I'm living in a nightmare," he continued, smiling ruefully at the foxgloves as he sat next to me.

"Oh Dad, are things that bad?"

"Worse."

Once again, I thought he was going to cry.

"It's like I'm walking on eggshells the whole time. She can tip at the least thing, you know."

"Have you considered going to a psychiatrist with her? She obviously needs help."

Just then, Neil appeared at the door with drinks on a tray, two G & T's for us, whisky on the rocks for Dad. He walked towards us, saying "Cocktail time!" and handed the whisky to Dad.

"Can I ask you a favour?" Dad said, savouring the taste of his drink.

"Of course."

"When you talk to her on the phone, if she rings here… "

"She never does," I said, "only when you're staying with us."

Dad made a 'Not now' face and ploughed on.

"Well, when she calls again, could you not tell her that I watch TV with you?"

"What do you mean," Neil said, glancing at me, "not tell her?"

Dad did his embarrassed little laugh.

"You told her that we'd been watching telly last weekend when she rang, and when I got onto the phone she grilled me about what we'd been watching."

"And why is that a problem?" I asked him.

"Well, if she knows we've been watching something which has a bit of violence or maybe even a bit of, you know, sex in it… "

"What, you mean like Coronation Street?" Neil laughed.

Dad just winced, looking annoyed.

"Whatever I tell her, she'll go and check the Radio Times to see if it tallies. There's no getting away with it!"

I stared at the man who with every passing year lessened in my estimation, and yet for whom I felt a deep sorrow. Totally useless domestically, he was one of the last breed of Northern men who needed a woman to balance his world, to cook and clean for him and provide the solace of being looked after, fed and mothered. Every woman he'd dated after my mum died had been a potential wife, rather than a girlfriend to have some fun with.

Ironically, the one he'd married had completely turned his world upside down, providing nothing but misery and regret, albeit within an extremely clean house.

I wondered aloud if she'd ever been physically violent with him after he'd done something which had annoyed her.

"No, no! Nothing like that!" he protested. "She's just… I just… well, you know, I just want… "

"A quiet life. Yes, I know, Dad. Mum always used to say, 'Your father hangs a Do Not Disturb sign on the door to his world.'"

"Your mum said that?"

"Several times. But she loved you."

He looked for a moment lost in memories, swilling the ice around in his whisky.

"Does Sybil love you, Dad?"

"Ee! That's a bit personal!" he said, looking mildly affronted.

"Well, does she?"

He knocked back his drink and said, "She does her best for me."

I shook my head. He was beyond help.

"Another drink, Bert?" Neil said.

"Only if you're having one," he replied.

Dad's last visit to see Neil and me was in the late Summer of 2006, at our house near Haverfordwest in Pembrokeshire which we moved into in 2001. It was a large 1970s upside-down detached house in three-quarters of an acre of garden, and while we loved the place, it had become too large for just the two of us and we'd put it on the market a few weeks earlier.

The original idea was that Neil's parents, Nell and Ike, would move in with us at some point of their choosing. However, Ike had died within weeks of us arriving in Pembrokeshire and Nell had passed away unexpectedly while staying with us in 2004.

Having got rid of our mortgage when we'd sold the cottage in Lewknor and bought our current place for half the price, we'd worked out that, by selling the Pembrokeshire house at a reasonable profit, we could buy somewhere in Southern Spain outright and still have good savings left to keep us going indefinitely, in a country where the cost of living was so much lower and yes, provided more blue skies to wake up to.

We'd just had word that a couple who'd viewed the house that afternoon had put in an offer, which we'd accepted, and were sharing a bottle of Champagne with Dad to celebrate.

As we sat in the front sitting-room watching the sun going down through the silver birch trees by the window, I explained to Dad why we'd decided to leave the UK.

"I think it's a great idea!" he said, quaffing his champers and holding up his glass for a refill. "I'm looking forward to coming to see you in Spain, sitting in the sun all day on your patio, eating home-grown olives and drinking a nice Rioja!"

Although there were no worries about Dad's health at that point, I'd become a little concerned during his stay that he was beginning to act a little strangely. I don't mean regarding his life with Sybil, which certainly bordered on the bizarre, it was more that he'd become obsessed with, for instance, playing Sudoku whenever he was in the house. As soon as we'd return from a trip out, within seconds he was back on the sofa, Sudoku book in hand and almost manically playing another game.

I asked him once why he seemed so taken with it.

"Keeps my mind agile!" he'd replied before becoming absorbed once more, studying the page, pencil in hand, like it was the most important task he'd ever undertaken.

I'd also noticed, especially when he was sitting in the back of the car, that he'd started sniffing all the time, blowing his nose, then sniffing again, as though his nose was constantly blocked. I'd asked him on one of our journeys out to Marloes where we'd sit and watch the seals and their babies playing on the rocks below the cliffs, if he had a cold coming on.

He'd looked surprised, shook his head and replied, "No. Why?" Then he began sniffing again.

A few weeks later, having completed on the sale, Neil and I moved out of the house to rent a small cottage nearby while we planned our visit to look for a house in Spain. I called Dad to give him our new temporary address and began chatting about how we were looking forward to his first visit "to our new house in the sun!".

"It won't be long, " I told him, "before you'll be sitting on our veranda with a glass of Sangria in your hand, Dad!"

His response shocked me.

"I'm not coming!" he stated.

"Why ever not?" I asked him.

"I don't want to come to Spain. I don't want to fly. Flying frightens me!"

This was from the man who had happily, nay excitedly, flown to Singapore three times a year in the '80s, had dreamed as a teenager of being a pilot before his poor eyesight robbed him of that ambition, and was the father who had insisted Mum, me, Sue and him fly to the Isle of Man in 1961 when we could just as easily – and more usually at that time - have got the train and the ferry.

"You'll love flying," Dad had told me as he drove us in one of our old jalopies to Manchester airport.

Once on the plane, he'd pointed out of the window at the white billowing clouds floating by.

"They look like you could step out and walk on them, don't they, son?" he had said, wonder in his eyes.

So this sudden change of heart about flying to Spain – especially after our conversation just a few weeks earlier - was bemusing to say the least.

Six months later, I rang Dad a couple of days before Neil and I were due to leave the UK en route to our new home in Murcia. Before I'd had a chance to even ask him how he was, he told me that a friend of his, Don, a singer in his jazz band, was going to ring me and explain why he'd hated living in Spain.

"Don may be able to change your mind!" he said.

"But Dad," I replied, "we've bought the house there now, we're going. You know that."

"Yes, but let Don explain! He really *hated* it there!"

He sounded almost desperate.

"Dad?" I said, "Why are you suddenly so against me going? You said you loved the idea when we'd talked about it last time you stayed."

He ignored what I'd said.

"Don will call you today," he said, "hopefully talk some sense into you."

With a curt "'Bye", he put the phone down.

Of course, Don just complained bitterly about how "everything closes in the afternoon, just as the wife and I want to go shopping!"

"It's called their Siesta," I replied.

"I know! It's ridiculous!"

It seemed to be his only bugbear of his five years living in Valencia.

Once Neil and I had settled in our new home, I called Dad a few times to chat about the house, what we were planning to do to it and – more from hope than expectation - how much I was looking forward to him coming to stay with us. But each time he became more hostile, more angry, in the end refusing to even react to what I was saying, giving me the silent treatment every time I mentioned my new life in Spain.

Our phone calls became increasingly about what Sybil had done and nothing about what Neil and I were up to. Over a period of a couple of years, Dad no longer answered the phone, which was unusual. Sybil had started picking up, explaining each time, "Your dad's asleep. He sleeps a lot more during the day now."

On one occasion she'd told me, "He's not sleeping well at nights anymore."

"Why is that?"

"He's having bad dreams and night sweats. We're going to the doctor tomorrow and see if they can give him something."

Finally, after weeks of beating around the bush, I asked her what was wrong with him. She left a pause before saying, "He's had tests, John… it's Alzheimer's. Your dad's got Alzheimer's."

* * *

On one of my visits to see family in 2009, Dad seemed quite contented if a little bemused, as Sybil dashed around making tea and wiping down surfaces.

As she was busying away with a mop and bucket in the kitchen, he tapped his head and said, "Something's not right… in here, John. It's not working right."

"What do you mean, Dad?"

"I don't know. I just know something's going wrong… " he tapped his head again, "… in here."

Sybil had booked us into their favourite restaurant, run by a friend of hers. The last time I'd accompanied them there, years before, I'd had a contretemps with the waitress about the one slice of toast we'd been given with our paté. I had clearly embarrassed Sybil – and infuriated the waitress - when I insisted on an extra two pieces of toast with which to finish my starter. This time, however, such matters paled into insignificance.

As the three of us sat in the small bar area waiting to be seated, my dad looking around the room with an expression which said, 'Not sure where we are, but it's very nice,' Sybil turned to Dad and, in a kind of Les Dawson stage whisper, said, "John's not like us, is he?"

Dad stared at his wife, then at me, then back at Sybil, "You what, love?"

"I said," she nodded over at me, raising her whisper to a rasp, "John's not like us, he's not a *racist* like us, is he?"

Dad leaned into her, cupping his ear, trying to make sense of what she was saying.

"I'm sorry, love, what are you saying?"

Eyes popping out of her head and staring around the room, she repeated it again, her voice now an exasperated growl.

"I *said*! John's not a *racist* – like *us* – is *he*?!"

The buzz of conversation in the bar stopped. Curious glances shot across the room at us. Sybil tried a friendly chuckle back but her face had turned crimson.

Dad began laughing to himself, shaking his head as though she'd said something funny and muttering, "Ee, she's a one, isn't she?".

I'd had enough.

"No, Sybil," I said. "I am not a racist. Though I'm fully aware that you are. But, unless you want a row right here, right now, I suggest you drop it."

She glared at me, her face turning a dangerous beetroot colour. Her mouth hanging open in disbelief, she turned to Dad in silent comment about his son's downright cheek. Dad just smiled at her, then at me, nodding his head as one would at a complaining toddler.

"Ee, tha' lad's getting a bit irksome, ain't he?" he said, his Salford accent sounding more pronounced than it had ever been.

Another surreal night out with my father and his wife had begun.

* * *

As my father's condition worsened and Sybil could no longer have a proper conversation with him, she oddly turned to me for some kind of comfort, clearly enjoying our now weekly phone calls. They always had to take place on a Thursday, "as I go to the hairdresser's on a Friday," she'd explained. I guessed the other days were full of various cleaning and polishing duties on her rota of numerous 'things to do round the house'.

Although I didn't like the woman, I did respect how she'd rallied to look after Dad through all the changes in his personality and behaviour. Most disturbingly, he'd started saying someone had bugged the house, telling Sybil to be careful what she said because 'they' were listening.

She no longer knew who she'd find when she walked into a room. He'd sometimes be looking frightened and suspicious of her, other times frustrated and annoyed with her, and then, on better days, benign and affectionately grateful to her for looking after him.

He'd even occasionally become boyishly playful. One afternoon when she'd been taking him to Rochdale for a haircut, he'd suddenly broken away from her and started play-boxing with a mother and her two kids walking past them.

"They were terrified!" she told me. "I didn't know where to put myself!"

Sybil voted for Brexit in 2016, telling me on the phone on the day of the Referendum, "Well, we have to stop all these *Asians* getting in the country, don't we?"

When I pointed out that leaving the EU would have no effect whatsoever on 'these Asians' she was having such a problem with, she replied, testily, "Well! It might help anyway!"

As I was wondering how to end the call politely, she uttered the words I had been expecting for weeks. "That Nigel Farage! Ooh, he's wonderful! I could listen to him all day!"

I promptly told her that Farage was basically a Nazi, and if he ever got into power he'd have people like me and Neil locked up in concentration camps.

Instead of even pretending to sympathise, she made a strange whinnying noise.

"Well, maybe… ," she said. "But I still think he's wonderful!"

In spite of my ambivalence, I'd listen each week as she mostly chattered away about things her and my dad had done in the past, holidays they'd taken, and how she'd loved listening to him play in the band at the jazz club, which, she told me, "was why I fell for him, I loved the way he played piano!".

If he was awake, she'd hand the phone to my dad "for a quick hello", but he was often the boss of a factory sorting out a problem with his staff, or just on his way to London to take part in a BBC Radio broadcast with the band. I never tried to bring him back to reality, just let him ramble on happily about some adventure or task he was in the middle of. A couple of times he thought I was his cousin John, who he hadn't seen since he was in his teens, other times he'd ask me to "give my love to your wife."

Dad became more confused as time went on, wandering around the house looking, Sybil told me, "like a lost little boy". Most days he'd ask Sybil who she was; was she his mother?; were they in the pub? (his parents had been publicans); and, rather ironically, was she the cleaning lady?

While I let her tell me "what he got up to this morning!" and pour out her heart on the difficulties of looking after "a child really", I'd also divert her onto happier things. She especially loved reminiscing about the time I had taken her to see Barry Manilow in concert.

"Ooh! I'll never forget that night, John!" she said. "It was a dream come true, meeting Barry!"

By the summer of 2017, Sybil's health was failing and she found it increasingly hard to cope. She told me that she was getting very little sleep, lying in the dark listening to Dad whispering that there were demons in the room or shouting out in the midst of a nightmare.

By day she had to watch his every move, especially after she'd found him in the garage shredding all his manuscripts of musical arrangements he'd written over the years.

Even with Dad going to a day-care centre twice a week, allowing Sybil to get some shopping done without leaving him alone in the house, she was clearly exhausted and I was particularly concerned that her health might collapse before his. I called her several times to check how she was, alarmed at how increasingly ill she sounded on the phone, even more so when she informed me she was only eating ice cream now. I offered to fly over and help out.

"No! You don't need to do that!" she told me. "What can you do anyway?!"

Still, I insisted, if I was needed, I'd be there.

I decided to call her daughter, Christine, to discuss Sybil's failing health and whether she could now properly look after Dad on her own. We both felt that the best option was that Dad should be moved to a permanent care home, but Sybil was refusing to consider it, saying it would "break his heart!".

Sybil eventually agreed to put Dad into a temporary rest home for a couple of weeks to give herself a break. However, while he was there, Christine rang me to say her mum had been taken into hospital, diagnosed with severe pleurisy and possibly pneumonia. The slightly better news was that she had finally accepted that she could no longer look after Dad and he should go into a permanent care home. I offered to go over and help Christine find somewhere.

"No, don't you worry, John, I'll find something," Christine assured me, "and when Bert's settled in, then come over and see him. Till then, you can't really do anything."

Sybil returned home a couple of weeks later, by which time Christine had found a permanent place for Dad near Rochdale.

On the day after he'd been admitted to the home, I received an alarmingly abusive email from Sybil. In it, she vented her dislike and obviously long-held resentment of me. Page after page of the venomous text spouted vicious accusations, each one more offensive - and inaccurate - than the last. It was the outpouring from a clearly disturbed mind.

I read it to Neil who suggested that I forward the email to her daughter, asking her to speak to her mother about it. Christine rang me a few hours later, sounding as shocked as I was by what her mother had written.

I had by then composed a reply, which I read to Christine over the phone. She sounded genuinely touched.

"Oh! What a lovely reply to such a horrible email!" she said.

"Should I send it to your mum?"

"Oh yes! I'm sure it will make her think again about what she's written to you."

The next morning, I received a reply from Sybil, but it was even more venomous than the first email. More accusations, more vitriol and she added in a threat this time, "You're not getting any of our money! You're not worth a penny of it! You sit there in your ivory tower in Spain, never worked a proper day in your life! I'm giving your share to the Dog's Trust!"

The fact was, for years I had told her and Dad that I didn't want their money, that they should spend it on enjoying themselves. But Dad had replied each time that, "It's what's due to you. It's only right, son. You and Neil have been fantastic to me. We'll see you right. You and Christine get half each of whatever we both leave."

Unbeknownst to my sister, Sue, she had been written out of the will years before after she and Dad had an unresolved falling out – something my mum would have sorted out very quickly, but without her influence the disagreement had festered, preventing any chance of apology and forgiveness from either of them.

Dad had wanted me to be the executor of the will until I told him I'd give half of my share to Sue.

"You can't do that," he'd told me, "it's not our wish she gets anything."

"But after you've gone, Dad, I'll do with the money what I like, which means half of it will go to Sue."

"Then we'll ask Christine to be the executor!"

I told him that would be fine, which annoyed him even more.

Anyway, I decided not to reply to Sybil's second missive, forwarding it to Christine and telling her that I no longer wished to hear from her mother. And I didn't.

Neil and I flew over to the UK and went to see Dad several times in the care home. He was in a world of his own but seemed well looked after and clearly pleased to see us. He especially enjoyed looking at the photograph album Neil had suggested we put together for him of special moments in his life, some he remembered, pointing at old jazz band friends and even telling us their names.

Occasionally though, he would be in a darker place, one time saying the nurses had burnt all his things on a bonfire in the yard.

"I managed to pack some of my things before they got 'em, though," he said triumphantly. "Someone's sending a car for me later, so I can finally get out of this prison!"

Back at home, I'd ring him twice a week, and let him tell me about whatever fantasy world he was inhabiting that day. If Sybil was there when I called, he'd try to get her to speak to me but she always refused, even when he begged her, "It's my son!" I'd hear him say. "Why don't you want to talk to him?"

"I don't!" I'd hear her say. "I don't speak to him anymore!"

He'd come back on the phone, telling me, "She's one of the workers here. Nice lass, but she's very shy."

One morning in the May of 2018, I received an email from Christine telling me Dad had been admitted to hospital with a burst bladder, clearly very poorly.

I rang the hospital to find out how he was but, instead of telling me, the nurse said, "Wait a moment, please."

The next thing, Sybil was ranting at me down the phone.

"You should have been here!" she yelled. "You should have been here!"

For five minutes, she railed at me, accusing me of this and that, venom once again spewing out. I finally managed to interrupt her flow and demanded to know how dad was.

"Well he's *dead!*" she said and then continued to rant at me for another five minutes.

As calmly as I could, I said, "Sybil, would you ask Christine to let me know when the funeral is?"

"I hope you're coming!" she shouted. "You better had!"

"Of course I'll be there," I replied. "He was my father."

As I put down the phone she was still yelling, "You should have been here!"

At the funeral, her daughter came over to speak to me for about thirty seconds while Sybil and her friends, some of whom I knew, completely ignored me. I sat at the back of the room with Neil, as the minister read out a Sybil-composed eulogy which made her life with Dad sound utterly idyllic. It only mentioned me and my sister once in passing and sounded as though his life had only really begun in 1976 when they'd got married. Anything pre-Sybil had been whitewashed out of Dad's story.

After the service, Neil told Christine that we would not be joining them at the reception.

"We wouldn't be welcome," he told her.

"Okay then!" she replied.

"John really did try with your mum, you know," he said, "but she is an extremely difficult woman."

Christine was non-committal, obviously forgetting my conversations in the past with her, when she'd complained about how impossible her mother could be.

As Neil and I were leaving, I saw Sybil walking towards me with a friend in tow. She handed me a jiffy bag which contained Dad's (broken) St Christopher medal and a CD recorded at one of his Singapore gigs, which I already had on cassette, a gift from Dad years earlier.

I thanked her and, as she turned to walk away, she said, "He suffered you know! Oh! He *did* suffer!"

As she rejoined her friends who gathered around her, Neil said under his breath, "Yes, he did suffer. He suffered for forty years!"

Back at the hotel, I lay in a long hot bath and composed the eulogy I wished I'd had the foresight to write and read out. It wouldn't have dissed Sybil, but would have brought into focus that he'd been my father for sixty-five years, and that he'd had a life pre-Sybil, which only I could tell. I would have shared things Dad and I had enjoyed together, long before any of the people sitting before me had come into his life. I'll always regret not doing it.

During my last visit to Dad in the rest home, after we'd spent a couple of hours looking once again at the photo album, I'd taken hold of his hand to say goodbye. He'd pulled it up to his mouth and kissed it, moaning with affectionate pleasure and rubbing his cheek against my skin. He'd looked up at me and, beaming a truly loving smile, said, "Been great to see you, son. Your visit has made my day, my week, my year! Thank you, son! I love you!"

I would have mentioned that in my eulogy too.

Chapter Ten

Long Since

In the Autumn of 1995, I flew out to Atlantic City with Alfie Shore to see Connie Francis in concert, staying at the Caesar's Palace, a gaudy, plasticised celebration of everything awful. Enormous chandeliers, which hung above sweeping golden-banistered staircases, did their best to look chic and pricey but failed miserably. Gift shops offering plastic tourist trash fascinated yet repelled; canned lift music played incessantly everywhere you walked, sat, waited, wandered through.

The 'politeness' from staff, which met you at every turn, was delivered in a tone of voice which implied they'd been up for hours having to deal with idiots like us.

What intrigued me the most was that no-one smiled. Everybody, staff and visitors, looked tired, fed-up, bored or simply mind-dead. Perhaps it was the sheer size surrounding us which left one speechless and drained, feeling unimportant and dispensable. Everything was wide and huge - the corridors, the escalators, the gambling casinos, the cafés, even the people staying there were larger than anybody I'd met before.

On my first morning, I found Alfie in the breakfast bar and helped myself to a small bowl of muesli, some toast with honey, a glass of freshly-squeezed orange juice and an Earl Grey tea. As I munched away, listening to Alfie happily nattering about how great it was going to be to meet Connie Francis, I watched with fascinated horror as family after family, mums, dads, kids and grandparents, repeatedly visited the buffet bar not once, not twice, sometimes up to four times.

Each time they'd pile their plates up with enormous waffles covered with lashings of maple syrup, bacon, eggs, occasionally even giant-sized steaks, and always with a massive side helping of chips. They'd struggle into optimistically narrow seats, and cover the ghastly mess on their plate with oodles of ketchup. It was all washed down with oversized paper cups of Coca-Cola, which were refilled at least twice during their gastronomic nightmare.

When I'd visited New York in 1975, I was struck by how lean, fit and healthy the people who walked briskly along Fifth Avenue were. They looked purposeful, bright-faced and readying for their day. Either things had changed in twenty years, or maybe just along the coast from The Big Apple lives and expectations were different.

After breakfast, needing some air, I left Alfie looking forward to the show later that evening and made my way towards the nearest exit. What I hadn't expected was that one had to walk through the casino, past a roomful of people sitting at endless rows of fruit machines, plastic bowls full of tokens in their hand while the other hand yanked the one-armed bandit handle. Occasionally the sound of winnings falling like broken china accosted you, but more often than not it was the cursing of the foiled gamblers, who once again dug into their bowls for another token which may bring them the riches they desired. I soon learnt that they were there when I left the hotel, and still there when I returned hours later. Still losing; still cursing; still looking bored as hell.

As I strolled outside and onto the boardwalk, I automatically began humming The Drifters' apt and beautiful 1964 hit. I'd smiled during Bette Midler's film, *Beaches*, when her character spent her childhood hiding with friends under the clicking heels of the famous wooden walkway above.

But times had obviously changed. The boardwalk was dirty and covered in green mould and everywhere smelt of dog shit. It permeated the air, blanketing even the scent of the salty sea which struggled to waft by and offer some nostalgic consolation of days out at the beach with my parents in the 1950s.

'Oh my,' I thought, 'how would Lieber and Stoller react if they saw *this?*'.

I began singing 'Avoid the boardwalk!' to myself, which kept me amused at least. After about ten minutes, I found a side street and thought I'd have a wander away from the patrolling tourists. Within five minutes, I was regretting my detour. Groups of three and four people, huddled on street corners and clearly doing drug deals or something equally shady, stared at me as I walked past.

Deciding I needed to get back to the seafront and quick, a hooker suddenly appeared out of nowhere offering me "a bit of quickie fun, darlin'?" I politely refused and hurried back towards the boardwalk, where I'd at least feel safe again amidst the crowds who were taking in the dog-poo air.

* * *

After a long sleep and a hot bath, I ordered an early dinner in my room and got ready to meet up with Alfie in the foyer of the hotel. He was waiting with a tall blonde chap who, smiling broadly and extending a positive handshake, introduced himself as Stuart Colman. Full of the energy of success and an obvious enjoyment of life, I liked him instantly.

Alfie led us outside and hailed a cab, chatting excitedly about the Liverpool talent contest I'd attended the week before.

"John was a real pro!" he gushed, as we got in.

"I should hope so!" Stuart said, winking at me.

"*And* he picked the winner!"

"Now that *is* good to hear!" Stuart replied, giving me a mock salute.

Alfie laughed a deep throaty laugh.

"You guys are gonna get on real well!" he shouted, clearly thrilled with himself that everything was going to plan.

It only took us about five minutes to reach the theatre. The foyer was packed and we happily followed the burly Alfie who politely but firmly pushed through the melée, showing our tickets to the usher who led us to our seats about halfway back in the stalls.

I noticed that most of the audience were elderly, a mix of chattering blue-rinse ladies and balding excited men who'd no doubt bought all of Connie's singles back in the '50s and early '60s during her pop heyday. The air of anticipation was almost tangible.

After a half hour delay, the band suddenly struck up a rousing 'Who's Sorry Now?' and the pop legend finally appeared, entering rather oddly from a side door. She made her way slowly up the steps onto the stage and turned to face her fans, arms outstretched, soaking up the adoration as people stood, cheered, screamed and yelled.

She was a surprisingly tiny woman, dressed in a crocheted black outfit with matching head covering. She looked more like an Italian lady in mourning rather than a once-massive star celebrating her return to the stage. Only her glinting necklace, bangles and earrings betrayed her starry past.

Connie clasped her hands in prayer-like supplication, Our Lady of The Broken-Hearted, there for her pilgrims to worship and pay homage to the woman who, with several million-selling tearjerkers, had helped them through disastrous love affairs forty years earlier.

The conductor waved his baton grandly and the orchestra kicked in with 'Lipstick On Your Collar'. The place roared as hundreds of cheated souls sang along with Connie, joining in with the 'ticking-off-finger' thing she had done on numerous TV pop shows back in 1959.

For an hour she performed all her greatest hits, 'Happiness', 'Mama', 'Carolina Moon', 'Stupid Cupid', 'Everybody's Somebody's Fool', 'Among My Souvenirs', 'When The Boy In Your Arms Is The Boy In Your Heart' and the gay anthem of 1961, 'Where The Boys Are.'

When she went into 'V-A-C-A-T-I-O-N', everyone – even me – clapped and sang along, joyfully spelling out the word as we'd done as kids and teenagers beside our Dansette record players.

Her voice was certainly not what it was and she began to sound increasingly more worn out with each song, her voice fraying alarmingly on some of the top notes. Regardless, the audience screamed and shouted 'Bravo!' at the end of every number, as though knowing their waves of love would keep her going.

And of course, she finished with her biggest smash and signature song, 'Who's Sorry Now?', which had sold millions around the world in 1958.

It felt like the triumph of perseverance over physical frailty to me, but her ten-minute standing ovation clearly showed I was in the minority. Connie touched her heart and appeared to be in floods of tears as the noise from her fans reached fever pitch. Finally, she was rescued from the growing hysteria – and the possibility of an encore - when two sturdy minders appeared from the wings and gently escorted Connie off the stage.

With a signal from Alfie, the three of us quickly made our way to the foyer ahead of swarms of fans who were pouring out behind us shouting Connie's praises, one of them yelling out, "She breaks *and* fills my heart!"

As we reached the street, I quietly voiced my concerns to Stuart about the state of Connie's voice.

"Don't worry, John!" he said. "With good production and the support of The Crickets, she'll sound fine on the album. Trust me. It'll be great!"

He turned and pointed at the hundreds of people happily milling out of the theatre.

"And look at these guys, John!" he said, laughing. "They'll buy the album for sure! Connie is a goddess to these people – and thousands more around the world!"

"Okay!" Alfie said. "We're due at Connie's house in ten minutes! I have the cab waiting around the corner!"

We were welcomed into Connie's oddly named 'Rest House', a sizeable chalet in a gated community of about twenty identical houses, by a breezy young chap who beamed at us and led us into a little hallway, where he invited us to sit on a range of comfy sofas.

"The Queen of Pop will be arriving very soon!" he said, efficiency oozing out of every pore. "Can I get you guys anything to drink? Tea? Coffee? Fruit juice?"

We politely declined, preferring to watch the urgent milling about of several busy people, nervously chatting amongst themselves before dashing off to deal with some important task.

After about ten minutes, a sudden flurry of activity kicked off as everyone rushed to the front door. Four burly bodyguards stood aside as Connie, looking even tinier than she had on stage, wandered into the hallway, smiling around her in a sort of Queen Motherly way. Several chattering P.A.'s and what looked like a couple of medics dashed forward and took over, encouraging their charge to make her way past us and towards a settee situated in a kind of ante-room at the end of the corridor.

The white-coated duo helped her down onto the settee and then sat on their haunches, looking up at her, holding her hand and apparently consoling a clearly exhausted woman.

"Maybe we should go," I suggested, which was met with a stony silence from Alfie and Stuart. "It feels like we're intruding on a wake," I insisted.

However, my wry wit wasn't cutting it with these guys, obviously intent on meeting the legendary pop star.

Finally, after another ten minutes of watching Connie being given cups of tea and sympathy and then being helped up and led out of view – 'to a bed?', I wondered - a clean-cut, bleached-toothed chap, dressed from head to foot in a matching white cotton outfit, walked up to us and said, "Connie is ready for you now, gents!"

As he chatted away happily about "what a *star* she is!", and, less diplomatically, how "my mother would *kill* to be here tonight!", we were led into the chintzy little room, all net and flowered silk. Connie was standing by a huge dining table, inviting us to sit down as she offered a tiny hand to each of us.

"Hi guys!" she said, remarkably enlivened. "Have you been offered tea?"

Before we could tell her yes but we'd turned it down, she looked up at the white cotton'n'tooth man who sort of bowed, before sweeping out in search of three teas.

"Thanks so much for coming to my show!" Connie enthused. "I hope you enjoyed it!"

"Your fans clearly *adore* you!" Alfie replied diplomatically.

She sat up a little straighter and beamed at him.

"They do don't they?" she said, as our teas arrived on a silver tray.

White-Tooth placed it reverentially on the table and went to sit in a chair at the end of the room, positioning his head in a sort of praying-at-the-floor mode.

As I poured milk in mine and offered the jug to Stuart, I said, "You sang a lot of your hits tonight!"

"I did! The fans want to hear the golden oldies!"

She chuckled and sipped at her tea like a grateful rescued bird.

"Okay, Connie," Stuart began manfully. "I think you know why we're here!"

She beamed at him coquettishly, suddenly looking forty years younger.

"Yeah! To make a new album with you guys!"

She put her cup in the saucer and leaned forward.

"I recorded one a few years ago for another British guy," she looked into the middle distance, "I can't recall who now... "

I recalled it perfectly, the 'British guy' was a colleague of mine who had his own record label.

"I hope she doesn't ask you to hire a Thames barge!" he'd said when I told him about my forthcoming adventure to meet The Queen of Sobs.

Puzzled, I'd shaken my head.

"When she did an album for me about ten years ago," he said, "she insisted I hire a barge to sail down the Thames." Eyebrows raising as I leaned in, he continued. "Connie, with not a trace of irony, told me to, 'Book your Queen to stand on deck next to me, we can both wave at our British fans lined up along the river!'. When I explained that our Queen was not for hire she seemed most put out."

I was still inwardly chuckling at the memory when I heard Stuart saying, "As you know, Connie, it will be sixty years since Buddy passed next year and we..."

"Oh, darlin', *darlin'* Buddy!" she said, sitting back and smiling at her recollections of, "That *dear* boy!".

Stuart had told me earlier that Connie had apparently been with Buddy's wife, Maria Elena, when news had come through of Holly's plane crash on February 3rd 1959. I expected her to tell us about that, but instead she said, "So! You want me to record some of his songs for you!"

She began to reel off the titles of his most popular hits, naming 'Heartbeat' as her favourite and trilling a few lines for us.

"Gorgeous, Connie," Stuart cooed. "That would definitely be one of the songs we'd do."

She nodded and then looked at me, "And you, honey, *you're* the A & R guy, I guess?"

I nodded.

She nodded back.

"Which company?"

"Carlton Records," I replied.

She shook her head, obviously not recognising the name, then, without warning, began an angry rant about a major label she'd once been signed to.

"They were *fuckin' bastards!*" she shouted, causing White-Tooth to look up from the floor and shoot an alarmed glance down the hall at the medics who were hovering nearby.

"Well, Connie," Stuart jumped in, "Carlton isn't a major record company like *that* one. It's an independently-run label, part of the Carlton Communications Group."

"Hm!" she said, sitting back in her chair, "I'll have to look into them!"

She smiled beatifically at me.

"You seem like a respectful young guy, honey. I like you!" She giggled and reached her hand across the table towards mine. "You know, I would *love* to make the album for you! And working with this great guy… " she glanced at Stuart fondly, "it'll be *fun!*"

"*And* with The Crickets!" Stuart added.

"Yeah! I *love* that idea!" She looked at me. "Was that your idea, honey?"

"No, no, it was Stuart's," I replied.

"Honest too!" she murmured. "I admire honesty."

She threw her head back and laughed.

"Oh, I *love* those guys! Haven't seen 'em in years!"

She smiled at each one of us and began to stand up.

"We'll have a ball!" she told us. "For *Buddy!*"

She touched her heart and took out a tiny lace hankie from her sleeve, dabbing her eyes. We all nodded in empathy and stood up.

With a final girlish chuckle, she waved regally and two of her minders rushed over.

"Okay guys!" she said, twinkling at each of us, "It's my rest time! The old girl needs some sleep!"

She shook our hands and gave us affectionate pecks on the cheek, the scent of lavender water and face powder wafting up.

"We'll speak soon, Connie!" Stuart said as she wandered off down the hall, disappearing into another room before the door was closed behind her and the beaming welcomer was at our side once more, chatting excitedly as he led us out to our waiting taxi.

* * *

A few days later, I stood in the control room of AIR Studios, watching Elkie Brooks recording the opening track of her new album. The studio occupied a spacious converted church in North London which was owned by George Martin and his business partner John Burgess.

John was an old friend of my former manager Stuart Reid and I'd often see John and his wife Jean at parties at the Reids' home in the 1970s and '80s. I always enjoyed chatting about the smash hits he'd produced for Manfred Mann, Adam Faith, Peter & Gordon, Matt Monro and Freddie & The Dreamers. Alongside Martin, John was one of the most successful producers of the 1960s.

Elkie was standing at the mike surrounded by the RPO, and as she soared through 'Nights In White Satin', accompanied by Tony Britten's beautiful arrangement, I got shivers down my spine. She looked so tiny but my, the huge sound which came out of her mouth made her a giant.

When she'd finished her vocal, the musicians clapped, banged their bows and cheered her.

"Was that alright?" she said, coming through the enormous door to the control room followed by a delighted-looking Tony.

"It was fucking fantastic!" her husband shouted, going over to hug her.

As we all listened to the playback in wonder, Tony leaned towards me and murmured in my ear, "This is going to be a beautiful album, John."

A week later, I sat with Nigel Wright listening to the first track he'd just mixed of Maria Friedman's album. Nigel had been my first stop when we'd signed the contract with Maria. He'd done a great job on Des's *Portrait* album, but more importantly for Maria, he had the musical theatre credibility of producing million-selling albums of some of Lloyd Webber's biggest hit shows.

One of her contractual stipulations was that she had to meet and approve the producer who must have standing as a successful, recognised figure in the music business. She and Nigel had hit it off immediately and the chemistry needed in any recording situation was clearly working like a dream.

Cole Porter's wondrous 'I Happen To Like New York' began like a slow-moving steamboat arriving at the port of the city. Then Maria's remarkable voice kicked in, slowly building to a Streisand-like climax. I was utterly blown away.

"She's not bad is she?" Nigel smiled at me.

"She is truly a star!" I replied.

"Yep. She is. Thanks for asking me to make this album. It's going to be a blinder!"

* * *

By the close of '95, we had Maria's album completed, Elkie's album done, Sonia had just finished her first single from *The Philly Album*, a cover of Harold Melvin & The Blue Notes' 'Wake Up Everybody' and Hazell Dean had delivered her fantastic Abba Album, *The Winner Takes It All*. Singer-Songwriter John Wilson had also brought me the tapes for his album, *Tell Me Something New* and Stuart Colman was sending very positive messages about the Connie Francis and The Crickets sessions.

Meanwhile, Lonnie Donegan was in the midst of recording his album, *Rock Island Line* and, as the sessions had progressed, he'd invited me several times to his apartment in Paddington to hear the tracks as they were finished.

I was astonished at how 'now' they were. I'd always seen Lonnie as a Skiffle star from the '50s, a big influence on many burgeoning artists from that period, but his massive chart success had been too early in my childhood to really have an effect on me. Now, listening to the breathtaking new songs he'd written, I completely altered my rather one-dimensional view of this fascinating and enigmatic man.

Lonnie treated me like a favourite nephew, with great respect and often amiable joshing, but always keeping that veneer of seniority. You were forever his audience, never the other way round. His stories fascinated me so that wasn't a problem.

For instance, I'd had no idea that he owned the publishing to 'Nights In White Satin'. I told him that Elkie Brooks had just recorded it for her upcoming new Carlton album and he smiled as he recounted how its composer, Justin Hayward, had been a young wannabe at his publishing office in the mid-'60s and had played the song to Lonnie to see what he thought.

"I knew it was a smash as soon as I heard it," he told me, "and so I offered Justin a deal. It's paid quite a few electricity bills over the years!"

I did recall that Lonnie had written Tom Jones' massive '67 hit, 'I'll Never Fall In Love Again' which had stayed at No.2 in the charts for four weeks.

"Yeah!" Lonnie laughed. "Bleedin' Engelbert kept Tom off the top with 'The Last Waltz'!"

"But it did end the year as the seventh best-selling single of 1967," I said, "ahead of several No.1s like 'A Whiter Shade of Pale', 'I'm A Believer', 'Massachusetts' and even 'All You Need Is Love'."

"Blimey! You know your stuff, don't you?" he said, staring at me.

"So, your starter for ten, my son, which record also kept Tom off the top with my song?"

"Scott McKenzie's 'San Francisco!,'" I replied.

"Bingo! You're a flippin' walking encyclopaedia!"

I marvelled at Lonnie's success and mentioned, a little cheekily, how his incredible tally of hits in the '50s must have made him a rich man.

"Nah!," he scoffed. "You joking? Never earned a penny from my big hits. My record label were very sneaky. They put me and my band on at the Shepherd's Bush Empire for an evening, which was packed, and paid us a performance fee. And, of course, they recorded the show, which I had no problem with. But then… " he wagged his finger at the memory, "but then, they released the live tracks as singles didn't they? Without having to pay me a penny in royalties!"

"Bastards!" I replied.

"Too right, my son. I think I said something similar to the boss man at the label. Didn't go down too well!"

It impressed me how artists like Lonnie had survived such situations, huge success with little financial reward, but still managing to keep his head and self-belief above the water of lessening sales and unrenewed record deals as the years went by. The limos may no longer have been taking him to another awards ceremony, but he knew that he was still special, still hugely talented and still able to fill concert halls.

*　*　*

Gary Glitter was true to his word and invited Neil and me to his show at Wembley Arena. When Neil and I visited him in his dressing-room after a packed crowd had cheered and stomped him through all his hits, yelling 'Leader! Leader!' like a football chant, Gary gave me a red rose, kissed us both on the cheek and told us to, "Look after each other."

I'd gone to the studios a few days earlier to hear the new single, and as the track had begun with that famously anthemic, 'Hello! Hello! Hello!', he jumped up from his seat, leapt into my face and began miming to the track. I couldn't help smiling at this man's sense of fun and amazing energy.

He made a great video for the single, sitting on a massive throne and holding a ridiculously oversized telephone while he vamped like mad at the camera. 'Hello, Hello, I'm Back Again! (Again!)' hit the Top 50 at the end of 1995, giving him his first hit for three years. It turned out to be his last ever chart success.

A few years later, Gary became more famous – indeed infamous - for something much less glittery, far more sordid and decidedly disturbing. When the news of his arrest for having sex with minors was announced, I asked a friend of mine, who'd been in The Glitter Band, if he'd ever had any inkling of Gary's penchant for under-age girls.

"No, not at all," he told me. "The only thing I remember is that he liked his girlfriends to wear little white ankle socks, schoolgirl stockings, it turned him on, so... "

I never reconciled in my mind the man I'd met and got to know - the charming, courteous star - with the sneering, smirking predator the press described during his court proceedings. He seemed the personification of Jekyll and Hyde.

One of the results of his arrest and imprisonment was the near ruination of a music business associate of mine who ran a successful record label, specialising in third-party licensed recordings. Months before the arrest, in what at the time was considered a coup, he had licensed Gary's entire back-catalogue for two million pounds.

On the day *before* the TV and newspapers were full of Gary's disturbing exploits, enough *Best of Gary Glitter* albums to ensure a Top Ten placing the following week were shipped out to all the major chain stores.

Forty-eight hours later, every album had been returned to him. He was left with hundreds of thousands of CDs which he would never be able to sell and a catalogue which was virtually worthless. As the song says… 'What a difference a day makes'.

Chapter Eleven

Return Visit

Gordon Lorenz had been producing Pickwick's *The Shows Collection* series since 1990, during my first stint at the company. The range had grown to over thirty albums in the five years since we'd started it, and, now part of the new Carlton catalogue, it was still selling in the thousands.

We'd recently hit the one million sales mark, which we'd celebrated with a Platinum Disc presentation in Covent Garden, with Stephanie Lawrence, Paul Jones, Carl Wayne, Jess Conrad and Fiona Hendley being our recipient guests of honour.

l to r Gordon Lorenz, Jess Conrad, Carl Wayne, Stephanie Lawrence, Paul Jones, Fiona Hendley and John Howard

One morning, Gordon rang me, with a different project on offer. "John?" he began, in his breathlessly conspiratorial tone he always adopted. "How would you like to release a single featuring *Judy Garland's* daughter singing 'Have Yourself A Merry Little Christmas'?"

"Liza?!" I shouted down the phone, like an excited queen about to meet one of his idols.

"No," he demurred, coughing a little, "not Liza, John, but... her younger sister, Lorna – Lorna Luft!"

I'd seen Lorna performing in the mid-'70s at the gay nightclub Country Cousin in King's Road. She'd put on an excellent show but, for some reason, had never broken through into the big time like her younger half-sibling.

Gordon ploughed on. "She's on tour every year in the UK, John, performing some of her mother's greatest hits to packed houses!"

I remained unconvinced, unsure if Lorna had the pulling power in terms of record sales. Gordon, however, was not about to give up.

"Lorna was *actually featured on TV with her mum* when she performed 'Have Yourself A Merry Little Christmas' back in the '50s, John," he told me, waiting for my impressed response. Getting none, he continued in a slightly louder voice, "And I can get hold of *the original footage*, which we could use in a promotional video for our single. And here's my big idea, John... we could overdub Lorna's voice onto Judy's original recording of that song, turn it into a duet, and have it out in time for Christmas!"

Immediately I thought of the issues of getting MCA to clear Judy's recording.

"I've spoken to Lorna," Gordon continued excitedly, "and she assures me that she knows the people who own it!"

"So do I, Gordon. It's MCA Records. I used to work there."

Gordon made a hissing noise, which I took to be a laugh.

"Of course you did, John! And yes, you could speak to them... but Lorna would also speak to her dad, Sid Luft, who produced those shows for her mother."

"But it's MCA who would have to clear the recording."

"Yes, John!" Gordon said, a little miffed at being out-manoeuvred, continuing in a torrent of words impossible to interrupt. "But, think about it! If you can license Judy's original recording from your old mates at MCA, and I overdub Lorna 'duetting' with her mum and Sid clears our use of the video with Lorna filming her parts which we can insert into it, well, it could be a *huge* Christmas smash!"

I didn't wholly disagree. When Natalie Cole had done something similar with her father's voice for the *Unforgettable* album, it had hit the British Top 20 with ease. While Lorna wasn't anywhere near as well-known as Natalie, the association with Judy could be a similar winner, especially at Christmas.

"Lorna's over here at the moment, John," Gordon gushed on, "and I can arrange for *the two of you to meet* and chat about it!"

I met Lorna outside the apartment she was staying at off the Euston Road, and we wandered along to a chic little café she'd become fond of during her stay there. She was the essence of polite showbiz and looked great, with porcelain-like skin which seemed to radiate from within her shiny copper-red hairdo. She chatted easily, in that Californian languid way, putting you instantly at ease and making you feel like her best friend. It's a talent many Americans I know possess, but those from L.A. do it better than anyone. Compliments came thick and fast and sounded utterly genuine, and even possibly were.

Lorna was clearly excited about recording the single with Gordon and ventured the possibility – "if it's a hit!" – of recording an album for Carlton.

She invited me to dinner at The Atlantic Rooms, a cavernous West End ribs and steak joint near Piccadilly.

"Bring your partner along!" she'd said, telling me in the same breath that "my sister was married to a gay man, you know."

"Peter Allen," I ventured.

"That's right, John!" Lorna replied, her eyes widening then immediately darkening within seconds. "Such a talent, such a loss, gone too soon."

"He died of AIDS in… "

"1992," Lorna said, shaking her head. "And his partner Gregory died in '84. So tragic."

"Neil and I have lost a lot of friends in the last few years," I told her, as I signalled to the waiter for the bill.

"Me too," she replied. "Really terrible."

I walked her back to her apartment and arranged to meet her that evening at eight o'clock.

Neil and I joined Lorna and her surprise companion for the evening, the songwriter Charles Hart, who looked skinnily elegant as he stood to shake our hands. Hart had written the lyrics for Andrew Lloyd Webber's *Phantom of The Opera* and *Aspects of Love*, making him a very rich man and no doubt ensuring for Lorna that I would be impressed by her showbiz contacts.

As he rattled on about his love of piloting small aircraft, no doubt now able to buy several, Lorna hugged him in that all-encompassing Judy way, beaming at me as if to say, 'isn't he *adorable*?'. However, after about five minutes, she managed to interrupt him by inviting us all to her forthcoming wedding. It was taking place, she told us, in a castle "somewhere in Scotland!" and we would be "my guests of honour!".

On the drive home, Neil and I chuckled about how green with envy some of our friends would be.

"Start the conversation with 'we've been invited by Judy Garland's daughter to her wedding!'," Neil suggested, "changing the subject before they ask which one!"

A couple of days later, a barbecue arrived 'By Special Delivery' at our house. There was a red rose and a pink ribbon attached and a handwritten note from Lorna, thanking me for giving her the opportunity to make records again.

In the end, MCA licensed Judy's recording once I'd explained what we planned to do.

"A Judy's Greatest Hits album wouldn't be a bad follow-up idea…" I'd suggested to Norman Griffin, my successor at the company. "And Carlton would be happy to release it!"

"So would MCA," Norman countered.

I couldn't complain, it was exactly the same response I'd've given me.

Gordon did an excellent job dubbing Lorna's voice onto the fifty-year old track. He added some new strings and gave it an effective radio-friendly '90s gloss, also sending me a rather effective video featuring Lorna sitting by a grand piano miming to the song, segueing into a clip of the young Miss Luft listening to her mom singing the seasonal evergreen back in the '50s.

The Lorna/Judy single was released at the end of November and started to get some Radio 2 play. However, within days the producers there decided they actually preferred Judy's original and playlisted that instead for their Christmas selection.

The video got a couple of airings on breakfast and midday TV shows and Lorna stepped up to do any interviews we could get her, but, sadly, none of it helped to shift any records. The single absolutely stiffed. Which meant that an album was now out of the question. The invitation to Lorna's wedding never did arrive.

* * *

One of the hangover projects from before I rejoined Pickwick/ Carlton, and another of Gordon's productions, was an album by The Beverly Sisters. It was recorded to celebrate the 50th anniversary of V.E. day and featured popular songs from the 1940s performed with the trio's trademark three-part harmonies. They'd enjoyed several hit singles in the '50s and early '60s and were a regular act in TV variety shows when I was growing up. The album itself was pleasant enough and fitted into our budget range perfectly.

The press department's Trinny pulled off something of a surprise coup, getting The Bevs a guest spot on the BBC's Breakfast show, so while I drank my coffee before setting off for work, I sat and watched as one of the show's presenters introduced 'the girls'.

On sashayed Joy with the twins Teddy and Babs. They were a fabulous, if slightly unnerving, times-three creation from an age long gone. Dressed in matching baby-doll pink and white outfits topped off with pink ribbons dangling from enormous blonde curls, they offered the viewers glowing white smiles which were dazzling enough to have most people rushing for their sunglasses so early in the morning. It was akin to seeing a trio of grandmothers in clothes they wore as children, Baby Janes with candy floss.

The two presenters began by asking them about their early careers when they'd – briefly - become national treasures, Joy particularly something of a British icon when she'd married national football hero, Billy Wright in 1958. But, true pros that they were, the sisters only wanted to talk about their new album.

Joy held up a copy of the CD for the camera and told Great Britain, "This is our new album, viewers! We've recorded it to celebrate fifty years since V.D. Day!"

Both presenters went a bit red, shuffled their bums about on the sofa and tried to break in with more questions, but Joy was having none of it.

"We are so proud of this CD, aren't we girls?" she gushed on, leaning forward to give the camera a better view.

"Because we all remember V.D Day, don't we, girls?" Joy said to her sisters, who nodded away happily, their curls bouncing buoyantly, their pink ribbons jogging along in unison. Joy smiled at the camera and waved the CD around.

"The whole nation celebrated V.D Day!" she laughed. "And V.D

Day is still very special to everyone in Great Britain!"

At that, the twins produced little Union Jacks and waved them at the by now clearly stricken presenters, who both resembled rabbits caught in the headlights of a thirty ton truck.

"You must be very proud," one of them jumped in, hoping to shift the conversation away from more mentions of STDs on a family show.

"Oh we are!" Joy replied. "Who wouldn't be, releasing a new album which celebrates V.D Day?!"

"And tell us, girls," the presenter had another go, "when was your very first hit record?"

The Bevs looked unsure for the first time since they'd sat down.

"Well!" the presenter said to the camera, happy to shut them up, "it's an amazing *forty years* since the girls' first album, 'A Date With The Bevs', was released, which included this hit!"

A grainy black and white clip appeared of the youthful trio singing 'Sisters', before cutting back to the present day ladies all giggling on the sofa at each other. Then, as Joy held up their new CD once more, one could almost feel both presenters flinch.

"That was Then!" Joy said. "This is Now! Celebrating *Then!*" She was clearly thrilled at that well-rehearsed headline. "Fifty years since *V.D Day!*"

There was no escape for the hapless presenters who watched the car crashing – along with their careers – right into millions of homes.

"Hooray for V.D Day!" all three sisters chimed as one, and happily waved their Union Jacks again.

After chuckling for most of the drive into work that morning, I met a clearly distraught Trinny on the stairs.

"Hooray for V.D Day!" I shouted.

"*Don't!*" she said. "Just *don't!*"

* * *

On a February morning in 1996, word was quickly going around Carlton that, after an angry row with Paul McGrane, Tel, the Head of the TV Albums department, had suddenly stormed out of his office and left the company. Within minutes of the rumour becoming a memo'd fact, Paul popped into my office and sat down.

"As you'll know by now," he said, his mouth still holding that half-smile, "Tel has gone, leaving several projects unfinished, which we'll ditch. But there's one which he completed and I think it would be a good fit for you, John. If you'd like to take it over, that is."

Gary Wilmot's album, *Showstoppers,* had been recorded with the London Symphony Orchestra, arranged and produced by Mike Batt, with an accompanying TV series to promote it. It certainly had potential and I agreed to add it to my roster of releases.

I and several members of Carlton staff were invited by Gary to watch the recording of the first episode of 'BBC's Showstoppers', which featured Cliff Richard performing songs from his forthcoming musical *Heathcliff*. As I enjoyed Cliff and Olivia Newton-John singing their hit duet from the show, 'Had To Be', I remembered how Tim Rice had chatted to me about the musical when I went to his house in Barnes in 1994.

We met Gary after the show and I found him utterly charming. He invited me and Trinny to a playback of his album at the recording studios, with Mike Batt hosting.

I hadn't seen Mike since I'd accompanied Stuart and Patsy in 1974 to a Christmas party at his vast house in West London. He was riding high in the charts at the time with The Wombles' seasonal smash, 'Wombling Merry Christmas' and had a few weeks earlier visited my recording session at Apple Studios to listen to the just-completed 'Family Man', which he'd loved.

Twenty-one years later, he hadn't changed very much, his carrot-red hair was now flecked with grey here and there, but as ever he was affable, chatty and happy to play us an album he was clearly very proud of.

While quaffing champagne and nibbling on canapés, we listened to Gary's album featuring some of the classics of musical theatre, and I was most impressed. Gary had a great voice and Mike's production and arrangements were first class.

Unfortunately, the advertising budget which Tel had agreed with Gary's management was nowhere near anything my department could afford – especially since the BBC had refused to allow us to use *Showstoppers* as the album's title. In fact, TV-advertising of any kind was no longer an option. I'd guessed that this had been the reason for Tel's blazing row with Paul McGrane, and wondered momentarily if the high hopes Paul had spoken of when he'd wooed me away from MCA less than a year earlier, were beginning to look more like hopeful optimism than definite expectation.

This meant that the renamed *Gary Wilmot – The Album* sold or failed on its own merits, with the hope that the TV series, whose star we did share, would help shift the number of copies Woolworth's had ordered. However, the chainstore's chief buyer was mighty pissed off that the TV campaign had been pulled and Gary's album didn't even register in their first week in-store chart.

Within a couple of weeks it was clear that the album had bombed. Tel had been expecting (and had no doubt promised the singer and producer) a Top Ten smash but Gary's much-anticipated release didn't even tickle the Top 75.

Although it wasn't a record I'd commissioned or even been much involved with, it still felt like a blow. Firstly it was a lovely album, but more importantly for me and my staff, it was a decidedly poor start to Carlton's planned assault on the mainstream albums market!

* * *

On a cold and snowy February night, Neil and I travelled into Earl's

Court for the 1996 Brits Awards. I'd last attended the event in 1992, as a guest of Polygram, when it had been held at the Hammersmith Apollo.

That evening, we'd all sat in the theatre watching great performances on stage, a respectful audience enjoying an evening of the nation's top talent, including Lisa Stansfield, Curtis Stigers and Seal.

Four years later, the BPI, who organised the event, had decided to stage it on a much bigger scale, in the cavernous Earl's Court Arena, turning what could have been a great evening into a total shambles.

The place was full of large round tables, at which sat various record company execs and their chosen minions. By the time Neil and I arrived at the Carlton table, the gathered music biz royalty were all tanked up and shouting abuse across the room at each other.

I went to the loo shortly after we arrived and was faced with every cubicle, doors wide open, full of people sniffing coke off the top of the cisterns. One by one they'd stand, shake their heads, laugh hysterically from faces going a bizarre shade of puce and walk out looking like they could take on the world.

As the evening progressed, the coke-fuelled mass began heckling anyone from a competing record company who stood up to receive an award. Instead of applauding the winners walking to the stage, the losing tables shouted "Fuckers!" at them like a yobbish football crowd. Of course, the winning tables responded with "Fucking losers!".

By nine p.m. the place was in riot mode. The now deafening noise from the audience threatened to drown out the artists who appeared to either give or accept a Brit. Luckily for the performers, the track they mimed to was so loud it managed to mute the catcalls and abuse being hurled their way.

What should have been the highlight of the evening - David Bowie performing 'Hallo Spaceboy' with Pet Shop Boys - was an embarrassment over which the music business should hang its corporate head in shame. Bowie gave an energetic performance of his forthcoming Top 20 hit, stoically batting away the wall of noise clamouring before him. The Petties just looked their usual doleful selves, staring out at the 'crème de la crème' of the music industry blithely showing themselves up to be nothing more than drug-addled thugs. I felt like walking on stage, grabbing a microphone and yelling, "Listen, you fuckers! This is a legend in your midst! Shut the fuck up!".

One particularly amusing moment, which I will always treasure, was when Tina Turner, there to present the award for Best International Female Solo Artist to Bjork, descended the stairs as her massive hit, 'Simply The Best', rang out around the arena. She stood at the podium, waved the Brit in the air and, leaning into the mike, said, "So! Why are you playing 'Simply The Best' when I have *never* won one of these?!"

It was the only moment which reduced the crowd to shocked silence. The music industry had been royally slapped in the face by this amazing woman. It highlighted the futility of the whole event.

However, no-one there had prepared themselves for the spectacle about to unfold, as Bob Geldof strode to the mike and (no doubt already regretting it) announced, "Ladies & Gentlemen! The King of Pop! Michael Jackson!"

On stage came a 'choir of angels' in diaphanous white chiffon gowns, which failed to hide the fact that most of them were burly bodyguards, flailing their beefy arms around like vestal virgins on steroids.

Michael then appeared, also in white chiffon, adopted a crucifixion pose and mimed to 'Earth Song', which had topped the charts the previous December.

As his minders in disguise shimmied, swooped and danced

around him, the Arena quickly became filled with jeers, catcalls and cries of "Get off!". Even the ghostly panstick and mask-like face could not hide the fact that The King of Pop was not amused.

Then, something wonderful happened. Jarvis Cocker, who had been sitting near the front on his record company's table, jumped on stage and wiggled his bum, first at an aghast Michael then at the audience and TV cameras. As one, Michael's 'angels' morphed into the beefy bodyguards they actually were. Chiffon flowed hilariously around their muscled frames as they lunged and grabbed hold of Cocker, dragging him off the stage. It was the only point in Jackson's whole performance which drew cheers and cries for "More!". In just a couple of delightfully rebellious minutes, Cocker became the darling of a nation.

* * *

In spite of the Lorna Luft setback, Gordon Lorenz still regularly rang me to suggest new recording projects. Some I rejected but others, like *Lionel Bart and Friends Sing Lionel Bart* had great potential.

Gordon arranged for us to have afternoon tea with Lionel at Brown's Hotel, and I was entranced by the man. He was such easy company, full of great stories, extremely witty and disarmingly attentive when asking me about myself.

There was a pianist playing in the coffee lounge who, seeing the great man just yards away, couldn't resist playing a medley of songs from *Oliver!*. Lionel smiled, stopped chatting, lifted his finger and cocked an ear as excellent renditions of 'As Long As He Needs Me', 'Reviewing The Situation' and 'Where Is Love?' floated around the room.

When the medley had finished, Lionel stood and applauded and went over to the pianist, who looked near to fainting.

"Would you like me to sign that for you, young man?" Lionel asked his gobsmacked fan, pointing at the sheet music.

As he rejoined us, winking and murmuring, "Bless 'im," he looked at me and said, "John? Would you like to come to a workshop performance of my musical, *Quasimodo?*"

He explained it was written in 1963 about the Hunchback of Notre Dame but had never been performed on stage before.

"I thought it was going to be a real winner," he told me, "but no-one was interested."

He chuckled to himself.

"I sent the script to Noel Coward and he replied, 'Brilliant, dear boy, but were you on drugs when you wrote it?'."

He laughed again, "I replied, 'Probably, Noel, yeah!'"

He told me that his friend Cameron Mackintosh was hosting the workshop.

"Frances Ruffelle, Peter Straker and Ray Shell are starring in it. It should be pretty good!"

How could I resist?

Arriving at the workshop studio behind Selfridge, I saw the great and good of musical theatre convening to acknowledge a genius. I gave the guy on the door my name and was handed a specially created scroll-poster and a letter of welcome signed by Lionel.

I was wandering through to make my way upstairs to the performance area, when I noticed Mike Batt chatting with a group of people. I went over to say a quick en route 'Hi', offering my hand but, to my surprise, was met by a red-faced angry man who, with hands wedged firmly in his pockets, glared at me.

"How are you, Mike?" I asked him.

"Very pissed off, actually," he replied, "Your company really let me and Gary down. A complete fuck up!"

I could have told him it was a project I'd unexpectedly inherited, one which I'd chosen to take over and see through to release. I could have also told Mike how we'd done our best but events had conspired to thwart us.

I could have finally told him how much I'd loved the album and wished it had sold better. But, instead, I just replied, "Mike, this is neither the time nor the place. Today is Lionel's day."

He continued to glare at me for a few seconds then, still clearly fuming, went back to chatting to his friends.

I made my way upstairs and, sitting alone, enjoyed the next couple of hours of a musical which, if it had been staged when it was first written, would have been the precursor to *Les Miserables*, indeed would have most likely made the French-written smash redundant. A chance to add another blockbuster musical to his name had eluded Lionel, simply because of a lack of vision by people who should have jumped at it.

Half an hour later, as I was driving out of the multi-storey car park in Poland Street, Lionel drove past me, opened his window and shouted, "Alright, darlin'? Enjoy it?"

"It was fabulous, Lionel!" I said. "Congratulations!"

"Thanks my friend!" he said, "Toodle-oo! Speak soon!"

Waving happily, he drove off.

Sadly, news of Lionel's increasingly failing health began to seep through the grapevine, and in the end meant he never made the album for me. I'd noticed how breathless he'd seemed at Brown's, but his spirit appeared so strong and positive I assumed that would push him on. Unfortunately, what could have been a lovely project never got off the ground. He died three years later of liver cancer.

* * *

Over the next few weeks, I arranged for various members of Carlton staff to meet, see and hear some of our artists.

I first of all took a group of people to watch Maria Friedman's one-woman show at The Whitehall Theatre. It clearly opened their eyes to her enormous talent, the younger members of staff being particularly taken with Maria's beautiful interpretation of Kate Bush's 'The Man With The Child In His Eyes'.

I then arranged a playback of Elkie's album, attended by the artist, during which, when 'Nights In White Satin' burst into a vocal crescendo which could have broken glass, Gerry Donohoe shouted, "Fucking hell!". Elkie smiled at me and nodded approvingly.

Finally, I hosted an evening at one of John Wilson's gigs, to build excitement about an artist many of my colleagues wouldn't know. They all went home gobsmacked at his talent and his ability to connect with an audience.

One of the highlights that night was when Bruce Welch of The Shadows walked up to me and said, "I am so pleased this guy's got a champion at last. Superb talent. Well done for signing him, John!"

He told me he'd been a fan of John's ever since Cliff Richard had recorded three of his songs for his 1993 chart-topper, *The Album*, which Bruce had co-produced. One of them, 'Never Let Go', gave Cliff his 115th Top 75 hit.

I was tempted to tell Bruce that my sister had Cliff & The Shads wallpaper in her bedroom in 1961, and how much, even at the tender age of eight years old, I had fancied the group's rhythm guitarist like mad. But I didn't.

* * *

As well as producing Connie Francis's *With Love To Buddy*, Stuart Colman also brought me a beautiful new Crickets album, *Too Much Monday Morning*. It featured Nanci Griffith on a couple of tracks and became a personal favourite of mine of all the Carlton releases.

It set us up nicely for Connie's album, with which I'd been pleasantly surprised. Featuring The Crickets on backings and vocal harmonies, there was a lovely warmth to the recordings. 'Heartbeat' especially, Connie's favourite Buddy song, stood out as the best track.

Hearing her voice ringing out really well, I guessed she'd been simply exhausted that night in Atlantic City.

Two more projects were also underway, both produced by Rod Edwards, who had been the musical director on *Blood Brothers*. Stephanie Lawrence, whose *Footlights* album had done well for Pickwick in 1992, was recording *Songs from Marilyn*, the musical in which she'd starred a decade earlier; Rod was also producing *Black To Broadway* by Monroe Kent, who I'd seen and been much impressed by in *Five Guys Named Moe*.

The Carlton roster was looking increasingly exciting, musically diverse and suitably eclectic.

One afternoon, I was listening to some of Lonnie's new tracks in my office when Gerry Donohoe walked in and sat down.

He nodded with approval then said, out of the blue, "Paul McGrane told me that you once released an album."

"I did, yes. In 1975. *Kid In A Big World*."

"Could I hear it?"

"Well, yes, if you like but… "

"Bring it in."

"It's an L.P., Gerry. That's how old it is! Have you got a record player?"

"Bring it in!"

The next morning, I popped into Gerry's office with the L.P. He shut his door and took it off me, smiling at the sleeve showing the twenty-one year old me staring wanly out of a window.

He put it on his hi fi and signalled for me to sit down. While he was studying the tracklisting, the chorus of 'Goodbye Suzie' kicked in. He sat back in his chair and yelled, "Fucking hell, John! What a voice!"

I just nodded.

"Can you still sing?" he asked.

"Yeah, though I don't much these days."

He turned the volume down and said, "How do you fancy singing in a band?"

"Which band?"

"The band I'm forming with Paul McGrane and a couple of the other guys here. We need a keyboard player and a good singer to complete the line-up."

He smiled at me.

"We've been asked by Music Week to take part in a Music Biz 'Battle of The Bands' night at the Shepherd's Bush Empire. We've accepted the offer but we need a singer. In other words, *you!*"

We called ourselves Chance Would Be A Fine Thing and a week later duly turned up at the Shepherd's Bush Empire for the competition. A lot of Carlton staff were there and, though we performed well and got a great reaction from the audience, we weren't even placed in the final five. Still, I got to perform at one of the most famous theatres in London and for the first time in my life sang a Rolling Stones number, in fact two, 'Honky Tonk Woman' and 'Brown Sugar'.

I'd wanted to do a couple of Beatles songs but Gerry had refused, saying, "I'm a Stones guy. You can't be both!"

The morning after the gig, Gerry stopped me in the corridor.

"We woz robbed!" he laughed.

"It was fun though!" I replied.

I was about to carry on to my office when Gerry stood in front of me. "How do you fancy making an album for Carlton, John?"

I laughed.

"I'm serious," Gerry said. "So is Paul. Come with me, I want to talk to you."

I followed him to his office and sat down.

"Look," he said. "If you did an album for us it would be such a great back story for the label. Think about it."

He mimed a headline in the air, "'Carlton's A & R Director, John Howard, releasing his first album for twenty years!'"

He grinned at me.

"What fabulous PR, John! Our guys would have a ball promoting it!"

I wasn't sure and said so. My main concern was how my artists would react if they were told their A & R Director was competing with them in the albums market. But he persisted.

"I think they'd be knocked out, John! It would be amazing publicity for their albums too! And what music magazine wouldn't find your story absolutely fascinating?! We need an angle, John, and you're it!"

When I got home that evening, I rang Keff. He'd been nagging me for years to do an album with him but I'd always dodged the issue. Those days were for me over, in the past, and I'd moved on, more happily than I would have expected twenty years earlier.

Our demo of 'Blue Days' in 1992 had led to great things for a brief period, but that had been as far as it went. Unsettlingly, my conversation with Gerry had got my creative – and my ambitious - juices flowing again.

"How do you fancy producing a John Howard album?" I asked Keff.

He laughed.

"Well, I'm going to have to check my diary, but… "

"Fuck off! I'm serious!"

"Then my diary is suddenly quite empty!" he said. "At last! I get to make a record with John Howard!"

186

John performing at Shepherd's Bush Empire 1995

Chapter Twelve

The Pros & Cons of Passion

As I hadn't written any new songs for years, Keff and I decided that some of the tracks on the new album would have to be covers. So, I put together a list of songs written by my musical heroes which I fancied interpreting and sent it to Keff:

Walk On The Wild Side (Lou Reed)
Don't Talk (Put Your Head On My Shoulder) (The Beach Boys)
Something (The Beatles)
Barefoot (k.d. lang)
Birds (Neil Young)
Ram On (Paul McCartney)
Not A Day Goes By (Stephen Sondheim)

I also wanted to record my own version of a song I'd fallen in love with when I'd seen the musical, *Elegies* in 1993, which Neil had been in during its run at The Drill Hall in Tottenham Court Road. 'Angels, Punks & Raging Queens' had opened the show and had blown me away.

I left Keff to get on with putting together arrangements and backing tracks while I addressed a far more pressing dilemma; to come up with some of my own songs to complete the tracklisting. I no longer had a piano, hadn't owned one since I'd left my former partner, Bayliss, in 1986, so I had to make do with a tiny Casio thing Keff lent me.

I looked through various box files of scraps of lyrics I'd written and abandoned over the years then sat at the keyboard and worked some of them into full-grown songs. Often, I put together three or four scraps into one lyric and then added a new hook or middle eight to fill it out.

There were also a couple of songs I had on cassette which I'd written in the '80s which, with a bit of work, would be fine. Finally, I sent Keff very rough demos of:

'The Pros & Cons of Passion' (from a 1986 poem)
'Neil (You Can Depend On Me)' (a 1989 song)
'Stormwatch' (started in 1988)
'You Breathed New Life Into Me' (made up of scraps of lyrics)
'Don't Look Back' (written in 1989)
'Who?' (from a 1986 poem)
'Another Time, Another Place' (a song I wrote for a Steve Levine session in 1986 which was never completed)

About two weeks later, he delivered a cassette of all his backing tracks, listening to each one with me. I was beside myself with joy, they sounded beautiful and I couldn't wait to get going on routining the vocals and recording them.

Keff booked Red Bus Studios off Edgware Road for the sessions which began in early April. I would be at Carlton during the day, then I'd drive down to the studios every evening to work on the album.

I recorded 'Don't Look Back' first. It was an easily-pitched number, without too much soaring or 'big' singing required. When I'd recorded the first take, I waited to hear what Keff thought and, for a few seconds, silence from the control room had me worried.

"Oh my God!" he finally said. "I have never heard you sing like that before!"

"What do you mean?"

"Well, you sounded so in the moment. You just sang it, completely naturally. Beautiful, John."

"But it was more a kind of first guide vocal," I said, readying myself to do a second take.

"No! It's perfect," he almost shouted. "That is the vocal! Next!"

In the same mode was 'Birds', and we got that done in a couple of takes, with me and Keff adding some backing vocals here and there.

Over the next few nights, I recorded all the lead vocals, the most complex and rangey being 'Don't Talk' so we left that to last, Keff and Tracey joining me to add some multi-harmonized backing vocals.

The second week was taken up with Keff bringing in extra musicians. When Dave Mattacks walked in to overdub drums, I was taken back to the Nicky Graham sessions at CBS in 1980 when Dave had also added drums to the rough mixes of 'I Tune Into You'. He had not only been the drummer with Fairport Convention, but had also worked with one of my songwriting heroes, Nick Drake.

Brass players and finally a small string section all contributed "to add texture and air", as Keff put it.

By the third week of April, it was mixed and ready to play to Gerry and Paul. I nervously sat in Paul's office as the tracks, one after the other, rang out around the room. Finally, as the reprise instrumental of 'Walk On The Wild Side' finished, Gerry declared, "Fucking brilliant, John!"

Paul nodded in agreement.

"You're not bad, are you?" he said, winking at me. "Ever thought of taking this up professionally?"

"Now!" Gerry said, jumping up from his seat and pacing the room. "Arrange one of your company playbacks, John. *Everyone* should hear this!"

The album, titled *The Pros & Cons of Passion*, was scheduled to be released at the beginning of June, with a great sleeve design done by the Carlton art department which featured a pair of footprints walking away in the sand which halfway along became a single set of prints.

My old friend Angus Hamilton, with whom I'd done the Roy's

Restaurant revues a few years earlier, interviewed me about the album for Gay Times. Promo copies were sent to Radio 2 producers and music reviewers, and I also sent out cassettes, along with a personal letter, to all the artists who I had signed to Carlton. Letters and copies of the album were also sent to the artists' managers. I wanted them all on board and to know about it before they heard second-hand. I was prepared to cancel the album's release if the artists had been unhappy about it.

Recording The Pros & Cons of Passion album

I also sent a copy to Des and Jodie, because they had been so supportive of my songwriting and, of course, it was Jodie's brother-in-law who had produced the album. In truth, I also hoped Des might choose one of my songs from the album to record for his next release!

Within just a few days, I received some really lovely notes back from my artists and their managers, telling me how much they'd enjoyed the record, many of them pleased to have signed with "such a creative, musical guy!", as one of them put it. We were a team. Gerry's idea had worked. Maria Friedman even gave me a big hug when we met up in Bristol the following weekend, where she was appearing in a play, to discuss her upcoming release.

"I love your album, John!" she said, looking at me in a beguilingly different way. "You should be very proud of it!"

"Thanks Maria," I replied as we settled in the theatre coffee bar for cakes and tea. "But you know the reason I made it was to help promote the label and its new releases."

"Sure, of course, but I'm even more pleased we know each other now." She squeezed my arm. "You dark horse you!"

Jodie sent a message via Keff to say how much she loved the album, especially 'Neil (You Can Depend On Me)', which, Keff told me, "she thinks could be a huge hit!"

One evening, my mobile rang as I was driving home after the company playback of the album, on a high as it had gone really well. Everyone agreed that 'Walk On The Wild Side' should be released as a trailer single. One of the production girls had particularly liked my interpretation of George Harrison's 'Something', which I'd sung from the point of view of a man singing to another man: "*Something in the way he moves attracts me like no other lover…* ".

"Hi John! It's Des!" his usual cheery voice rang around the car.

"Des! How are you?"

"Fine young man! Jodie and I got your cassette. Thank you for sending it to us!"

"No problem, Des. Jodie said she really liked it. I hope you enjoyed it?"

"Yeah, she really loves it, particularly your song to Neil on there. She thinks it could be a hit record!"

"Yeah, Keff told me! Fantastic!"

"But, John… it wasn't that I wanted to discuss with you. I have a question for you."

"Okay!"

'Here goes,' I thought, 'I wonder which song he wants to record?'

"I was wondering," he said, "*why* did you record this album?"

I was stumped.

"Not sure what you mean, Des?"

"I mean… you are the A & R Director of Carlton, right?"

"Ye-es."

"And you have several new albums being released on the label by artists who need your care and attention, right?"

"Of course."

"And yet, John, you go and record your own album for the very same label! How do you think your artists will feel about that?"

He sounded decidedly tetchy, and I had a job not sounding just as irritated back.

"Well, as a matter of fact, Des, I've had great responses from my artists – and their managers. I sent them all copies of the album and -"

"And how will that make them feel, John?"

"Sorry?"

"Don't you see how it could make them feel? As though you've stolen their moment. Their spotlight."

The traffic was at a standstill on the M40, as was my comprehension of what he was saying.

"No, I don't see that at all, Des," I replied as calmly as I could. "And, for your information, I was actually invited by Carlton Records'

Managing Director to make the album! It wasn't my idea."

"Oh?"

"Yes! He suggested it would be great publicity for the new label, which our Chairman *wholly* agrees with!"

"Great publicity?... How?"

"Well, for one, it would give the label a different image for journalists; a record label run by a guy who's also a singer-songwriter with his own back story. It could potentially give us that extra ingredient other labels don't have. A different hook, and everybody needs a hook, Des. Nowadays more than ever."

"But it's all so *wrong*, John," he persisted. "An A & R Director releasing his *own* album on the label he *works* for, it's... well, it just isn't *done!*"

As the traffic began to move along again, I said, "Maybe not in the UK, Des, but what about Smokey Robinson?"

"Hm?"

"Smokey Robinson! He's the Managing Director *and* A & R Director of Motown Records. He continues to release records of his own on the label as well as signing and mentoring other Motown acts!"

"It's *not* the same thing, John!" Des said, his voice going up a couple of notes. "For heaven's sake, Smokey was already a recording artist! He was making records years ago. He has a right to... "

"Er - you're probably unaware of my own history as a recording artist?"

"Eh?"

I'd never discussed my 'previous life' with him. He knew I was a songwriter but I'd never told him much else.

"I was signed to one of the biggest record companies in the world, Des – in fact the same one you're signed to now."

I let that sink in.

"I performed in major London theatres with top artists and appeared on prime-time TV with Johnny Mathis and Lynsey De Paul; I recorded with people like Rod Argent, Trevor Horn, Tony Meehan, Biddu, and Culture Club's producer Steve Levine; I wrote and recorded the theme song for a Peter Fonda movie, which the director, Peter Collinson - who directed The Italian Job - commissioned me to write."

It had gone quiet on the other end of the line. I carried on while all this new info about myself had seemingly stunned him into silence.

"My Managing Director's idea is that my story will help to bring a higher profile to Carlton Records, *and* give a different promotional slant to brand new records by Elkie Brooks, Lonnie Donegan, Maria Friedman, Sonia, Gary Glitter, Hazell Dean, Connie Francis, The Crickets - all of whom I've signed. What's wrong with that?"

I'd reached my turn-off and, as I sped down into Lewknor, I said, "Des, I'm nearly home now. I'm going in for something to eat after a long and extremely exciting day. Tomorrow I'll be meeting up with Elkie to discuss *her* new album and then I'll be visiting Lonnie at his London flat to discuss *his*. The following day, I'm having a meeting with Shakin' Stevens' producer Stuart Colman, who's bringing over the tapes from America for the Connie Francis and Crickets albums he's produced for me. Oh yes! Sonia's due in this week to meet everyone at Carlton before her first single - produced by Steve Levine - is released. And in a few days' time, I'm getting together with Gary Glitter to chat about a follow-up to his first Top 50 hit for three years which Carlton released."

I parked outside the house.

"By the way, do let me know if you want any of these top acts on your show and I'll ask our promotions department to contact your producer."

I got out of the car holding the mobile to my ear as I locked up.

"So, with all due respect, Des – and I have a huge respect for you - *you're* wrong. Times have changed."

As I reached the front door, he said, "Okay. We'll see, John."

* * *

In May of 1996, shock waves went around the company when Paul McGrane's secretary, Bobbie, delivered redundancy notices without warning to various members of staff. Most of my own department was wiped out in just a few minutes of brown envelopes being delivered. Other less fortunate divisions were closed down completely.

I wondered what had happened to the exciting new beginning Paul had talked about when he'd wooed me away from MCA just over a year earlier and went straight along the corridor to ask him what the hell was going on.

He smiled ruefully at me and said that the company was not proving to be the instant cash cow Michael Green had expected.

"There will probably be more redundancies to come, John," he said with disturbing emphasis. "Even I'm not safe. My advice is to submit your bonuses invoice as soon as possible. You've earned every penny. But, do it soon, mate."

I walked back to my office wondering what had happened to the old businessman's motto: 'Speculate to accumulate'. Clearly, having 'speculated', Michael Green wasn't prepared to wait for the second bit.

Over the next three weeks, even though imminent releases went out, Elkie's album immediately hitting the Top 50 and Maria's getting heavy rotation play on Radio 2, the redundancies had sapped our collegial energy. The positive vibe around the building had gone. We now went about our jobs expecting another visit any moment from the no longer sparkling Bobbie, who cried on my shoulder one morning, saying "everyone's blaming me! I'm just the messenger, John!"

Our previously bright and expectant future was suddenly clouded by uncertainty. Morale was at rock bottom.

One morning in June, I walked into Gerry's office for one of our regular update chats. Although things had definitely changed at the company - certainly walking past lines of empty desks and closed, darkened offices began each day with a heavy heart - my get-togethers with Gerry were still something I looked forward to.

But, as I sat down, my heart began to beat a little bit faster, and not in a good way. For the first time ever, he wouldn't make eye contact with me, and instead of inviting me to have a coffee with him, just said, "John? Can you come and see me at, say, four o'clock today?"

"Sure, Gerry! Is everything okay?"

He lifted his head and almost met my eyes, "We'll have a talk at four o'clock, John. Thanks!"

His sign-off was clearly a 'You can go now'. As I got up, he pulled out a spread sheet on his desk and began studying it, slowly tapping his finger on the desk.

When I got back to my office, the sales notes for the new releases were waiting for me, my usual preparation for me to go along and do my spiel for the sales team the following day. It felt rather odd seeing 'The Pros & Cons of Passion by John Howard!' at the top of one of the sheets.

I'd already made a few notes before the redundancy announcement, which were full of positivity and vision. Now, I began making changes, and having huge misgivings about going ahead with the album. How would I put a positive spin on an album by the A & R Director of such a depleted team, which had been reduced by a third already, with the axe hanging over all of us of still more staff losses. The doubts, never there before, were nagging at the edges of my mind. As were Des's recent sign-off words, "We'll see, John."

When I walked into Gerry's office later that afternoon, Nina, the Human Resources lady, was standing beside him, an ominous folder with my name on it in her hand. As soon as I'd closed the door, she handed it to him. He asked me to sit down, opened the folder and read what was on the page.

"Okay mate," he began, with a sigh, "there's no easy way to say this, John. We are going to have to let you go."

Nina stared fixedly at the Carlton paperweight on Gerry's desk. Meeting my eyes for the first time that day, Gerry said, "I'm so sorry, John. We just can't afford to go on with the label."

"What happens to the June releases?"

"Cancelled, mate."

"But the May release went so well!"

I looked at Nina who clearly didn't care.

"Elkie Brooks," I said, "immediate chart entry."

Then, counting them on my fingers for her benefit; "Maria Friedman, Connie Francis, John Wilson, they've all had fantastic reactions, great orders from all the chain stores, fantastic reviews are a certainty!"

Nina shuffled her feet and sighed. I almost expected her to start studying her nails.

"It's crazy, Gerry," I went on, "the company will get back what we've spent from sales alone. On top of that, there's the third-party licensing income, which is already coming in, and there'll be more. Judy Legg's really excited about what we have coming up. She's lining up deals as we speak."

Gerry went a bit pink and started fiddling with his pen, clicking the biro in and out.

"Lonnie will be devastated," I said. "Your childhood hero, Gerry! *Such* a great album!"

"Your album is also fantastic, John," he replied. "Losing that's very disappointing."

"And it was your idea," I couldn't help saying.

He flinched slightly and glanced up at Nina who was now looking out of the window. Finally, I gave in to the inevitable and smiled at him.

"I'm used to it, Gerry," I said. "My recording career has been littered with what-ifs."

He leaned forward and smiled back at me.

"That's why you'll bounce back from this, John."

"What do you mean?"

"Because you stay positive and never *expect* anything. It's what keeps you grounded, it's what makes you... *you*."

Ten minutes later, I drove out of the car park and called home. Neil's breezy voice chimed through my dark mood.

"Hi love!"

"I'm leaving Carlton," I replied.

"Okay, you'll be home in about an hour then?"

"No, what I mean, darling is, I am *leaving Carlton. Now.*"

The phone went quiet.

"Oh! You mean... ?"

"Yep. I've just been given my marching orders by Gerry."

"Why?!"

"They're closing the whole thing down. The dream is over."

"So what now?"

"We'll chat about it when I get home."

What amazed me was how many phone calls I got that evening from the artists I'd signed, who'd all been given the news of my departure by poor old Bobbie. Lonnie, Maria and Elkie were particularly lovely, saying they'd already instructed their solicitors to put into action the Key Man Clause they'd insisted on in their contracts. It meant that if I left the company at any time, Carlton would be contractually obliged to give them their albums back. I'd found it flattering that they'd insisted on the clause, but never imagined it would be acted upon so soon after they'd signed with us.

"I've really enjoyed working with you, my son," Lonnie said. "I am so sorry about what's happened."

"I'm really gutted about your album, Lonnie," I said.

"Don't you worry. I've already got a label interested in putting it out. Thank you for all your help in making it happen. You've been great. Take care, boy."

The following morning, Hazell's manager rang to tell me that they'd received the artwork for her album.

"Your credit we asked for isn't there," he said. "So I just called someone in the design studio to ask why."

"What did they say?"

"Just that they'd been instructed to take your name off the back of the sleeve. Hazell's livid. She specifically asked for a 'Thanks to John Howard' credit."

In effect, Carlton was already air-brushing me out.

A couple of days later, the manager of Stephanie Lawrence rang me.

"I went in to see Gerry Donohoe this morning," she told me, "to find out what Carlton is going to do with my artist's album now you've gone."

"What did he say?" I asked her, intrigued.

"Well, within minutes of me sitting down, Gerry began bad-mouthing you. Saying it was 'all John Howard's fault the label has closed down' and that you had completely mismanaged it."

"Really?"

"Yes. So I held up my hand, stopping him in mid-bitch. I not only told him that you are a *very* good friend of mine, I said that *you* were the only reason I'd brought Steph to Carlton – and that I knew many others like me felt the same. I told him he was crazy to sack you, that you should be feted not fired for what you'd done for his company."

"What did he say to that?"

"He just went a delicious shade of red and his top lip started sweating profusely."

"Fabulous! I wish I'd been a fly on the wall!"

"Well, darling, I certainly swatted *that* little bug into submission! You're better off out of it, dear."

Another call that afternoon was from Fred Dellar, who wrote for Mojo Magazine. He'd been sent a review copy of *The Pros & Cons of Passion* a couple of weeks earlier.

"I'd given it a rave review, John," he told me sorrowfully, "and when I called your office just now to interview you about it, I was told you'd left the company. Is that true?"

"Yes, Fred, I'm afraid it is."

"And your album?"

"Pulled."

"Ridiculous!" he said.

"Yeah, seems to be the way it goes with my albums!"

"They're *fools*! The album's great. It could have done really well. They should have released it, even without you there."

I went to bed that night full of mixed emotions, one minute sad, the next angry.

The following morning, I opened the front door, a little bleary-eyed after very little sleep and collected the milk from the doorstep. As I straightened up with the bottles in my hands, I nearly dropped them again. My company car, which I'd been allowed to keep for a further two weeks, had been spray-painted with 'Poof' on the doors, bonnet and boot.

I went inside and yelled *"Neil!!"* at the top of my voice.

Chapter Thirteen

Home Is Where The Heart Is

"It's okay," Neil was saying, as I sipped the very sweet tea he'd made me. "I'll go and see Mike at the pub and ask him if he has anything which can remove the paint. He may also have an idea who's done this."

I was shivering slightly and found myself rocking to and fro.

"We're leaving!" I said. "We're selling up and moving!"

"No, we're staying and facing this down," he replied. "I refuse to run away from homophobic cowards."

Kissing me on the top of the head, he made me a second cup of strong tea and took the car around the corner to the village pub, The Leathern Bottel, to show the landlord, Mike, and anyone else there, what had happened. Ten minutes later, he returned with a pot of paint cleaner and proceeded to remove as much of the spray-paint as he could.

"Mike thinks he knows who it might be," Neil was saying as he scrubbed away at the graffiti. "He's going to have a word with some local lads and tell them to pass the message onto their mates that the village does not take kindly to things like this being done to friends and neighbours."

The pleasant-sounding policeman I reported the vandalism to, Constable Green, told me he'd be around within the hour. Meanwhile Gerry's secretary, Rhani, had faxed me a damage report form within minutes of my calling her.

As I was filling it out, Neil came back in and said, "The spray-paint has gone completely now. I've managed to wipe it all off. So just report the scratches on the form, you don't need to mention the graffiti."

Ten minutes later, I opened the door to Constable Green, a bespectacled chap in his fifties, who smiled paternally at me and asked if I was okay.

"I've also had my car vandalised by local hooligans," he told me as I led him through to our back garden, where he sat with his little notebook on the patio, admiring our pretty walled garden.

"Amazing isn't it?" he mused. "Such a tranquil and picturesque village and yet it can harbour such nasty little tykes?"

"Do you think it's local?" Neil asked him, offering him a biscuit with his cup of tea.

"I do. And these kids are not poor or under-privileged. They're just bored. Their parents have great jobs and work long hours, so they're left to their own devices – which always means trouble."

One imagined Miss Marple wandering down the lane with a basket of freshly-picked wild flowers, seeing the vandalism and muttering, "Such wickedness!", shaking her head sadly.

When the policeman had gone, Neil said, "Let's go for lunch to the pub."

I was horrified by the idea.

"Honestly," he said, "the sooner we show just how little this has affected us, the better."

So, we wandered up the lane and into the beautifully maintained beer garden which overlooked the road to the local church, which just a few nights earlier we'd sat in listening to the local choir, an annual event arranged and conducted by one of our neighbours. As we approached the pub, everything looked as it always did, a quiet, rural idyll Neil and I had come to love very much.

Mike rushed up to us to see how we were, took us inside and gave us two pints "on the house!", ushering us to our favourite window seat. I had to admit, I was beginning to feel better just being out of the house.

One of the regulars came over to us, patted my shoulder and said, "Terrible, what happened to you, we are so sorry!"

He was quickly joined by the lady who organised the Harvest Supper every year.

"We hope this doesn't put you off our little village," she said, her eyes tearing up. "We like having you here!"

"Quite right!" Mike shouted from the bar.

A couple by the door lifted their glasses and cheered us.

I could have cried. It was as though the whole community was wrapping its protective wings around us.

Later that afternoon, as I was snoozing on the sofa after a hearty pub lunch, the phone rang. Neil had driven to the shops to buy us more much-needed gin, so, feeling a bit groggy, I ran to get it.

An unfamiliar, East End-sounding voice said, "Is that John Howard?"

"Yes it is," I replied, "who's this?"

"Oh, you don't know me, John. My name's Brad. But I know you… and I know all about how your car was vandalised this morning… "

He sniggered as my heart sank.

"Very sorry to hear about the *scratches* on your *lovely* new Audi!" Brad continued. "And, John, I know who did it. Would you like to know?"

Writing down on a pad what he was saying, I tried to keep my voice amiable and calm.

"Yes, that would be useful, Brad."

"I thought it might. Now, you're friends with Greg Church, aren't you?"

Greg had worked at Carlton in the TV Division and, when that had closed, had migrated into promoting the company's audio and video releases. I'd always found him pleasant enough, albeit in a shady, barrow-boy kind of way.

He'd once confided in me, on one of his daily walkabouts, that he had several gambling debts, owing a lot of money "to some very dangerous people." Looking slightly ashen, he'd told me that Den, a chap in production, had been badly beaten up the previous night in the car park.

"It was meant for me," he'd said, sitting down.

"How do you mean?" I'd replied.

"Think about it. He and I are both stocky blokes in our fifties with silver grey hair. From the back, in a dimly-lit car park, he could easily be mistaken for me. I was threatened a few weeks ago that if I didn't pay up they'd get me. Looks like poor Den has paid the price."

"So," Brad was saying, "let your mate Greg know I've called, will you? Tell him from me that, if we don't get what he owes us, then other friends of his'll get more than just a few scratches on their car!"

He chuckled unpleasantly.

"Greg is not my mate," I told him, "we just worked at the same company."

"Well, that's not what I've been told, John. Apparently, you always looked very matey when you were at Carlton."

"Then your information – from whoever it comes – is wrong," I said, feeling a little less threatened by a man who was clearly relying on inaccurate third-party reports.

He sniggered again.

"Well, John, I hope you'll be happy in your lovely little cottage in *Church End Lane*! It would be a shame to ruin all that, wouldn't it, John?"

As I put the phone down, I realised that Brad had only mentioned the *scratches*. *Not* the spray-painted 'Poof' which, being far more personally upsetting, he would have certainly mentioned if he'd known about it.

I thought through the events. I'd faxed a vandalised car report to Rhani that morning which contained my name, address, phone number, the make of the car and details of the scratches. She'd said she would pass it on to Carlton's accounts department. So, someone in accounts, for whatever reason, must have passed that info onto Brad. Maybe someone who disliked Greg and knew Brad? Or someone who wanted to unsettle me?

Needless to say, I never heard from Brad again and, to this day, I've never gotten to the bottom of what it was all about, nor who vandalised my car that morning.

* * *

Neil and I flew off a week later for a very welcome break to Mykonos. We'd last visited in 1987, shortly after Neil and I had first met. Like me, he'd been entranced by the island.

However, this time we found it completely transformed, and not in a good way. Someone had obviously pumped an enormous amount of money into it since our last visit. Everything looked brighter, more expensive, swishier, but somehow it now looked much more trashy, tourist resort gaudy.

The little old houses in the village we'd wandered by on our way to the cafes and restaurants each evening were now neon-lit American-style ice cream parlours and over-lit jewellery and gift shops. And the place was decidedly noisier, disco music thumping out of shops and bars. It even felt less gay now, lots of young, fashionable straight couples danced in tree-surrounded courtyards, shouting and whooping as they knocked their bottles of beer back.

Even the cute old taverna on the thankfully still-gay Super Paradise Beach had been replaced by a hilltop flashy bar, where swanky fashionista queens sat around an infinity pool drinking cocktails.

Pierrot's Bar, the gay night-life hub of Mykonos for years, had been gutted and turned into a cavernous chill-out disco called Razzle.

There was a glitzier feel everywhere we went, and it was awful.

Happily, Kastro's Bar, our old nightly haven of soft classical music and great views of beautiful sunsets over the sea, was still there and looked exactly the same. We wandered in ready for a cosy chat with our old friend who ran it.

"Kostas!" I cried, ready for the big bear hug he always gave me. "How lovely to see you again!"

"Er... hi!" he said unsurely, backing off from my outstretched arms.

"Don't you remember me?" I asked him.

"Er – no, no I don't, I'm afraid," he replied, trying to place me.

Beginning to feel like George Bailey from *It's A Wonderful Life*, I explained who I was, introduced Neil and told him how many years I'd been coming to his bar.

"I first came here in 1978," I said, "I was with Bayliss then."

Studying me again, he shook his head.

"Sorry no, I don't know you at all."

He glanced at Neil and narrowed his eyes.

"I think I remember your friend, but from quite a long time ago... "

"We were last here in 1987," I offered helpfully.

"Hm, yes, I think I do remember you," he said, continuing to look at Neil, "but you... ", he looked at me again, "no, I don't recognise you at all. I'm very sorry!"

As I undressed for bed that night, I was feeling like a stranger in a strange land I'd once thought of as my second home.

"I told you, darling," Neil said. "You look nothing like you did before. I'm not surprised Kostas didn't recognise you!"

I saw my seventeen-stone muscled frame in the mirror and sighed.

"Maybe I should have brought an old photo with me," I said, getting into bed.

As I turned off the light and lay in the dark, I mourned my lovely old Mykonos. It - and I - had been transformed since those halcyon days of my many previous visits. We were no longer on good terms. I never went back.

* * *

When we got home, I found the latest Music Week amongst the bills and circulars lying on the doormat. Neil made us a coffee and we sat down to resettle ourselves, Neil to check the electricity bill and me to have a look at the weekly charts, one of my lifelong pleasures associated with being a devoted pop fan.

I noticed that Hazell Dean's single, 'The Winner Takes It All', the title track of the Abba album she'd done for me at Carlton, was bubbling under the Top 75.

Feeling a mix of both pride and regret, I turned the page and there, to my utter surprise, was a half-page ad for a new Carlton album, *Dancing In The Street*. I'd known nothing about it till then and stared at it in disbelief and rising anger.

While the label hadn't spent a penny on advertising *any* of the albums I'd brought them – and which the company *owned* – it had now decided to place an ad for an album which contained *entirely* licensed-in tracks. It truly beggared belief.

Even more infuriating, someone at Carlton must have been putting the album together while I'd been working there, without my knowledge. They'd have had to pay a fortune for some of the big hits on it, extremely high royalty rates and no doubt several advances. It was the final kick in the teeth for me.

My fury, however, galvanised me into action. I phoned Music Week's advertising manager and placed my own ad in the following week's issue. It announced my new freelance availability for licensing, compilations, A & R advice, sleevenotes and concept creation. Its headline read:

'Are you ready for a brand new beat? Summer's here and the time

is right'. Direct quotes from 'Dancing In The Street'. Bitchy? I'll say!

Within a day of the ad going in, my phone starting ringing. Most of the calls were from potential new clients, but several others were from former Carlton colleagues.

"Gerry was *enraged* by your ad!" one told me delightedly.

"He couldn't get over your *cheek*!" another said, "It was delicious!".

"He was *furious* when he saw your ad!" yet another informed me.

"Good! Hell hath no fury like a queen scorned!" I replied.

Chapter Fourteen

And The World

Through the Autumn of 1996, freelance work was going well with quite a few projects coming my way. As I worked away at home, the income I'd enjoyed at Carlton was in no way being equalled, or likely to be for the foreseeable future, but it was a good start. Word-of-mouth - and my ad - was paying dividends, albeit smaller ones than I'd been used to.

My worry was that, even with Neil's additional income from his acting work and driving jobs between plays, we were in danger of not being able to pay our mortgage. The house had been bought when I'd been offered the Carlton job, suddenly able to afford a beautiful period cottage in a gorgeous commuter-belt village. It was the typical Young Executive Dream and we had embraced it with gusto, increasing our mortgage to match the dream.

However, it was becoming clear that we may have to, at some point, consider selling up and downsizing to a more manageably-priced house. That particularly depressed Neil who loved the cottage. It was, he'd declared when we'd moved in during the summer of '95, "the kind of house I've always wanted to live in."

Then, in early November, I got a call from a Belgian chap who ran the Brussels-based International Music Division at Reader's Digest. He wanted to offer me a job which seemed at first like manna from heaven.

I'd first met him in January that year when I was at the MIDEM music festival in Cannes with Carlton. He'd strode onto our stand accompanied by his Belgium-based assistant, Charles Meyer, and his American boss, José Perez, all three of them keen to talk about the artists I was signing up.

Charles, who I'd licensed from a few years earlier when he was the Repertoire Manager at Decca, seemed oddly breathless, a bit sweaty and out of sorts, but he'd brightened somewhat when I showed him the just-published Carlton Recordings catalogue.

"Some really top names here!" he declared, showing José who beamed at Charles then at me.

"Fantastic, John!" José murmured, browsing through the pages.

His constantly twinkling, and recognisably searching eyes whenever he looked at me was a sure sign that we played in the same garden.

"And these would be available for a flat fee?" Charles enquired.

I hadn't come across this kind of licensing before and asked him to explain what it meant.

"It's very simple!" he said. "We pay you what could be a substantial amount of money upfront, which would allow us to use the recordings, royalty-free in perpetuity on our collections!"

"It's non-exclusive, of course!" his boss added, nodding at Charles.

"Of course it is!" Charles said, sweating a little more. "It doesn't conflict with your other licensing deals at all. It guarantees Carlton a large swathe of money in one lump, and all you have to do is send us copy masters!"

He beamed at José.

"Then we'd disappear from your life," he continued, pushed on by José's encouraging smile, "and get on with putting the tracks on our various box sets! It's a win-win situation for us both, John!"

Over the following hour, going through the catalogue, they listed the recordings they would want. For each title we agreed that RD would pay Carlton £250. The proposed deal amounted to tens of thousands of pounds.

Meanwhile, Gerry and Paul were watching from a corner of the stand. When the RD team had left they came over.

"Nicely handled!" Gerry said, shaking my hand.

"Of course!" Paul grinned. "Why do you think I brought John in?!"

"Odd little chap though, the Belgian," Gerry said.

"Yes," I replied, "and Charles seems terrified of him. He's obviously difficult to work for."

"Who cares, if they pay us the money!" Paul laughed. "A celebratory lunch at the Grand Hotel, I think? On me!"

So, ten months later, on this November morning, as a light snow was beginning to settle on the Buddleia outside the study window, here was Charles's boss, offering me a job.

"You would work with me here in Brussels," he was telling me, "acting as my assistant."

"Assistant?"

"Well, your title would be International Music Manager, but yes, you would in effect be my assistant here in Belgium."

"So... what happened to Charles?" I enquired.

"It – er – it didn't... work out with Charles," he said vaguely. "He no longer works for me. In fact, he passed away shortly after I'd fired him."

"Oh! I hadn't heard! Poor Charles! That's dreadful! How did he die?"

"He fell down the stairs of his apartment," he explained briskly and without any sign of regret.

"Dear me! That's awful!"

"Yes. But he... had problems... and simply wasn't what I required."

I was about to ask why when he ploughed on, explaining what the job entailed, " You would be dealing with not only our music licensors, but also helping many of RD's twenty-six international branches to get the best deals for their collections."

He chattered away happily about what he'd achieved in his twenty-five years at the company and how "so many RD employees" depended on him for his invaluable help and advice. After just five minutes he was getting on my tits.

"I would like to invite you to come over to the Brussels office," he went on, "where you could get a feel for what I require. We will, of course, pay for your travel and accommodation while you're here."

Having decided I didn't like this man at all, I told him I'd discuss it with Neil. Most importantly because, if I took the job, it would mean my moving to Brussels, initially on my own.

"Please call me when you have made a decision!," he said and put down the phone.

Later that evening, Neil and I agreed, over a bottle of wine and a home-made chilli, that it was worth me at least going over to Brussels to suss things out. Though I already had misgivings, the job itself sounded right up my street.

The next day, I called a friend of mine who worked at the UK branch of Reader's Digest Music. I told him about my conversation with his Belgian colleague and asked him for an honest opinion of the man.

"Oh God, he's an *awful* person!," he said. "He's known as Shitface here. We call him SF for short. But, John, you would be *perfect* for the job! Please say yes!"

A week later, after a speedy Eurostar journey, I arrived in Brussels and got a cab to SF's office. It was, disappointingly, not in the city itself but situated on a drab industrial estate in a run-down suburb in the sticks.

"You caught a *cab*?" he said when I walked in, decidedly displeased. "Why didn't you take the bus?"

"Because I had no idea that there *was* a bus or, in fact, where I could catch it."

His hooded eyes told me he didn't believe me.

"I thought I had clearly instructed you where the bus station was!"

'Yes,' I thought, 'you did, but I had no intention of faffing around with that when there was a handy line of cabs available.'

He began to explain, as to a child, where the bus station was but I waved away his detailed instructions with an excuse that I needed the loo.

"Of course!," he declared. "It's down the corridor, turn left and the lavatory is on your right. I'll be waiting for you at my desk!"

I purposely took an age, washing my face, freshening up, checking myself over several times before returning to SF's smiling secretary Marianne. Her knowing wink convinced me she'd enjoyed my making her boss wait. With a wink back, I entered his chaotic lair.

He directed me to a chair opposite him, from where his head was just about visible above precarious piles of folders on his desk, which he pushed carefully aside so as to give me a better view. I was tempted to push them back.

Not looking at me, he extracted a folder from one of the piles, opened it and studied it as though he'd never seen it before. With a pencil poised in his hand not a little camply, he underlined something, as though marking someone's homework.

Finally, coughing and putting down his pencil, he located a piece of paper under another of the piles and gave me a typed-out list, explaining that they were all the heads of licensing at each RD company.

"You would be their main point of contact," he told me as I perused the list. "They all have so many questions!" He chuckled. "I seem to spend all my days answering them, guiding them, like children!" He glanced over at me and nodded. "That's why I need an assistant!"

After a couple of hours of going through numerous ongoing projects, with endless explanations of what each one entailed, I explained that I was rather hungry. Having risen at five and eaten very little on the train apart from a bag of crisps and a cup of coffee I was famished.

"I prefer to work through lunch," he said rather disapprovingly. "A glass of milk suffices for me! But! For today, for you, we will eat in the canteen!"

I followed him down to the huge basement eaterie, where we queued with our plastic trays and cutlery, reminding me of school dinners. Everyone waited patiently to be served by unsmiling ladies in polyester housecoats and hats.

As we neared our turn, I told him I was vegetarian, so needed to know which of the dishes had no meat or fish in them. He threw me a mystified stare, coughed and told me that there were *no* vegetarian dishes on offer.

"None?" I asked incredulous.

"No. You should have sent me warning beforehand."

"Or even better, the canteen should get a selection of vegetarian meals on their menu!."

I saw a couple of people ahead of us smiling to each other.

With a purposely prolonged sigh, I chose a salad and a piece of apple pie. I refrained from asking if it had gelatine in it.

When we finally sat down, I took my plates off the tray and leaned it against the table leg. SF stared at me horrified.

"No, no!" he said angrily, shaking his head so much I thought it might fall off. "You *must* keep your plates *on* the tray! We *all* do!"

I looked around and, sure enough, he was right.

"But I find it uncomfortable eating off trays," I replied. "So, I'll do it my way if you don't mind."

He coughed again, clearly a nervous tick, twitched his shoulders up and down as though his back had an itch and glanced vexedly around the table, trying to gauge our neighbours' reactions. Ignoring him, I tucked into my salad and rather delicious warm crusty bread.

The girl next to me, her eyes fluttering through gorgeous pink glasses, nudged me and giggled.

"You are a man who knows his own mind!" she said, beaming at me while checking to see if SF was listening.

"I try to be," I replied.

"So *rare* here!," she said, and got on with sipping her Oxtail soup, giggling to herself.

It was a brisk half-an-hour for lunch, conversation with SF decidedly stilted, then back in silence to his office where he handed me a small pile of folders.

"These are the ones I would want you to take over," he told me, adding pointedly, "should you take the job, of course."

At about three o'clock, my eyes beginning to droop, he announced, "We are now going to look at possible apartments for you to rent, once you have moved to Brussels, should you... "

"... take the job, of course."

His shoulders danced up and down and off we went.

I was very grateful for some fresh air and the chance to stretch my legs. I followed SF as he marched into the company car park, pointing out a dilapidated people carrier parked next to his car.

"That would be your company car," he told me.

"Why would I need an eight-seater people carrier?" I asked him, staring at the sad old thing which obviously hadn't been washed in months.

"Charles required it for his family."

"But I don't have a family, just my partner Neil and several cats - and they won't be accompanying me to work."

SF shook his head vigorously, his chin pointing to the heavens.

"Well, I'm afraid I don't have the budget for a new car, so this..." he waved his hand dismissively at the abandoned vehicle, "would be yours."

The thought, 'we'll see about that,' went through my head as I got into his Peugeot and was whisked out onto the main highway and off to the suburban outskirts of the city. He'd arranged viewings of half a dozen apartments, which all had large, unfurnished wood-panelled rooms, high ceilings and a total lack of any sense of ever being loved or indeed lived in for months. I wandered through each room like a ghost surveying someone's past life, becoming more depressed with each viewing.

At around five o'clock, SF dropped me at the hotel he'd booked me into, and, shaking my hand, told me he would call me at home in a couple of days.

"When I have the details of your proposed salary from my accounts department, we can discuss it."

As soon as I'd shut my door, he sped off without waving and I walked into the hotel's small reception area where an unsmiling girl checked me in, handed me my key and told me to take the lift to the second floor.

A rather incongruous couple were waiting for the lift as I got out. He was a very large, sweaty man wearing a smelly suit and a guilty stare. She was a tiny lady in her forties, with a short frock and frilly see-through blouse, which purposely revealed extremely voluptuous boobs.

I nodded at them as they walked into the lift, and just as the doors were closing I saw him tweak her bum which elicited a giggle and a saucy glance at me. Where they were going I had no idea; what they'd been up to I could certainly imagine.

Reaching my basic but pleasant room, I put the suitcase down and went to run a much-needed bath. But, as I was about to turn on the hot tap, to my horror I noticed several tiny crabs walking along the bottom of the tub. Although I didn't like washing them down the plughole - they'd done me no harm - I simply had no choice. I ran the tap and they disappeared like tiny creatures in a devastating flood. I then emptied one of the sachets of shower gel onto a rag hanging on the shower head and scrubbed furiously around the tub. I rinsed the suds away and filled the bath with steaming hot water along with the second sachet of shower gel. Finally, with a welcome G & T from the mini-bar, I gratefully climbed in.

After a crab-free bathe, I drank a second gin and tonic, got dressed and, after calling Neil to report the odd events of my day, took a pre-dinner walk along the avenue outside my hotel. Within five minutes of me stepping into the street, I was accosted by a lady offering me her wares "to nice man like you!". I politely declined and wandered on but, during my ten-minute walk, was approached three or four more times, once by a teenage boy who was the most insistent. He seemed shocked to the core when I told him he wasn't my type, spat out some unintelligible profanity and minced off.

Finally, I reached the end of the avenue, which opened out into the truly impressive Grand Place, my intended destination.

It was certainly grand. The cobbled central walking area glimmered in the gathering mist; sauntering couples and ladies with tiny dogs on sparkly leashes passed me by, miniaturised characters against the enormous gothic buildings which surrounded us. It looked like a De Chirico painting, and for the first time in years I wished I had a sketchbook and pastels on me.

I found a busy cosily-lit street café off the square and enjoyed a tasty cheese omelette and fries with a very good cup of strong coffee. It steeled me for the return journey to my hotel, which held the same propositions from the four street-workers who had clearly forgotten that I'd turned down their offers not much more than an hour earlier. The teenage boy actually spat at my feet this time, but I managed to avoid the missile and swiftly made my way back to the hotel as he yelled some insult at my back.

Feeling exhausted and oddly depressed, I went to bed and turned off the light. Lying in the dark listening to the busy traffic outside, I cursed SF for booking me into a knocking shop in one of the red light districts of Brussels.

***

The day after I arrived back home, SF called me with a salary offer. It was half of what my basic salary at Carlton had been. I had no idea what the tax rate in Belgium would be, but I'd heard it was much higher than in the UK, along with swingeing deductions from monthly incomes which went towards national healthcare. My potentially ever-dwindling wage was the final straw which convinced me it would be impossible to accept the job.

Although I'd decided to turn him down, out of sheer curiosity – and, yes, a little perverseness - I questioned SF about how much of my salary would be left after deductions. He stammered something about not yet having that information.

"Surely you know how much of my income would go towards tax and healthcare deductions?" I said. "Don't you know what *you* pay in tax and healthcare each month?"

"Well, yes, but that isn't applicable to your salary."

"No, but you must be able to work out the percentage of your gross salary against your actual earnings each month and then do a comparable calculation for me?"

He wittered on nervously, becoming increasingly flustered as I refused to accept his vague explanations.

Finally, after about ten minutes of this nonsense, I told him, "Look, I need to get proper calculated figures from you. I need to know how much my salary would be after deductions. That doesn't seem like an unreasonable request."

Sounding like a scolded child, he promised to call me back the following day, which he did, his calculations working out at a third of what I'd been earning at Carlton. I had to tell SF that, regrettably,

I couldn't take the job.

However, the following morning, he called again.

"I have spoken to José in America," he said, "and he has told me that he definitely wants you to take the job."

"But I can't," I replied. "I couldn't afford to."

"Yes! Of course, I am aware of our conversation yesterday. But, after discussing it with José, I have agreed that you would be based in London rather than Brussels. I have also agreed that your salary, which would be paid by the UK company - as my budget will not allow for it - would match what you were being paid by Carlton, plus travelling expenses and an annual performance-linked bonus. Would you consider taking the job in those circumstances?"

"Yes, I would," I replied, giving Neil a thumbs-up.

Later that day, I got a call from José.

"John!" he shouted down the phone. "So pleased you're coming to work for us! After having met you in January I *knew* you were the guy I wanted!"

"How did you manage to persuade SF to allow me to work in London?"

"No persuasion necessary, John! I simply instructed him that it was what I wanted! I always intended that you would be based in our London office. He changed the goalposts without telling me." He chuckled. "You'd be no use to us at all in Brussels – as his *'assistant'*!" He laughed derisively at that. "As our *International Music Manager*, you will need to be in London where the record companies are! *And* I also want you to be the go-to guy for all our music people. You'll be visiting them on a regular basis and getting to know what they need. I always believe a face to a name is imperative in our business. Now that you're aboard, we can really get going on making our music division a global power-house. It's a no-brainer!"

"And the revised salary? Was that your idea?"

"Of course! It will be a high profile, extremely pressurised job you're taking on, for which I believe we should pay you accordingly. You get monkeys when you pay peanuts!"

"I am so glad you stepped in!"

"I will always do that, John, *anytime*! I'm always here if you need me. When are you starting?"

"In two weeks. First week of December."

"Excellent! I'll get a letter of confirmation off to you and I look forward to working with you! It'll be a blast! The both of us have to get this company ready for the 21st century! Otherwise *it will sink*!"

As I put the phone down, I realised that José and SF had entirely different agendas, and I wondered which one would prevail. I knew for sure that a Battle Royal lay ahead.

As I lay in bed that night, I thought back to my time at MCA. During my two years there, I'd licensed a lot of recordings to Readers Digest. It was clearly suffering from an outdated arrogance and misplaced belief that the music business owed it a living. There was an endemic company malaise, leading it to think that it could rest on the laurels of its huge successes in the '70s and '80s, ignoring how music licensing had changed radically in the previous ten years.

Aggressively marketed TV-advertised compilations on labels like Telstar, Sony and Polygram were enjoying huge sales figures. They'd helped to increase MCA's licensing profits five-fold by 1995. In addition, getting just one or two brand new singles on TV-marketed releases was a huge boost for our A & R Department, who used the albums' high profile to build a burgeoning hit at radio.

But as well as those frontline companies, budget and mid-price licensees also had to up their game – and their royalties. MCA's and every other major licensor's attitude was, "We've got the hits, you pay accordingly."

By contrast, Digest's slow, archaic way of licensing and releasing box sets of old, over-used recordings not only bored my young staff to pieces – "Oh God, it's Reader's Digest!", Keren, my TV albums manager, would groan whenever she saw their number on her phone – it also resulted in increasingly lower income from them. RD was at the bottom of our Earner's List. But they still expected to be treated as a priority.

"But we are Reader's Digest!" was their response whenever I'd turned down their requests for more recent tracks.

"And we are MCA/Universal," I'd reply. "And my job is to make as much money for the company as I can. There is no way our head office in LA would accept what you're offering for these kinds of artists."

"But we need to find some newer material, John," one of the RD chaps had pleaded.

"Then, why don't we meet up to renegotiate the deal? Increasing the royalty you pay and offering advances would make it much easier to get your requests cleared."

The offer was never taken up.

Once a year Keren and I were invited to have lunch with RD's music team. While other licensees wined and dined us at happening, buzzing Soho restaurants, Digest insisted on 'entertaining' licensors in their company's private dining-room, a cavernous, featureless space on the edge of Mayfair. It was completely empty, except for one overlong, highly-polished dining table plonked in the middle of the room. Every murmur echoed around the beige walls full of silver and gold discs awarded to RD twenty years earlier.

Our pre-ordered meals were served by a solitary waitress in her Lyons Corner House black and white pinnied uniform. She rarely spoke and almost bowed as she cleared away our dishes. I once made a slightly camp, totally harmless comment about an oddly phallic-looking dessert she'd just placed in front of me.

"Well! *That* looks tasty!" I cried, pulling a face at her.

It was met with a beetroot-reddening face and an uncomfortable shuffling in the seats of our hosts.

If, during the meal, the conversation dipped, as it usually did at some point, the room would be full of the din of embarrassed silence. You actually felt your voice getting quieter as the meal progressed, unconsciously matching the libraryish whisperings from the opposite end of the table.

"I *hate* going to lunch with Digest!" Keren once said to me, when our annual dreaded pilgrimage was imminent. "Can't I do a sickie?"

"No, you can't!" I replied. "I need you there for moral support – *and* to have a laugh with when we finally get out!"

So, as 1996 was coming to an interesting close, my mission, at least in José's eyes, was clear. Readers Digest simply *had* to change or face the consequences of being left at the bottom of the pile of music licensing. As I turned over in bed and began to drop off to sleep, I mentally rubbed my hands at the challenge – and my word it was certainly that.

Footnote: Although 'SF' was addressed and usually referred to by his real name, for convenience and anonymity I am giving him the moniker SF whenever he's mentioned in the book.

Chapter Fifteen

Oh, Do Give It A Rest, Love

On December 9th 1996, I walked into my new office in the Reader's Digest building, which was just across the road from St Paul's and a couple of doors away from the Central Criminal Court. I loved this part of London, so much history and atmosphere, and in a street famous as the backdrop on news programmes whenever there was a high profile court case going on.

My excitement was doubled when I opened a letter on my desk from Thomas Shand, RD's Chief Executive Officer.

He heartily welcomed me to the company, saying, "So looking to forward to working with you and José on growing RD's global business!". Interestingly, he failed to mention SF anywhere in the letter.

That afternoon I received congratulatory calls from José and the various members of his music team in Manhattan, all saying they were looking forward to meeting and working with me. I became increasingly excited at this new job, then SF called.

"I need you to come to Brussels tomorrow," he said, sounding edgy, "to collect all the files you will be working on. I wish to go through everything with you in person."

There was a definite tone of annoyance in his voice, no doubt after being shot down in flames by José over where I would be located, how much I was being paid and what my mission at RD was.

I'd already decided I'd try to diplomatically straddle these two disparate points of view, for the time being at least. I'd do my best to put up with SF's shenanigans, he was my direct boss after all, but knowing I had the backing of José *and* Thomas Shand helped me prepare myself for coping with the little Belgian's 'tricky' behaviour. The job had the potential of being very exciting, and one which, if I could at least sidestep SF's power-play hurdles, could propel me to a winning finishing line.

I told SF I would arrive at 11 o'clock the following morning adding, "I've had a really lovely welcome letter from Thomas Shand," thoroughly enjoying SF's reply, i.e. the discomfited cough.

Two days later, I returned from Brussels, laden down with several heavy folders which I'd lugged onto the Eurostar train, transferred to a cab bound for Paddington and then onto the train to Oxford. Neil picked me up at the station and listened amused as I told him all about my trip. Thank goodness I had him to laugh away the annoying Belgian and his finickity demands.

Chuckling away as we sped through the gorgeous Oxfordshire countryside, he said, "Just remember to say to yourself, darling, every time SF gets on your tits, that you got the job you wanted, the pay you wanted and the location you wanted, and he could do nothing to stop it. Just think of that every time you want to slap the stupid man across the face!"

Leaving the numerous folders at home, planning to take them to the office in ones and twos over a week or so and have a look at them when I was ready, I caught the train into London the next morning.

I was beginning to enjoy this mode of travel. Every few days, I'd stop off at WH Smith's in the station and peruse the best-selling paperbacks section. Reading the latest Patricia Cornwell, Joanna Trollope or Maeve Binchy made the twice-daily 45-minute journey fly by.

As I was walking towards my office, a bespectacled chap in his forties who resembled a Geography teacher stepped out of the lift. He beamed away at me, strode forward and offered his hand.

"You must be John Howard!" he said.

"Yes, I am he!" I replied, shaking his hand.

"I've heard all about you! I'm Andrew Winstanley, Head of RD

Music UK, over at Berkeley Square!"

"Oh yes," I said, not mentioning I'd never heard of him.

"If you have time, do come and join us this afternoon, John!" he said, still holding onto my hand. "It'd be lovely to have your input at our next product meeting!"

RD UK was situated just across the road from Morton's restaurant, where I'd played piano several evenings each week back in the mid '70s. Still remembering those times when I'd serenaded customers with Sondheim, Jimmy Webb and Streisand classics, I gave my name at reception and was handed a laminated 'Visitor' badge. Instructed to go to the second floor, I was met at the lift by a small group of smiling faces.

"Why are you wearing a Visitor's badge?" Martin, the company's Head of Music, enquired.

"The girl on reception asked me to pin it to my lapel," I replied.

"But you're one of us!," a lady who introduced herself as Claudette, Head of Production, shouted.

"We'll make sure you're on the RD Employees List in future, John," Martin said, "then we can dispense with such silly formality."

As we arrived at the meeting room, we immediately made for the snacks table, tucking into warm croissants and very good coffee. It felt extremely convivial as we chatted amiably, everyone asking how I was settling in, before Andrew arrived with a cheery, "Morning chaps!" and we all sat down.

As I watched proceedings unfold, I could see that while there was a strong team atmosphere, an interesting but gently competitive edge developed as various upcoming releases were presented by the originator and then discussed by everyone there.

It was particularly heart-warming to see how ready people were to listen to any ideas I offered. This was a tight-knit team, but one eager to allow in differing views.

At the end of the meeting, as folders were closed and people got up to return to their offices, Andrew turned to me and said, "So, John! How are you finding working with SF?"

Several pairs of eyes stared at me expectantly. My unintended pause made him chuckle.

"Yes, John, join the club!" he said, smiling knowingly at his colleagues. "He's a total pain in the ass. But! – and we can all agree on this - he does know his RD product!"

I decided to jump in with the question I had been keen to have answered for weeks, "Why did SF not get on with Charles?"

A concerned murmur floated around the room, and I wondered if I'd overstepped the mark. People stopped packing away their things and stood waiting for Andrew's reply.

"Why does SF not get on with anyone?" Andrew replied. "He considers everyone but himself useless at their jobs. If he doesn't drive you crazy within a few weeks, John, you're a better person than any of us here!"

"At least I won't be based in Brussels with him!" I said, walking out into the corridor with everybody else.

"Yes! A definite plus!" Andrew said. "That was Charles' downfall really, he hated being in Brussels having to work so closely with SF every day. You will enjoy the job so much more being based in London, without a doubt!"

"I was so sad to hear what happened to Charles," I said. "He was such a different guy when I knew him during his Decca days. Really confident and sure of himself. That had gone completely when I last saw him."

There was again an uncomfortable silence, a couple of nods and then people began drifting off.

As if to lighten the atmosphere, Andrew said, "It's good to have you aboard, John!"

He shook my hand and, as he wandered off down the corridor,

the rest of the team waved goodbye, went into their offices and I walked to the lift.

Wandering into a sunny Berkeley Square, I mulled over how the malign, ghostly presence of SF seemed to hover over everything within this organisation.

* * *

In late January, I flew to Brussels, the day before SF and I were to leave for MIDEM. He was keen to know how I was going on with the various projects he'd given me, and actually appeared pleased that I'd managed to clear several of the tracks already.

Then, as the atmosphere became almost convivial, I told him I'd arranged several trips abroad through February, to meet the various global teams and to discuss their needs. To my surprise, instead of giving me his hearty approval at my initiative, SF went bright pink and thrust out his little beardy chin at me.

"Travelling is *my* job!" he told me angrily. "*You* are meant to stay at your desk and proceed with projects I have given you to complete! If you need to talk to RD colleagues you can quite easily do it on the phone or, much more efficiently – *and less expensively* - by email!"

Taken aback but not cowed, I countered, "José has told me *specifically* that he wants me to travel to all the different RD companies, have meetings with the repertoire teams and their local licensors, and to get to know them all personally. He was most emphatic about that."

SF harrumphed, clicked his head towards the pile of folders on his still laden-down desk, twitched his shoulders up and down and coughed.

"I want to know of every trip you plan to make *before* you go there," he said, putting on his glasses which hung on a string around his neck.

He extricated a folder, causing the pile to wobble dangerously, opened it and stared at it, pencil poised in the air.

"Now! Let's do some work, shall we?" he said, motioning me to re-open the work ledger he'd instructed me to buy. "You can make notes as I go through what has to be done."

Any more talk of me travelling to RD companies was clearly banished from discussion, for now at least.

The following morning, I sat next to SF at the front of the tiny Sabena Airlines plane. My knees were jammed against the metal partition in front of us while his tiny frame had plenty of room. I complained I was uncomfortable, but he just shrugged in that oddly camp manner he adopted when brushing people off.

"It's not a long flight," he said dismissively. "You'll be fine!"

As the seat belt signs were switched off and the stewardess began coming around with drinks and snacks, I ordered a coffee and a cheese sandwich. She then looked expectantly at SF.

"Just a glass of water please!" he said curtly, as if interrupted.

He began peering through his briefcase on the floor at his feet, obviously looking for something.

"That should really go in the locker above your seat, sir!" she told him.

"Presently!" he replied, and continued searching through his bag.

Finally he brought out several folders, placed them on his knee and handed the case to the girl.

"If you would be so kind?"

With a look which said, 'I'd rather jam it in your face, bastard!' she smiled through gritted teeth and pushed it into the locker.

Once she'd gone, he proceeded to get out various piles of paper from the folders, place them on the table in front of him and study his spindly handwritten notes.

"Right!" he said. "Let's discuss who we want to see while at MIDEM!"

He droned on for half an hour about the projects and plans he'd brought with him, only briefly interrupted when my order arrived. I munched away his tedious little voice and then eventually feigned sleep, aware of a displeased grunt and cough beside me, mentally telling him to fuck off.

I'd assumed we'd be staying at one of the hotels along La Croisette. Or maybe at La Mediterraneo, by the glamorous sparkling marina, where I'd stayed in 1974 with Stuart and Patsy on my first trip to Cannes, just after I'd signed with CBS Records.

However, as we sat in the back of the cab on the half-hour journey from Nice airport to Cannes, where SF continued to witter away about his planned meetings ahead, I noticed that, instead of making for the centre of town the taxi suddenly turned off and sped up a narrow side street. It parked outside a dull little B 'n' B which looked like a run-down mid-'60s hostel, complete with soiled net curtains hanging in a window which also needed a damned good wash.

With sinking heart, I followed SF through to a dated and drab reception area where he checked us in.

"I always stay here!" he said happily as we stood in the cramped smelly lift. "I once brought my wife-to-be here for a special trip!"

'And she still agreed to marry you?' I thought.

We reached the top floor and walked to our rooms along a dingily lit corridor past a sad array of Woolworth's style framed pictures. When we reached his room, he opened the door and said, "We will unpack and meet downstairs in ten minutes! You are next door!"

When I walked in, I stared aghast that places like this still existed. Pine-covered walls surrounded matching bench-style seats with faded orange and yellow cushions. I made a note to self not to sit on them.

Against one wall was an enormous Balsa wood display cabinet, which displayed nothing except old Formica peeling off the shelves; against another wall was a tiny scratched dining table and one dilapidated chair.

In the pokey bedroom, a pine pull-down bed-frame stood against the wall which revealed a mattress and sheets stuffed inside it. The flooring was a kind of off-pink rubber tiling affair, from which pervaded the smell of musty feet and BO.

There were three rusty metal hangers in the rickety wardrobe which blocked half a bird-shit smeared window, through which I could just see the damp green back of an old office building. It gave out onto a weed-covered concrete yard, clearly unwalked on for years.

"Welcome to Cannes!," I said to myself, cursing the little man next door, who was no doubt already poring over folders and lists, pencil poised, notes for moi being made ready for our next meeting.

After nearly doing my back in pulling the frame down, I lay on the unmade bed which smelt of greasy hair and something unplaceable but unpleasant, and wondered how long I could stand working for this madman. Ignoring the smells which pervaded the place, I dozed off and dreamt of sipping Bloody Marys at The Carlton.

I was woken from a deep snooze by the bedside phone. A clearly annoyed SF was on the other end.

"Where are you?" he demanded. "I've been waiting down here for fifteen minutes!"

"Sorry, I dropped off," I told him. "I'll be down after I've freshened up."

He began wittering away, asking me why that was necessary, so I put the phone down and pattered into the tiny pink bathroom, where I took an absolute age to get ready. Finally, spruced up and smelling lovely from the gel and cologne I'd thankfully brought with me, I got the lift and walked into the lobby where a red-faced SF simmered on a pine bench.

To my surprise, he didn't mention my tardiness, instead suggesting we walk towards the Palais de Festivals, "rather than get an overpriced cab!".

He seemed to cheer up as we walked into a drizzly, grey street.

"I have arranged our first meeting already!" he declared.

I pointed at the rain, which was getting harder, and suggested we get a cab after all.

"No need!" he replied, with a triumphant shake of the head. "I have an umbrella!"

He pulled a minute ladies brolly out of his coat pocket, pressed the button on the handle and it unfolded above him. He then linked his arm in mine and proceeded to hold the brolly above both of us as we careered along like two old gaberdine-macked winos. I had to tilt my head under it to stay partially dry, which killed my back.

After five minutes of this, I suggested that I hold it.

"I'm the taller man," I explained.

Happy to agree to something which made logical sense, he handed me the umbrella.

I soon established a routine which not only suited me but was likely to prevent me from physically attacking SF in the street. Ignoring his initial protests over a crack-of-dawn breakfast, I arranged to meet him thereafter at ten o'clock every morning at the Palais. En route, I'd treat myself to a Herbes Provencal omelette and warm crusty bread at a great little café off La Croisette where I'd often bump into music colleagues and spend an hour laughing and nattering with like-minded friends. Surrounded by the marvellous noise and chatter, it reassured me that the sane and stimulating world I'd worked in, 'pre-SF', was still in place and there whenever I needed it.

Each evening, after a day wandering around the Palais from stand to stand, sitting in on his pre-arranged meetings and being weighed down with ever more catalogues and folders, I'd leave him at six-thirty when he'd busy off to at least three more appointments. I'd get a cab back to the B 'n' B where I'd take a shower, rest for an hour, select my outfit for the evening and meet SF – still in the clothes he'd worn all day - in reception at eight o'clock.

At my insistence, proffering my bad back as a good enough reason for 'the expense', we'd take a cab into the old town to savour some of the delights of good French cuisine.

While he wasn't happy about these arrangements, I managed to curtail his complaining by constantly bumping into various music colleagues at the packed eateries. He would immediately hand them a business card, muttering his 'flat fee licensing' mantra at them.

Happily, his twittering was usually drowned out by the cacophony of enjoyable conversations around us and my friends would nod respectfully at him, leaving him content in the mistaken belief that he'd impressed them.

I even began to imagine that he was actually enjoying himself, until one evening I suggested this to him while waiting for our cab back to the hotel.

With an impatient shake of the head, he replied, "It is purely business, John! We are *not* on holiday!"

At the end of the week, we flew back to Brussels from where SF drove us to his house on the outskirts of the city. He had invited me to spend the night with him and his family before we went on to Paris, to meet the French music team the following day.

His home was a large white clapperboard house, very much in the rural American style, which SF told me proudly he had built with his brother ten years earlier. I was pleasantly surprised that he had such an outdoor active side to him and, as he showed me around the garden, mainly planted out with vegetables and salad stuff, he looked suddenly younger and more relaxed.

His tiny wife, Tina, greeted me through the French windows and led me into a spacious sitting-room. Two doll-like children walked shyly towards me and shook my hand like miniature gentlemen, before scurrying off giggling. SF took me up to my room, a loft space which he'd converted into a small but comfy guest room, and told me dinner would be in half an hour.

I was planning on taking the opportunity to have a wash and lie down until then, but, as if reading my mind, he said, "I will be waiting for you downstairs where, in five minutes, we can go through all the meetings we had at MIDEM, and discuss the business cards we picked up during the week!"

No rest for the wicked, I told myself grimly, as I unpacked and hung up my clothes.

Thankfully, after about twenty minutes of his nattering on about some Bolivian flute music he'd done a deal on 'before you had joined me at the Palais', Tina quietly interrupted her husband to say dinner was ready. She had very sweetly made a mushroom risotto for me and given her family a meat variation. It was delicious. At one point during the meal, their oddly silent children whispered something to each other before the elder boy asked me, in precise, considered English, how long I had been a vegetarian.

"Only a few months," I told him, and praised his English.

He blushed up, whispered something to his brother who stared at me and nodded, then they both went back to eating their dinner in silence.

I managed to have a pleasant chat with Tina; about the house, what she did for a living – a nurse – and answer her questions about what I was hoping to achieve while at RD.

"I want to try and bring the company into the modern world," I told her, glancing over at a stony-faced SF. "I plan to discuss this with the various RD product managers around Europe."

She glanced at her husband, who carried on eating without looking up, and smiled nervously back at me. If her thoughts could speak, I guess they would have said, "Dream on, honey!"

After dinner, Tina went out for an evening with her friends, while the children disappeared up to their rooms. SF asked me to join him on the sofa, having poured me a glass of Belgian beer. As he extolled the virtues of the world-famous breweries, one of them just down the road from his house, he brought out a pile of photograph albums from under his seat. I settled down for a couple of fun hours looking at his holiday snaps.

"Here," he proudly announced, opening the first one, "are photos of *every* music meeting I have attended in my twenty-five years with Reader's Digest!"

My heart sank as he went from shiny page to shiny page, pointing out people I didn't know from across the decades. My boredom quickly turned to silent horror as, brushing a finger contemptuously across various people in different group photos, he told me how he'd got rid of them.

"I fired *her*, she was no use... I made sure *he* was sacked, hopeless!... *he* was useless too! And I ensured that *he* definitely didn't stay with the company for long!"

He made a gesture of snuffing out a candle.

"Phut!" he said, smiling smugly at me.

And so it went on, photo album after miserable photo album, a kind of maniacal, psychotic collection of all the RD employees he had managed to extinguish through the years. Each time he pointed at some unfortunate who'd met his wrath, he'd chuckle triumphantly. I wondered when *I* would be in one of these albums, and imagined my replacement sitting here years hence as SF pointed at me, saying, "Now he was *utterly* hopeless!".

I was very relieved when a tinkling, "Bonjour!" chirruped from the opening back door as his wife returned. Thankfully, they were early-to-bed people and I was fast asleep by ten o'clock, but not before almost breaking my knees as I jammed them up against the door of the smallest loo I'd ever used.

With an early departure of seven o'clock, we set off in SF's car for Paris. He chattered away the whole journey about who was who in RD Music France, who was useless and who was mildly better, while I did my best to doze off.

Alarmingly, he'd occasionally put his glasses on, so that, he explained, "I can see if there are traffic lights ahead."

He was obviously blind as a bat, with only memory guiding him on the motorway and through city traffic. I have never been so glad to arrive anywhere when we finally reached our hotel for the night.

***

Over the coming months, I discovered just how in need of help and advice some of the European music teams were, especially when it came to dealing with licensors. During my visits (insisted on by José who thankfully batted away SF's angry protests) various music managers explained how they'd send a fax to a licensor, listing the tracks they needed for a collection, and then wait for a response. They rarely followed it up with a friendly lunch out or even a phone call. Indeed, many of them hadn't actually met or spoken to any of their licensors.

"Take them for lunch," I told them, "get to know them, become their friends. Successful licensing is about building good working relationships. If a licensor clears some really important tracks for you over the course of a year, be sure to send them a gift at Christmas, a case of wine, or a food hamper. It worked wonders when I was Head of Licensing at MCA!"

During my first visit to RD Prague to meet Natalia, who was the sole music manager there, I'd done my usual 'get to meet your licensors' chat and was met with a shake of the head.

"I believe that is unnecessary!" she declared.

"Really? Why?"

"We are Reader's Digest!," she'd replied, sounding disturbingly like a female version of SF. "Our name on the headed paper is enough!"

"Do you get a lot of clearances?" I asked her.

She looked uncomfortable and went a bit pink.

"Not that many, no. The usual few get cleared, but nothing new. Nothing really big ever gets approved."

"You've never asked them why?"

Her puzzlement clearly grew. "No! I just try to get replacements from smaller labels."

"*Cheaper* replacements?"

"Well, yes. That is our brief from Brussels. Those are our instructions from SF!"

* * *

"You're just what this company needs!" Barbara Geldstein, Head of Global Music and Books, told me delightedly after my presentation at a music seminar in Coral Gables, Miami.

"Isn't he?" José said, grinning at me like a proud brother.

"Now, John," Barbara said conspiratorially, "you *must* continue to travel and visit our music teams on a regular basis. That's why José, Thomas Shand and I wanted you. You have the personality we need to inject some humanity into this company. You're a breath of fresh air!"

I saw SF had cornered Manfred, one of the RD Germany guys, who I knew he despised at the far end of the room.

"As much as I can, Barbara," I replied, "though SF hates me doing it."

Her eyes widened and then narrowed as she glanced over at SF, who was lecturing the poor chap like an angry headmistress.

"Why ever would he?" she said, shaking her head.

"He told me *he's* the one who does the travelling, and that *I* am his desk-bound assistant."

She moved closer into me, grabbing my arm *and* my attention.

"Listen to me, John, you have my, and Jose's, *and* Thomas's blessing to do as much travelling as you feel is necessary. I have spoken to our European colleagues and every single one of them has asked me when you're going over to see them again. They all really enjoy your presentations, but more importantly, they truly appreciate your invaluable one-to-one advice."

"It's been a slow process," I told her, "but I think the message is getting through, at least to some of them."

"It definitely is!" José said, beaming at me then at Barbara.

He moved in closer.

"I realise you-know-who isn't happy," José said quietly, "but as much as possible, John, try to ignore his complaints and just carry on doing what you're doing!"

Barbara shot a stare at SF who, having finished hectoring Manfred, was standing alone as everyone else chatted in little convivial groups. Barbara seemed to inwardly tut.

"We certainly didn't bring you in to be his *lackey!*" she said.

"Exactly!" José cried, laughing and patting me on the back.

"Now please don't worry, John," Barbara said, "and if SF gives you any grief, just let me or José know. Things simply *have* to change here."

* * *

In early 1998, Reader's Digest decided to close down its Berkeley Square and St. Paul's offices and locate all of its UK-based staff in a brand new building in the recently opened Canary Wharf.

With its tall grey skyscrapers and matching arcaded avenues, it soon became known as Windy Gotham City. I found the place fascinating, its expensive ghetto atmosphere purveying gleaming squares of slate-grey abundance where fountains playfully leapt and fell around people too busy to notice.

While I missed the history and architectural splendour of St. Paul's, I enjoyed the spanking brand new arrogance of Canary Wharf. It represented the smart, new business world's public hard-on, its glut of tower blocks seeming to thrust up and penetrate the narrow skies above. I could understand why some people found the business world sexy. Everyone I passed looked sharp, purposeful and ready for their day, indeed looking forward to what their day ahead held. Wealth, youth and modernity was showing off its confidence, its brazen power to a world ready for seduction.

Each morning and evening, I'd join the mêlée of rushing commuters busying past the oversized clocks at the tube station. I enjoyed being carried along in this New York City-like throng. Sometimes, en route, I would hum Sondheim's song from 'Company' – *"And another hundred people just got off-a the train"* – knowing that many of the people who dashed by would not have been born when Stephen wrote it.

Chapter Sixteen

The Reckoning

In the Spring of '98, I was invited by Thomas Shand to stay at Reader's Digest's head office in Westchester, a few miles outside New York, and attend a music meeting with the Manhattan team.

"I don't know why *you* need to go there," SF had complained when I'd told him about the invite.

"I guess because they'd like me to go," I'd replied.

No invitation had been extended to him, which was clearly the real bugbear as far as he was concerned.

I was picked up at JFK by a smart guy in his fifties who carried my bag to a pristine white limousine, told me to help myself with any of the liquor from the mini bar opposite my seat and whisked me off to one of the wealthiest areas of North America.

After a forty-five minute drive, out of the city into the tree-lined suburbs of New York, finally past huge mansions on either side of the road surrounded by conifers and beautiful gardens, we approached an enormous set of iron gates. As he slowed down, Martin the driver told me that The Clintons had a house just down the road from there. We were met at the gate by a heavily muscled security guard with a rifle at his side.

Once I'd shown him my invite signed by Thomas Shand, Hunk-Of-The-Year waved us through towards what, Martin told me, had been the home of the Wallaces, the benevolent wealthy couple who had started RD in the 1920s, "to inform, educate and entertain the people of America."

It was a large plantation-style house, complete with a wide veranda where I imagined Mr Wallace sipping his whisky decades earlier, as he read the latest Reader's Digest magazine. As I waved farewell to

Martin, who had carried my bag to a bright red polished door and rung the bell, it opened and I was greeted by a tiny lean lady who introduced herself as Bertha.

I'd been told by José that she had worked as housekeeper for the Wallaces in the '50s. Though now in her early seventies, she was still as bright as a button and dressed pristinely in a pretty three-piece pink and grey outfit. As she shook my hand and welcomed me, I immediately fell in love with her.

She offered to carry my bag which I laughed away and followed her into the large hallway. As we wandered into the beautifully-kept space – gleaming black and white tiled floor, white walls and lemon drapes, vases of lilies on white and lemon porcelain jardinieres in each corner - she seamlessly took on the role of tour guide. She waved her hand towards the sweeping Bette Davis-style staircase, telling me that Mr and Mrs Wallace would appear each evening at the top of the stairs, descending them together.

"After greeting all their staff they'd stroll into the dining room for dinner," she said, her eyes misting up at the memory.

"How divine!" I said, imagining the scene.

"Oh it was, John. They were!" Bertha said, smiling at me.

I looked around, admiring the splendid décor and smiled back at her.

"Would you like me to show you to your room, John?" she asked me, leaning her head on one side and twinkling up at me. "Then, when you're all unpacked and freshened up, I'll give you a proper tour of the place before we serve dinner. Okay, John?"

As her bright intelligent eyes sparkled at me, I wanted to hug her.

My room was both the grandest and the cosiest I'd ever stayed in. A large teddy bear sat on the lavishly embroidered pillow, which matched the heavy silk gold and mauve brocade bedspread on the king-size bed. An array of thick, soft white towels were laid out, along with a white bathrobe complete with a monogrammed 'RD' on the breast pocket.

There was an assortment of Christopher Wray-style lamps dotted around the room, giving a soft glow to everything. The windows were dressed with thick hessian curtains, again in a gold and mauve design, and matching silk tie-backs.

On the mahogany dresser was a bowl of fruit inside of which was a little handwritten note from Barbara, saying, "So great to have you here, John! Enjoy!". I quickly unpacked, had a wash in the ensuite bathroom and a generous head-to-foot cologne spray and went downstairs where Bertha was waiting for me.

"Oh my!" she said, breathing in delightedly. "You smell *gorgeous!*"

"Van Cleef & Arpels," I told her.

"I love a man with taste!" she declared, linking my arm and leading me off on our tour.

Over the next half an hour, she took me down corridor after corridor, proudly stopping at each Mondrian, Cézanne, Matisse, Van Gogh and Picasso which hung on the walls, all lit by tiny, focused spotlights.

"Are these all original paintings?" I asked her, gobsmacked.

"Yes they are, John. Mr and Mrs Wallace were collectors of great art. They were connoisseurs, and their mission was to try and bring some of their love of art and culture to the middle and working classes of America. God bless them, I loved them so!"

As I stared at literally millions of dollars-worth of paintings, she told me how, on her first day, the Wallaces had given her a welcome present.

"It was a specially crocheted scarf made by Mrs Wallace herself!" She put her hand to her neck. "I still have it and wear it of a chilly winter night. My! It's a delight! *So* soft!"

She smiled at the thought as we wandered along yet another corridor lined with works of art.

"Do you know, John, on the birthday of everyone who worked here, Mr and Mrs Wallace would give them a personalised gift. It always pertained to whatever that employee loved. If they liked cats, they'd be given a water-colour – painted by Mr Wallace himself! - of a big smiling Cheshire cat! If they enjoyed swimming, then a water-colour of a blue ocean against a summer sky was their gift."

She grinned at me, her eyes full of memories.

"And, John, they knew *everyone* by their first names, and always had a Christmas banquet for us here at the house – in what is now the boardroom."

She stopped and did a 'Voila!' with her hand.

"And, here we are!"

Her timing had been honed to perfection over many years. She threw open the large, polished satinwood doors to reveal not only an enormous boardroom, where a vast solid-wood table stretched back forever, but also, on the far wall, one of Monet's *Water Lilies* shone out gloriously under its specially-positioned spotlight. Its hues of purple, blue, pink and green seemed to glisten. It was the perfect climax. I actually gasped.

Bertha chuckled. "Yep! It is kinda breathtaking, isn't it, John?"

Her kindly eyes studied me as I stared entranced.

"Okay, sir," she said quietly, after I'd stared long enough, "that's the end of your tour."

She led me back down the corridor stopping once we'd reached the hallway.

"In half an hour, we'll serve you dinner, which will be in the room just to the left here. You're a vegetarian, right?"

"I am, yes, is that a problem?"

"No! Not at all, John. So am I! Those poor creatures which the human race kill and eat," she clasped her bosom. "My! I could not swallow a single piece of them!"

She seemed to momentarily pray to the high ornate ceiling, then opened her eyes, beamed at me and said, "You, sir, are a gentleman, I can see that. It has been a pleasure to meet and talk to you!"

She stretched up and gave me a peck on the cheek, her rose-scented perfume filling my nostrils like a warm Spring morning.

* * *

Back in London, two new projects were making my mouth water with anticipation; a brand new Dusty Springfield album, recorded specially for Reader's Digest, and a spoken word album featuring the three surviving Crickets talking about working with Buddy Holly.

The latter project came about when I was compiling a 3CD collection called *The Unforgettable Buddy Holly & The Crickets*. I thought that, to give it a unique marketing boost, I would try to arrange for Joe B Mauldin, Jerry Allison and Sonny Curtis to get together in a studio in the U.S. and chat about their memories of working with the great man.

My point of contact was, of course, Stuart Colman, who had produced two albums for me featuring the group when I was at Carlton.

Stuart was, as always, extremely helpful and organised a studio (free of charge) for the three legendary musicians to record in. It worked a treat, the guys chatting amongst themselves about recording and touring with Buddy. It had the relaxed easy atmosphere of three old friends sitting by the hearth reminiscing about 'the old days', their memories still crystal clear forty years later.

Sometimes Jerry would start to tell a story and Sonny or Joe would chuckle and take over, giving their own personal recollection of a gig or a recording session. I loved it. Jerry, bless him, even gave me a namecheck at the start of the recording.

Reminiscing With The Crickets was released as a standalone bonus CD given away with every purchase of the 3CD collection, which sold bucketloads. The album is still one of my most treasured possessions.

The Dusty Springfield project came about after I'd seen a TV commercial featuring Dusty singing a short snippet of 'Someone To Watch Over Me'. It was a brand new recording made specially for the ad and got my creative juices flowing. I rang an old friend of mine, Mike Gill, who had known Dusty since the '60s when he'd been her PA. He was still in touch with her, still referred to her as 'Madam', and loved the idea of her recording a new album of similar standards as part of a 3CD Dusty Springfield collection I was planning.

My concept was that CD1 would be her greatest hits, CD2 would be her most popular love songs (both CDs licensed in from Universal Music, who owned them), and CD3 would be the brand new recording.

Over lunch Mike told me not only did he think it was a wonderful idea, but he'd already spoken to Dusty and she loved it too.

"She'll record it in her own studio at the bottom of her garden," he told me, "which is where she made the TV commercial track. It's a large shed really but she gets superb results in there."

We agreed the deal – that the recordings would be paid for by RD but owned by Dusty. We would have the rights to feature the recordings royalty-free on the album within the 3CD set, as well picking tracks from it for future multi-artist collections, also royalty-free; she would have the right to license the album to whatever label she chose after six months of RD's release date.

I sent Mike a list of the twelve songs I'd love her to consider recording, agreeing that she would have final say, being free to include songs she herself wanted to record. The only stipulation from my side was that the songs would be recognised 'standards', like 'Someone To Watch Over Me', and that she would record that song in full for the album.

Mike popped into my office a few days later to pick up the contract. He also brought me a very special gift – a signed photo of Dusty, on which she had written 'To John, With Love'.

A few weeks later, Mike rang me. I was expecting good news but that was soon dashed by what he had to tell me.

"Unfortunately," he said, "a recent spate of tests showed that Dusty's cancer has returned and the prognosis this time is not good, John. She won't be doing any recording for the time being, she's simply not well enough, but I will keep you posted. She was so looking forward to it as well."

Over the coming months her health continued to decline and in March '99, six weeks before her sixtieth birthday, Dusty passed away.

At around the same time came more shock news. Thomas Shand had been, without warning or even hushed rumour, removed from his job. He had been replaced, José told me over the phone, by a "much more traditional, old-school guy."

"Something's happening here, John," he continued, "and it's not good. I'm not at all sure just how secure *I* am anymore!"

"Surely not, José," I replied, "you're doing such great things."

"Not according to the weather forecast around these offices I ain't! There are rumblings, my friend… Oh my, there are storms ahead!"

Sadly, his fears were well-founded. Just two weeks later, I got a call from Diane, who worked in the New York office, in tears because José had just been sacked by the new chairman of the company.

"There are rumours that Barbara's on the way out too!" she told me. "Oh John, none of us are safe!"

I emailed SF to let him know, but his reply implied he had known for some time about José's departure.

"It's sad," he replied, "of course, but RD had really gone too far down the modernising road. We were forgetting our core business. I have been saying this for months!"

His words hinted that at least he was safe. I shook my head at the idiocy of it all.

Barbara was indeed replaced a week later by a chap called Peter Chalport, who I soon found ensconced with SF in an office down the corridor from mine early one morning.

"Oh!" SF said, looking guiltily up from a pile of documents he and Peter were studying. "You have arrived much earlier than I expected!"

"And *you* are in London," I replied curtly, "which I certainly hadn't expected!"

He twitched his shoulders and coughed.

"Peter and I decided to meet here today as it was most convenient for us both."

He glanced sideways at Peter, who stood to introduce himself.

"Very nice to meet you, John," he said, in clear British tones.

"I assumed you were American!" I said, smiling at this librarian-looking chap, clearly at home in SF's company.

"I'm from Hampshire, but I now live in New Hampshire!"

I guessed he'd used that line several times.

"Well, good morning, gentlemen!" I said brightly, going to the door. "Very nice to meet you, Peter!"

I left them to their manoeuvrings.

Within a couple of weeks, José was replaced by Hester, who had previously headed the International Books division. A brisk, skinny lady with huge glasses which always looked on the verge of falling off her nose, she came breezing through my door one morning.

"Good morning, John!" she cried. "I am Hester!"

I stood and shook her hand.

"I am looking forward to working with you, John!" she said in a voice rather too loud for a small office.

"Nice to meet you too, Hester," I replied.

"So! What are your plans for acquiring further repertoire for Reader's Digest?"

"Well, my main plan is to continue to push RD into the 21st century," I told her. "Our traditional methods and attitudes must change."

She stood back a little and stared at me through her enormous lenses, her neck pinking up. Enjoying her surprise, I ploughed on, "It has to be about building good working relationships with our licensors if business is to grow."

She now looked like I'd slapped her face.

"We need to be friends with our licensors," I continued, "not combatants."

I'd purposely lobbed that last point at her just to watch her response. As I suspected, it went down like a lead balloon. She gave out a weird little hiss.

"Have you cleared this with SF?" she asked.

"He knows my feelings certainly," I replied. "It was what José and Barbara brought me in to do."

"But they are no longer with the company," she said, "my mission in to bring Reader's Digest back to its core audience."

I had no doubt that bringing Hester in was what SF and Chalport had been discussing the morning I'd arrived early. I imagined SF rubbing his hands at his folder-piled desk in Brussels, having successfully pulled RD Music back to the pre-José and Barbara time.

As Hester whisked out, aflutter with discontent, I realised that I was now The Last New Man Standing. The 'Exciting Global Dawn', previously imagined and planned for by Thomas Shand, had now been obliterated by the old grey clouds of traditionalism and Brussels-inspired malevolence.

* * *

In late April, my annual appraisal was, as usual, emailed to me by SF, and it took me aback. The previous appraisals had been, to my slight surprise, glowing, though I'd always suspected that was due to José checking and editing them before signing them off, making sure all

SF's negative comments were deleted. This time, I no longer had the windbreak of José to protect me from the gales of resentment blowing in from Brussels.

I read the appraisal with horror, mounting to disbelief and finally peaking at fury. SF criticised me for virtually all aspects of the job I'd done in the previous twelve months. He'd written, clearly delighted at the vitriol pouring from his poised pen,

"I'm afraid you are much too concerned about human relationships, rather than getting on with the day-to-day grind of clearing box sets. It may be boring, perhaps to your mind even beneath you, but it must be done and is why *I* employed you!"

It continued, "You are too wrapped up in promoting yourself rather than RD; more concerned that everyone likes you instead of getting the best deals for our company."

And the dig he could at last get in without censure, "You spend too much time travelling around the world rather than getting on with your job in London."

Finally - and the most insulting, if not downright ironic, "You are rather chaotic, I'm afraid. You need to be more disciplined in your approach to how you organise your work."

I read and re-read it, and each time I did my blood boiled more, thumping in my head as SF's insults and criticism jumped off the page like poisonous spiders.

Luckily, and clearly unbeknownst to SF, I had in fact been extremely organised over the last three years. Knowing what a malevolent and unpredictable creature he was, I had reams of emails from SF which I'd printed out and filed. All of them - copied to José - praised my work ethic and my efficiency. One of them credited me with clearing a particular collection 'extremely speedily!'. Another said that I was 'not only liked but highly respected by the global team'. Yet another stated that I was 'a hard-working member of staff, an excellent assistant!'.

While clearly written to enhance his standing in his then-boss's eyes, they all went to prove that this new appraisal was simply a hatchet job. It had been written by a bitter man no longer suffering the reins of America pulling him back from spewing vengeance and malice. SF was obviously now intent on finishing the job he'd started, getting rid of me his final coup.

Instead of replying to SF, or going down the corridor to speak to Hester, I decided to go over both their heads and sent an email direct to Peter Chalport, attaching the appraisal and asking to speak to him personally about what I saw as an unfair assessment. He replied rather quicker than I'd expected, telling me he was in London the following day and would come to see me.

Peter had a kind of friendly bank manager manner, rather dry and yet not entirely without humour or humanity. He appeared to be very concerned by what he'd read, and over coffee we went through the appraisal together. When we'd done that, I showed him the previous year's glowing appraisal.

"How could I go from this – to *this*, in such a short time, Peter?" I asked him, and he nodded as he read. "It doesn't add up, or at least it shouldn't."

He took a deep sigh, sat back and tipped his head on one side.

"How do you get on with SF personally?" he asked me.

This was a tricky (trick?) question and I was careful about what I said, trying not to get personal and bad-mouth my boss.

"He and I seem to get on very well," I ventured mildly, with a small measure of puzzlement in my voice. "To be perfectly honest with you, Peter, I had been told before I took the job that he can be difficult. But we have always, as far as I can tell, had a good working relationship. That's why this assessment is such a shock."

Peter nodded sagely and leaned forward a little.

"And how do record company people find him?"

He studied me, eyes narrowing in concentration as I answered this.

"Honestly?"

"Honestly."

"We-e-ell… everybody I deal with, both at major and smaller labels, have told me they find him obstructive, condescending, arrogant and presumptuous."

"Presumptuous?"

"He is still behaving in the old RD way – 'We are Reader's Digest. We should get the best deals, the lowest royalties, and not be asked for advances.'"

I couldn't tell if this was concerning Peter for the right reasons. But, I'd started, and he did ask, so I continued to quote SF's doctrine.

"His age-old mantra that 'We must always be treated as a priority' really angers our licensors. José specifically told me that I was brought in to make a change, to offer repertoire owners a more personable approach, to bring some humanity and yes, *humility* into things. To spearhead a more congenial and collegiate way of working with the record companies. The old RD arrogance simply does not work anymore."

Peter looked at the appraisal then up at me. His expression was suitably hard to read.

"Don't forget," I continued, "I was once a licensor at a major label!"

His eyes darted at me, a flicker of a smile crossing his lips.

"I was Head of Special Projects at MCA before I came here, and, I'm sorry to tell you this, but RD were a laughing stock there. Their requests were at the bottom of the pile."

Peter looked mildly affronted.

"Because, Peter," I told him, "we were earning *so* much more from *every* other licensee we dealt with."

Was I going too far? Too late now.

"RD wouldn't budge on deals," I continued. "They wouldn't raise the royalties they paid us, and always expected us to clear the best repertoire. It simply wasn't possible to do that when we sent in their requests to the Head Office in L.A. They were thrown back at us. Only the usual one or two tracks were cleared, that is the older and less interesting repertoire."

Peter sucked his teeth and studied me. I ploughed on.

"It was José who wanted me here, in London, as opposed to what SF wanted – that I work as his assistant in Brussels. Truthfully, I don't think SF ever really got over that, he saw it as an affront to his authority. But, after having Charles working for him in Belgium, and seeing how *that* worked out," ('Too far?' I thought), "Jose was insistent I was based here!"

I decided to shut up and let all this sink in. After a short pause, he said, "So, John! What do you propose we do?"

('Hurrah!').

"Well! First of all, Peter, I would like a new appraisal, to be reassessed on the positive work I've done in the last twelve months. Just talking to my RD colleagues will give you the proof of that."

That seemed to go okay. I pressed on.

"It's *very* important that I continue travelling to our RD companies in Europe – they have all told me how useful my visits are. It's much against SF's wishes, but, again, he was overruled - by Barbara - on that. For whatever reason, SF seems to resent me, and I truly haven't done anything to warrant that. In fact, I've always tried to be helpful and patient with him – and that's not always easy!"

Peter nodded.

"And?"

The door was open, I got radical. "I think we should split what I do from his authority. I shouldn't report to him. I know I can make this an even more dynamic area, but not with him constantly pulling me back and trying to rein me in. This appraisal is, I believe, another effort by

252

SF to do that. Slap hands, be a good boy and do as I say or else."

Peter couldn't hold back a grin. He said, "I *am* told by our US colleagues that you have a very winning way with our licensors, whereas SF… "

"Is disliked by them *all*, I'm afraid!" (Deep breath). "The Head of Polygram Licensing asked me to never bring SF to a meeting again. The Head of Licensing at BMG told me he used a photo of SF as a dartboard."

At that, Peter threw his face in his hands and moaned. When he looked up, his face had gone an odd shade of pink. I feared for his blood pressure.

"Okay!" he said finally, holding both hands up. "Leave it with me, John. I obviously have to discuss this with both SF and Hester as well as the U.S. music team. I may also chat to some of our other international colleagues. Thank you for your honesty. If you can be patient, I will have an answer for you presently."

When he'd left, I wondered if I'd gone too far. But he did ask!

In June, I was invited by the new RDUS team head, Rick Stenhope, to join him and his team in Miami for a music seminar of record labels and repertoire owners, NARM as it was known. A kind of American MIDEM.

I hadn't yet responded to SF about his appraisal - and was, disappointingly, still waiting to hear from Peter. I did send an email to SF to tell him I'd be flying out to Miami the following week to join Rick and the rest of the U.S. team. His reply was inevitably curt, asking me why I needed to go. I replied, as I usually did when he questioned my trips, "because Rick invited me, and clearly thinks I'll be a useful guy to have with his team at meetings."

I found Rick very personable and easy to get on with. A Canadian guy, he had come out of marketing, not particularly a music man as José had been, but I noted that, although his team still clearly missed their previous boss, they were happy it had been Rick who had replaced him.

I arranged several meetings at the music fair with various potential licensors, taking away their catalogues to study in depth. I also ran into my old MCA colleague, Bruce Reznikoff who greeted me with a bear hug. Over coffee, we had a long chat about my job at RD and updates on Bruce's team in L.A. It made me feel nostalgic for my days working for one of the majors, with none of the hassles SF had created.

On our final evening, Rick, his team and I were having dinner when one of the girls, Olga, turned to me and said, "So, how are you finding working for SF?"

"Difficult," I replied, and told her about my recent appraisal.

"How long have you worked for SF?" she asked me.

"Three years."

"Yep!" she replied. "That's SF's time limit with his assistants! He's never got beyond three years with anyone who's worked for him, apart from his long-suffering secretary."

Rick leaned in and said, "My advice, John, is to watch your back!"

The months passed uneventfully. I decided to keep my head down for a while, just getting on with obtaining clearances for new music collections and keeping travel to a minimum. Towards the end of the year, I finally received a new appraisal from SF, signed off by Peter. A lot of the original negative comments had been taken out, leaving a decidedly bland assessment of my worth. It was clear SF had had his hands slapped but was still unable to praise me any longer. I considered emailing Peter to thank him, but decided that would appear too smarmy and just let it ride.

Then, in late February, I got an email from Lisa, who ran the music division in South Africa. She'd blind-copied me on a round-robin report she'd written and sent to her bosses and global upper management. It detailed what she saw as the best way of improving business in her territory. My heart took a little leap - with admittedly wry amusement - when I read it.

"The most important thing," the email said, "is that it *must* be John Howard who comes here to meet record company people and licensors. On *no* account let SF anywhere near them! John is our people person – and this is a People Business. While SF is a great worker, with many years of loyal service at RD, he's a desk guy, not someone who endears himself or, more importantly, endears RD to the people we will always need on our side – our licensors!"

I glanced at the list of recipients: Rick and his team in the US office, Peter Chalport, Hester, Lisa's own bosses in SA...and right at the bottom of the list - *Oh No!* – SF! Instead of emailing her back, I picked up the phone and rang her.

"Hiyaah!" she said. "Did you like my email?"

"Well, yes, I did, darling," I replied. "I was extremely flattered, in fact, and thank you for your thoughts. *But*, are you aware that you included SF in the recipients list?!"

There was a gasp, followed by silence, then another gasp, followed by a lot of busy tapping on a keyboard – followed by a horrified yowl.

"Oh no!!" she screamed. "I've sent it to SF!!"

"Indeed you have, Lisa. He's probably reading it right now!"

"Oh *shit*!!"

"Yep! It's just hit the fan!"

A few days later, my office door opened and in walked Hester followed by SF. He stared at everything but me as they both sat down.

"We wish to tell you," SF began, still not looking at me, "that we would like you to leave Reader's Digest."

His eyes were riveted to the laptop in front of me.

"The fact of the matter is... " he wittered on, "what we would like... that is, what Hester and I... "

Finally, Hester jumped in, hissing impatiently.

"We have put together a very generous severance package for you," she told me, pushing a piece of paper across the desk like a secret agent in a café rendezvous.

I looked at it, they were offering me £35,000 to clear my desk.

SF began twittering away like a nervous bird.

"It simply isn't working any longer. You seem to be more interested in polishing your own star than doing the work I give you! You are simply *not* up to the job!"

"Lisa in South Africa *clearly* doesn't agree with you," I said, smiling broadly at them both, knowing neither of them were aware that I had seen Lisa's email.

SF coughed and froze in his seat as though goosed. Hester stood up and, leaning both hands on my desk, said, "When you have had a chance to consider our offer, please let HR know?"

She turned to go but stopped in the doorway.

"And, *most importantly*, any offer we make to you is conditional on you *not* speaking to anyone else here about this. Is that understood?"

"Perfectly," I replied.

SF jumped up and, tripping over the legs of his chair, escaped through the door as fast as his little legs could carry him. Hester marched past him and swept off down the corridor, SF scurrying after her like a tiny dog afraid of being left behind.

I sat alone in the silence for a few moments then picked up the phone and called Neil.

"Are you alright?" he asked me.

"I feel oddly liberated!" I replied. "The boil has finally been lanced!"

The following day, I sat in our solicitor's office in Oxford, showing her the pile of emails from SF which had praised my work since 1996, plus all my glowing appraisals. I then gave her the most recent damning one, along with the amended version following my chat with Peter Chalport. The final thing I gave her was Lisa's email.

"The last nail in my coffin, unfortunately," I said, as she read it. "Though it was never meant to be."

Smiling to herself, she looked up at me and said, "Well, John! We have them by the short and curlies!"

Chapter Seventeen

Preservation

I knew my Constructive Dismissal case would take a little time to progress. As with all these things, it meant letters being sent from Sheila, my solicitor, to RD's legal department, their reply being posted back, which was then read and discussed by me and Sheila, followed by our reply being posted back, and on it went over the coming weeks.

After Hester's warning as she'd left my office that I could tell no-one at RD about it, I kept the situation entirely from colleagues. It was difficult to do, but my solicitor had also advised me not to say a word to anyone, for the time being at least.

I'd arrive at RD each day, bid a cheery 'Good morning' to people I met in the corridor, get myself a coffee and chat casually to work colleagues who were also desperate for a caffeine injection.

I'd walk into my office, close my door and do whatever work I still could. I'd mainly fill my day replying to the myriad emails and product queries coming in from RD's international music managers. Giving them advice on royalty rates being demanded by their local licensors, suggesting track replacements for those which had been turned down, and basically acting as if nothing had changed at least kept my mind off what was going on elsewhere.

Sheila kept me abreast of discussions between her and RD's legal department, and, by the third week of May, they'd upped their offer to £38,000.

"Not nearly enough!" Sheila said on the phone one morning.

"It seems quite a lot of money to me," I replied. "Do you really think we could get more?"

"Yes, I do, John!" she replied.

258

I was happy to let her get on with it.

A couple of days later, I got a call from Brauna, a lady I knew from the Miami office. She was a wonderfully Bohemian lady who hated and distrusted SF. My kinda girl.

"John," she began. "I know I'm not supposed to know, and you certainly didn't tell me... but... I am fully aware that SF has made his move to get rid of you."

'My! What a village RD is!' I thought.

"I couldn't possibly comment," I said.

"Of course, not, darling one. But, even so, I thought some information I have, *first-hand* information, which came to me during last night's Product Managers' dinner here - which was attended by SF - would be of interest to you?"

"Do tell!" I replied, pen at the ready.

"Well!" she began with a wry laugh. "As unbelievable as everyone there found it, SF spent the entire meal bitching about you to anyone who was prepared to listen – i.e. *everybody!*"

"Really?"

"Oh yes! And I discovered afterwards that he's been wittering on about you not being 'up to the job' for weeks."

"Indeed?"

"And... get this! Last night, after dinner when we were relaxing with coffees, he actually told me – and several others sitting with us - that the main reason he wanted to get rid of you was because *you earned more money than him!*"

She shrieked with laughter, as did I. This was Manna from Heaven! I mentally hugged Brauna, thanked her profusely and bade a fond farewell. I then called Sheila. When I gave her Brauna's news, she actually whooped with joy.

"Fantastic!" she yelled. "What an *absolutely* crass idiot your boss is!"

"You have no idea!" I replied.

"It beggars belief, the stupidity of the man! Leave it with me, John. I do believe there will be something of a major progression to report. Very soon!"

The following morning, Sheila rang.

"Utterly wonderful news, John!" she said, barely able to contain her excitement. "I reported SF's latest gaffe to the RD legal guy last night, which got the most *delicious* gulp! Within half-an-hour, he called me back. He told me that they can no longer deal with the matter in-house, literally wiping their hands of it, and are handing it over to a top firm of independent music business lawyers, to sort it out once and for all."

I could tell there was more.

"Those lawyers have just emailed me and informed me that, as RD is *completely in the wrong*, the company is prepared to offer you the top amount for a Constructive Dismissal." She paused dramatically, relishing the next moment. "Now! If this had occurred a year ago, that amount would be £12,000... "

I began to stammer a shocked reply.

"*But!*" she stopped me. "Prepare to scream! That amount was raised a few months ago to - £50,000!"

I duly screamed.

"They're offering me *fifty grand*?"

"Yep!"

"Bloody hell!"

"Indeed, my boy! Now! You may decide that we could possibly get even more out of them, especially now they're running scared. And you may be right about that. We could turn the amount down and continue to fight for more. Personally, I think you deserve five times that amount! *However*, there is always the possibility that, after the seven years it could take to get a verdict, with a lot of potential unpleasantness and stress for you during that time, we could – possibly, *just possibly* – lose! Which would mean that you would go away with nothing."

I felt myself breathing hard.

"On the other hand… " she went on, but I didn't need to hear any more.

"Accept the offer!" I said. "I want to get away from this appalling place as soon as I can and wash my hands of them."

"*And* fifty thousand pounds better off!" I heard Sheila quickly tapping her keyboard. "Okay! I've just emailed their lawyers now to inform them that we accept their offer! Well done, John! You won!"

I was on the verge of tears.

"Just one more thing," Sheila said, bringing me back down to Earth. "One of the stipulations in the Constructive Dismissal Agreement, which they emailed over with their offer, is that you can *never* enter the RD building again. Once you have physically left the company, that's it."

"No problem at all!" I said, laughing my head off. "I have no intention of ever darkening their doors again!"

"I don't blame you! So! Go into your office tomorrow at, say, nine o'clock, clear your desk, and then make your way here to sign the agreement. I'll give you your cheque, and you can then consider yourself free of Reader's Digest - and that *dreadful* little man - *forever!*"

The next morning, bidding good morning as usual to people, I walked down the corridor to my office for the final time. It felt exceedingly strange, knowing this would be the last time I would see them, and that none of them knew it. I'd kept my side of the bargain, which Hester had insisted on, and had not breathed a word of my imminent departure to anyone. If SF's blabbing had spread to anyone in the UK building, nobody had said a word to me.

Even my secretary, Samantha, had been kept in the dark. The fact she was on maternity leave, and wouldn't be due back for another two months, meant I could call her when I got home that evening to give her the news, allowing her some time to decide on her own next move. She was fantastic at her job and I had no doubt that she would be asked to join another department very quickly, if she wanted to stay, that is.

I closed my door and busied about, packing up my music research books, which I'd carried from job to job for over a decade, and then sat down to write a final email to my global colleagues. In it, I told everyone how sad I was to report that I was leaving RD, that I'd loved working with them all, that the decision was not mine, and that I wished them all well in their future business dealings.

I then took all my ongoing project folders off the shelves and placed them in a pile on my desk. I looked around to make sure I hadn't forgotten anything and was just about to press 'send' on my laptop when the phone rang. To my astonishment, it was SF.

"Hello, John," he began, "First of all, I want to only wish you the best in your future life."

"Thank you," I replied curtly.

"You are, I believe, taking a vacation soon?"

"Tomorrow."

"For how long?"

"Two weeks."

"Right. Well, when you return from your holiday, I wish you to come into your office for a final meeting with me. I will fly over and be there at nine o'clock prompt. We can then go through all the projects you've been working on, and I can bid you a personal goodbye."

I almost laughed, but bit my tongue.

"Er - I'm afraid that won't be possible."

There was a pause at the other end.

"But why?"

"Because I am leaving the company today."

"Yes, I know you are! Of course I know that! But I need to go through everything with you, to know where you are up to with each project!"

This time I did allow a mild chuckle.

"Er – have you read the Constructive Dismissal Agreement?"

"No, I haven't."

"Oh! So you have no idea what the terms of the agreement are which your company has signed?"

"No."

"They haven't shown it you?"

"No. They haven't."

"Well, doesn't *that* speak reams?"

He coughed and stammered down the phone, "B-b-b-but I'm afraid I must insist! You *must* come back in – I must go through everything with you!"

I allowed a few moments pause, sighed heavily, and, as though to a small, confused child, said, "I suggest that you get a copy of the agreement - soon - and read it - carefully. When you do, you'll see there is a clause in there where RD stipulates that, after I have left the building today, I must never, *ever*, re-enter it!"

He was wonderfully, utterly speechless. I heard a mild wail and then he began again.

"But!..."

"No buts! It's there in the agreement, in plain English. As I say, I suggest you get hold of a copy, read it, and sharpish! Goodbye!"

He was still spluttering as I replaced the receiver.

I took a deep breath, pressed 'send' on my laptop and walked out of my office. As I was closing the door, my phone began to ring. It stopped as I turned to leave and then rang again. Walking down the corridor without looking back, I heard it stop and then begin ringing again. It was still ringing when I turned the corner towards the lift.

When I reached the ground floor and walked into reception I was met by Jane, the receptionist. In floods of tears, she rushed towards me.

"Oh *John*! I've just read your email! I can't believe it! *Why* are you leaving?"

"Thank you, darling," I said through her hugs and sobs. "It's best I say nothing."

I looked into her reddened eyes, "As I said in my email, Jane, it was *not* my decision to leave."

I blew her a kiss then walked out into the warm June air. Thrilled to be rid of SF and his machinations, my shoulders felt pounds lighter. I had to stop myself skipping down the street. I couldn't, however, prevent a flood of tears pouring down my cheeks. Relief, regret, joy and sorrow all flooded into me.

And so, one of the most confusing periods of my time in the music industry was over. I never worked full-time for a music company again.

* * *

On a lovely April afternoon in 2001, I wandered out onto the balcony of Ty'r Onnen, the Pembrokeshire house Neil and I had recently moved into. Drinking in the view of our half-acre of lawns, hedgerows full of ripening wild berries and abundant apple and cherry trees, I watched seagulls hovering over a small fishing boat which putted on down the Cleddau Estuary. The blue Preseli Hills in the distance seemed to merge into the cloudless sky.

"My," I thought, "Pembrokeshire is certainly as beautiful as we'd imagined!"

Sighing at the silence and breathing in the smell of freshly-cut grass, my reverie was interrupted when the phone rang. I went into our study and answered it.

"Hi!" a voice I recalled but couldn't quite place pealed happily at the other end.

"Hi," I replied, trying to sound just as pleased to hear from her as I racked my brains at who she was.

"It's Juliette!" she laughed. "From RD!"

Juliette worked in Reader's Digest's International Books Department, which was situated just down the corridor from my old office. She had been a welcome point of sanity during my time there. We'd often enjoyed a conspiratorial natter over coffee of a morning, me envying her having a really great boss, she sympathising with me about mine.

"I simply *had* to ring you, John!" she bubbled. "For the first time since you left, SF has *finally* arrived and just walked, like a man going to the gallows, into your office!"

She giggled deliciously.

"I decided that I *suddenly* needed a coffee and, as I passed by, I couldn't help a quick glance, as you do! He was sitting there staring at the pile of folders on your desk. I *almost* felt sorry for him. Almost."

I told Juliette she'd made my day and thanked her for letting me know.

"Have a great day!" she said as we signed off. "I'm sure you're going to have lots of great days!"

Ty'r Onnen, Pembrokeshire

As I put the phone down, Neil walked in and handed me a G

& T. We stepped outside to enjoy our drinks in the sunshine and I recounted Juliette's tale of SF's woe.

"Serves him right," Neil said. "The perfect closure."

We clinked glasses and laughed.

"Here's to us," he said, "and here's to the future!"

I had no idea then that, within just a couple of years, the New Millennium would bring me the kinds of artistic rewards I would not have believed possible thirty years earlier. But that's another story...

THE END

Author's Note

In The Eyeline of Furtherance is the third book in the trilogy
of my autobiographies published by Fisher King Publishing,
Incidents Crowded With Life and Illusions of Happiness
being the first two volumes. It's likely that this will be the
'final instalment' as what happened shortly after In The
Eyeline of Furtherance ends in 2001 has been very well
documented in the media, on my website and social media.

Which is that in 2003 my debut album, 'Kid In A Big
World', was reissued to rather wonderfully rave reviews,
and that springboarded me into a wholly unexpected second
career of recording and performing my music again.

So, with that in mind, I thought it was fitting that I include
herewith a list of all my record releases from 1975 – 2022.
It still amazes me to think that, when In The Eyeline's story
ended in 2001, I thought my sum total of record releases
would be 'Kid In A Big World' in 1975 and a handful of
singles through the '70s and early '80s. Never say never, eh?

John Howard Discography: 1975 – 2022

1974
Goodbye Suzie/Third Man – single, October

1975
Family Man/Missing Key - single, February
Kid In A Big World - LP, February

1976
I Got My Lady/You're Mine Tonight – single, January

1978
I Can Breathe Again/You Take My Breath Away – single,
February

1979
Don't Shine Your Light/Baby Go Now – single, October

1980
I Tune Into You/Gotta New Toy – single, March
Lonely I, Lonely Me/Gotta New Toy (Remix) – single, August

1981
It's You I Want/Searching For Someone ++ – single, March
Call On You/And The World ++ – single, July

1984
Nothing More To Say/You Keep Me Steady – single, March

1993
On Reflection: A Collection of Love Songs

- Rare Compilation Album CD, February

2003
Kid In A Big World – Reissue Album CD, November

2004
Technicolour Biography * – Album CD, August

2005
Can You Hear Me OK? ** – Album CD, May
The Dangerous Hours – Album CD, July
As I Was Saying – Album CD, November

2006
Same Bed, Different Dreams – Album CD, June

2007
Walk On The Wild Side *** – online EP, March
The Bewlay Brothers – online EP, April
My Beautiful Days – online EP, May
In The Room Upstairs – Live Album CD, June
Barefoot With Angels – Album CD, November

2008
Sketching The Landscape (Demos '73 – '79) – Compilation
Online Album, February
Creating Impressions (Singles & Rarities) – Compilation
Online Album, March
The Pros & Cons of Passion *** – Album, April
More From The Room Upstairs – Live Album, CD, June
Songs For The Lost & Found – Online EP, October

2009
Navigate Home – Album CD, April
These Fifty Years: The Best of John Howard – Compilation
Online Album, April
The Dilemma of The Homosapien/These Fifty Years – Online
single, June
Songs For A Lifetime – Online EP, November

2010
Making Tracks (Curios & Collectables) – Compilation
Online Album, April
Can You Hear Me OK? (Special Edition) ** – Online Album,
July
As I Was Saying (Special Edition) +++ – Online Album,
October

2011
Exhibiting Tendencies - Album CD, February
Dry Run – The 'Navigate Home' Demos –
Online Album, June

2012
The Ballad of Sam Mary Ann/Beautiful Poppies At Even –
Online single, May
The Deal (Revisited) – Online single August
You Shall Go To The Ball!! – Album CD, September
Atmospheres & Soundscapes – Online Album, November

2013
Loved Songs – Online EP, March
Front Room Fables – Online EP, May
I Tune Into You/Lonely I, Lonely Me – Online single, July
Storeys – Album CD, November

2014
Live At The Servant Jazz Quarters – Live Album, CD, March
Songs For Someone – Online EP, June
Hello, My Name Is – Album CD, November

2015
Intact & Smiling **** – Online single, June
John Howard & The Night Mail – Album, CD/LP, August

2016
Songs For Randall – Online EP, March
Not Forgotten: The Best of John Howard Volume 2 –
Compilation Online Album, April
Across The Door Sill – Album CD/LP, October

2017
From The Morning – Online single, December

2018
Songs From The Morning – Online EP, February
Kid In A Big World – Reissue LP, March
The Hidden Beauty ('73 – '79) – Compilation LP, March
Kid In A Big World – Reissue CD, Japan Release, September
Can You Hear Me OK? – Reissue LP, October

2019
Cut The Wire – Album CD, April
Four Piano Pieces – Online EP, October
Across The Door Sill (Special Edition) ++++ – Online
Album, October

2020
To The Left of The Moon's Reflection – Album CD, August

2021
Collected: The Best of John Howard – Compilation
Album 2CD, May
Dreaming I Am Waking: Piano Music For My Father –
Online Album, October

2022
LOOK: The Unknown Story of Danielle Du Bois – Album
CD, March
Kid In A Big World + The Original Demos (Reissue +
Demos) – Album 2CD, November

*recorded in 1974/5
**recorded in 1975, 1977 and 1978
++recorded as Quiz
***recorded in 1996
+++recorded 2005 and 2006
++++recorded 2016 & 2019
****recorded as John Howard & The Night Mail

For more information: www.kidinabigworld.co.uk

John's first two books, the acclaimed Incidents Crowded With Life and Illusions of Happiness are available worldwide online and via all good bookstores.

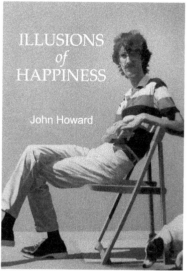

"Howard tells his story humorously, smartly, without lament."
Rolling Stone Magazine

"Insightful and witty, sad and sexy, I felt bereft when I finished this. A sequel beckons?"
Anthony Reynolds – Singer/Songwriter

"A great insight into the terrifying sex life of early 1970s Northern art students!"
David Quantick

"An authentic hidden treasure of eccentric pop: the kind of music that one could imagine had been reissued as a vestige of a time when Bowie still haunted the cabarets and Elton John preferred writing to shopping."
Celine Remy – French magazine Les Inrockuptibles

Lightning Source UK Ltd.
Milton Keynes UK
UKHW020642040322
399569UK00008B/400